# Mathematics

Paul Rigby
Clive Cowmeadow
Peter Sherran

Series editors: Graham Newman
Peter Sherran

# Extension 7

CAMBRIDGE
UNIVERSITY PRESS

CAMBRIDGE UNIVERSITY PRESS
Cambridge, New York, Melbourne, Madrid, Cape Town, Singapore, São Paulo, Delhi

Cambridge University Press
The Edinburgh Building, Cambridge CB2 8RU, UK

www.cambridge.org
Information on this title: www.cambridge.org/9780521722209

First published 2008

Book printed in the United Kingdom at the University Press, Cambridge

*A catalogue record for this publication is available from the British Library*

ISBN 978-0-521-72220-9 paperback with CD-ROM

# Contents

# Introduction

## Take advantage of the pupil CD

*Cambridge Essentials Mathematics* comes with a pupil CD in the back. This contains the entire book as an interactive PDF file, which you can read on your computer using free Adobe Reader software from Adobe (www.adobe.com/products/acrobat/readstep2.html). As well as the material you can see in the book, the PDF file gives you extras when you click on the buttons you will see on most pages; see the inside front cover for a brief explanation of these.

To use the CD, simply insert it into the CD or DVD drive of your computer. You will be prompted to install the contents of the CD to your hard drive. Installing will make it easier to use the PDF file, because the installer creates an icon on your desktop that launches the PDF directly. However, it will run just as well straight from the CD.

If you want to install the contents of the disc onto your hard disc yourself, this is easily done. Just open the disc contents in your file manager (for Apple Macs, double click on the CD icon on your desktop; for Windows, open My Computer and double click on your CD drive icon), select all the files and folders and copy them wherever you want.

## Take advantage of the teacher CD

The *Teacher Material* CD-ROM for *Cambridge Essentials Mathematics* contains enhanced interactive PDFs. As well as all the features of the pupil PDF, teachers also have access to e-learning materials and links to the *Essentials Mathematics* Planner – a new website with a full lesson planning tool, including worksheets, homeworks, assessment materials, guidance and example lesson plans. The e-learning materials are also fully integrated into the Planner, letting you see the animations in context and alongside all the other materials.

# Sequences

- Using symbols to represent numbers
- Exploring increasing and decreasing sequences
- Using a term-to-term rule
- Using a position-to-term rule

Keywords

You should know

explanation 1

**1** Each symbol stands for a number. Find its value.

a △ + 3 = 5     b ★ − 6 = 4     c ⬡ × 2 = 8     d 3 + ◆ = 15

e 9 − ♥ = 2     f 5 × ■ = 55     g ▼ ÷ 3 = 4     h ◇ ÷ 10 = 3

i 11 − ◀ = 3     j 14 + ♣ = 21     k ◗ + ◗ = 10     l ✷ + ✷ + ✷ = 60

**2** Each symbol stands for a number. Find its value.

a $\dfrac{⬡}{2} = 10$     b $\dfrac{▼}{4} = 3$     c ★ × ★ × ★ = 27     d $\dfrac{12}{✷} = 2$

e $\dfrac{16}{◀} = 8$     f $\dfrac{◆ + ◆}{4} = 3$     g $\dfrac{2 × ◗}{3} = 10$     h $\dfrac{△ × △}{8} = 2$

**3** ▲ = 7 and ● = 5. Find the value of these expressions.

a ▲ + 2     b 2 × ▲     c ▲ − 4     d 3 + ▲

e ● + 6     f 10 − ●     g 3 × ●     h ● − 4

i ▲ + ●     j ▲ − ●     k ● × ▲     l ▲ × ▲

m ● × ●     n ● ÷ ●     o ▲ ÷ ▲     p ▲ + ● + 6

**4** ★ = 6 and ♠ = 8. Find the value of these expressions.

a ★ + ★     b 2 × ★     c ♠ + ♠ + ♠     d 3 × ♠

**5** ✷ = 9. Find a quick way to work out ✷ + ✷ + ✷ + ✷ + ✷ + ✷ + ✷ + ✷ + ✷ + ✷.
Explain how you got your answer.

explanation 2

**6** ♥ = 20. What is each of these numbers?

  **a**  4 more than ♥        **b**  twice ♥          **c**  3 less than ♥

  **d**  half of ♥            **e**  ♥ less than 31    **f**  ♥ more than 4

  **g**  5 times ♥            **h**  ♥ more than ♥

**7** Repeat question **6** for ♥ = $\frac{1}{2}$. Which two pairs of answers will always be equal?

**8** ★ + △ = 10 and ★ × △ = 16. Write down a pair of values of ★ and △.

**9** Copy and complete the table. Use the completed entries as a guide.

|   | Start number | Change | Result |
|---|---|---|---|
|   | 3 | Increase by 5 | 3 + 5 = 8 |
| a | 7 | Increase by 11 | |
| b | 12 | | 12 + 6 = 18 |
| c | | Increase by 10 | 21 + 10 = 31 |
| d | ▲ | | ▲ + 5 |
| e | ♥ | Increase by 8 | |
| f | ◀ | Increase by 17 | |
| g | | Decrease by 4 | 16 − 4 = 12 |
| h | | Decrease by 20 | ☐ − 20 |
| i | ▶ | Decrease by 36 | |
| j | ✳ | | ✳ − 9 |
| k | | Double | 2 × ▩ |
| l | ✖ | Double | |
| m | ▼ | Treble | |

**10** Each letter stands for a number. Find its value.

a   $8 - e = 3$   b   $4 \times f = 32$   c   $g \div 3 = 11$

d   $k + k = 54$   e   $28 - i = 3$   f   $1 + j = 21$

g   $h \div 10 = 8$   h   $m + m + m = 75$   i   $t + t - 6 + t = 27$

**11** $m = 12$ and $n = 8$. Find the value of these expressions.

a   $m + 3$   b   $n - 6$   c   $4 \times m$

d   $6 \times n + 1$   e   $30 - m$   f   $24 \div n$

g   $2 \times m - 3$   h   $m \times n$   i   $n \times m$

**12** Copy and complete the table.

| Start number | Change | Result |
|---|---|---|
| $n$ | Increase by 5 | $n + 5$ |
| $k$ | Increase by 47 | |
| $p$ | Decrease by 12 | |
| $q$ | Decrease by 20 | |
| $w$ | Double | |
| $r$ | | $r + 6$ |
| $t$ | Halve | |
| $m$ | | $m + n$ |
| $w$ | Double and then increase by 1 | |
| $x$ | Multiply by 5 then decease by 10 | |
| $y$ | Multiply by 2 then increase by 7 | |

**13** Adam has $x$ pets. Bahavna has $y$. How many pets do they have altogether?

**14** Charlie has $x$ books. She gives three to her friend Daniel. How many books does Charlie have left?

explanation 3a    explanation 3b

**15** Write the next two terms of each of these sequences. State whether the sequence is increasing or decreasing.

  a  12, 14, 16, 18, ...       b  27, 24, 21, 18, ...       c  812, 712, 612, 512, ...

  d  24, 40, 56, 72, ...       e  318, 338, 358, 378, ...   f  79, 68, 57, 46, ...

  g  4, 8, 12, 16, ...         h  4, 8, 16, 32, ...         i  1, 10, 100, 1000, ...

  j  256, 128, 64, 32, ...     k  243, 81, 27, 9, ...       l  1, 1, 2, 3, 5, ...

**16** Copy and complete these sequences.

  a  1, 6, 11, ☐, 21, ☐       b  4, 7, ☐, 13, 16, ☐        c  2, ☐, 8, ☐, 14, 17, ☐

  d  8, ☐, 18, ☐, 28, ☐       e  40, 31, ☐, 13, ☐          f  52, ☐, 44, ☐, 36, ☐

  g  2.5, 3, ☐, 4, ☐, ☐       h  10, ☐, 9, ☐, 8, 7.5, ☐

  i  16, ☐, 19, ☐, ☐, 23.5

**17** Copy and complete the table.

|   | Term | Term-to-term rule | First five terms |
|---|------|-------------------|------------------|
| a | 1st: 10 | Add 4 | |
| b | 1st: 7 | Double and then take away 5 | |
| c | 2nd: 21 | Subtract 0.5 | |
| d | 2nd: 4 | Divide by 2 | |
| e | 2nd: 13 | Multiply by 3 and then add 1 | |
| f | 6th: | | 4, 9, 19, 39, 79 |
| g | 10th: | | 2.5, 5, 7.5, 10, 12.5 |

**18** Here is a partly completed train timetable. Copy it and fill in the missing times.

| Monday to Friday | | | | |
|------------------|------|------|------|------|
| Exeter Central | 1414 | 1533 | | |
| Pinhoe | 1419 | | | |
| Whimple | 1426 | | 1626 | |
| Feniton | 1431 | | | |
| Honiton | 1437 | | | 1707 |

**19** Odd numbers can be used to create sequences.

   **a**  Copy the pattern below. Extend it so you can see the first seven odd numbers.

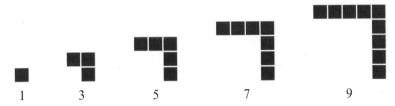

        1        3        5        7        9

   **b**  Write the first seven terms of a new sequence. The 1st term is 1, the 2nd term is the sum of the first two odd numbers, the 3rd term is the sum of the first three odd numbers, the 4th term is the sum of the first four odd numbers and so on.

   **c**  Is 144 a term in your new sequence? Explain your answer.

explanation 4a    explanation 4b

**20** The number of dots in the pattern below makes a sequence.

| Pattern | $\bullet$ $\phantom{x}$ $\bullet$ $\phantom{x}$ $\bullet$ | $\bullet \; \bullet$ $\bullet \; \bullet$ $\bullet \; \bullet$ | $\bullet \; \bullet \; \bullet$ $\bullet \; \bullet \; \bullet$ $\bullet \; \bullet \; \bullet$ |
|---|---|---|---|
| Position | 1st term | 2nd term | 3rd term |
| Term | 3 | 6 | 9 |

Copy and complete these statements.

The 4th term is   $3 \times \square = \square$      The 10th term is   $3 \times \square = \square$

The 50th term is   $\square \times \square = \square$      The nth term is   $\square \times \square$

**21** Write the first four terms of the sequences with these *n*th terms.

   **a**  $n + 5$        **b**  $n + 10$        **c**  $n + 100$        **d**  $n - 1$

   **e**  $2 \times n$        **f**  $5 \times n$        **g**  $10 \times n - 7$        **h**  $11 \times n$

   **i**  $3 \times n + 0.5$        **j**  $2 \times n + 2.5$        **k**  $3 \times n - 0.5$        **l**  $n + 9.5$

**22**   **i**   For each sequence, choose the correct *n*th term from the list.

   **ii**   Use the *n*th terms to find the 30th term of each sequence.

| *n*th term = *n* + 6 | *n*th term = *n* + 1 | *n*th term = 10 × *n* | *n*th term = 6 × *n* + 14 |

| *n*th term = 5 × *n* +5 | *n*th term = 2 × *n* | *n*th term = 4 × *n* − 3 |

| *n*th term = 3 × *n* − 1 | *n*th term = 2 × *n* − 1 |

   **a**   2, 5, 8, 11, ...          **b**   1, 3, 5, 7, ...          **c**   2, 4, 6, 8, ...

   **d**   10, 15, 20, 25, ...       **e**   1, 5, 9, 13, ...         **f**   10, 20, 30, 40, ...

   **g**   7, 8, 9, 10, ...          **h**   20, 26, 32, 38, ...

**23**   The 1st border (yellow) that surrounds the red tile contains 12 tiles, the 2nd border (green) contains 24 tiles and so on.

   **a**   How many tiles are in the 3rd border?

   **b**   Write the sequence that describes the number of tiles in each border.

   **c**   How many tiles do you think are in the 10th border?

   **d**   Find the *n*th term for this sequence.

   **e**   How many tiles are in the 50th border?

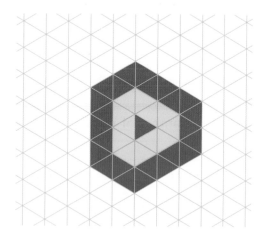

**24**   The first yellow border that surrounds the red square contains 8 tiles.

   **a**   How many tiles are in the second border?

   **b**   Write down a sequence that describes the number of tiles in each border starting with 8.

   **c**   Find the position-to-term rule for this sequence.

   **d**   How many tiles are in the 20th border?

   **e**   Which border contains 400 tiles? Is it a green border or a yellow border?

# Functions

- Using operations to make functions
- Applying an operation and its inverse
- Using algebra to describe rules
- Using a mapping diagram

Keywords

You should know

explanation 1

**1** Here is a function machine.

input → | × 5 | → output

**a** Write the output for each input value.
  **i** 3      **ii** 11      **iii** 7      **iv** ♠

**b** Write the input for each output value.
  **i** 20      **ii** 30      **iii** 35      **iv** 20 × ★

**2** Copy and complete these function machines.

**a** 4
7 → | + ☐ | → ☐   15, ☐, 27
☐

**b** 5
8 → | × ☐ | → 48   ☐, ☐
10

**c** 7
14 → | ÷ ☐ | → ☐   ☐, ☐, 3
21

**d** n
10 → | ☐ | → ☐   n − 8, ☐, n + 1

explanation 2a    explanation 2b

**3** Draw a function machine for each rule. Use the input values 0, 2, 8 and 12.

  **a** $x \rightarrow x - 1.5$      **b** $x \rightarrow \frac{x}{2}$      **c** $x \rightarrow 5x$      **d** $x \rightarrow x^2$

**4** Draw a function machine for each rule. Use the input values 0, 0.5, 4, and 10.

  **a** $x \rightarrow x + 8$      **b** $x \rightarrow 2.5x$      **c** $x \rightarrow \frac{x}{5}$      **d** $x \rightarrow x^2$

**5** Input and output values for some function machines are shown below.

Write the rule for each function machine in the form $x \rightarrow \square$.

a  $5 \rightarrow 8$  
    $10 \rightarrow 13$  
    $15 \rightarrow 18$

b  $12 \rightarrow 3$  
    $16 \rightarrow 4$  
    $20 \rightarrow 5$

c  $21 \rightarrow 15$  
    $27 \rightarrow 21$  
    $30 \rightarrow 24$

d  $2 \rightarrow 22$  
    $4 \rightarrow 44$  
    $5 \rightarrow 55$

e  $1 \rightarrow 101$  
    $2 \rightarrow 102$  
    $3 \rightarrow 103$

**6** Use algebra to write three possible rules that could describe this function machine. In each case copy and complete the machine.

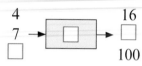

**7 a** Use a calculator to find $0.5 \times 0.5$.

  **b** Write three rules in the form $x \rightarrow \square$ that could describe this function machine. Copy and complete the machine in each case.

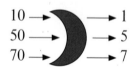

**8** Write the rule for this function machine.

10 →   → 1  
50 →   → 5  
70 →   → 7

Explain why there is only one rule for this function machine.

explanation 3

**9** Copy and complete these function machines.

a<br>
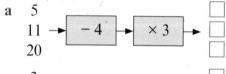

b<br>
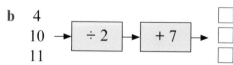

c<br>
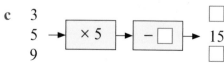

d<br>
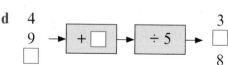

**10** Copy and complete this function machine to show $x \rightarrow 2x + 7$.

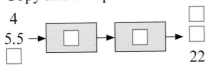

**11** Copy and complete this function machine to show $x \rightarrow 7x - 3$

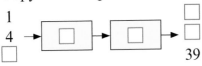

**12** Copy and complete this function machine to show

    **a** $x \rightarrow \frac{x}{5} + 2$      **b** $x \rightarrow \frac{2x}{5}$

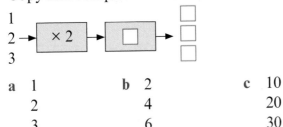

**13** Information about some function machines is shown below.

Work out the missing values.

**a**   $10 \rightarrow 2$      **b**   $27 \rightarrow 12$      **c**    $5 \rightarrow 5$      **d**    $0 \rightarrow \square$

        $12 \rightarrow 3$           $36 \rightarrow 16$         $8 \rightarrow 14$        $2 \rightarrow 23$

        $18 \rightarrow \square$          $99 \rightarrow \square$        $\square \rightarrow 26$       $\square \rightarrow 87$

        $x \rightarrow \frac{x}{2} - \square$       $x \rightarrow \frac{4x}{\square}$       $x \rightarrow 3x - \square$     $x \rightarrow \square x + 7$

**14** Copy and complete the function machine for each set of outputs.

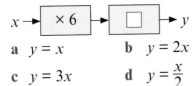

    **a**   1         **b**   2         **c**    10

        2              4              20

        3              6              30

**15** Copy and complete the function machine for each rule.

$x \rightarrow \boxed{\times 6} \rightarrow \boxed{\square} \rightarrow y$

    **a**   $y = x$         **b**   $y = 2x$

    **c**   $y = 3x$        **d**   $y = \frac{x}{2}$

explanation 4

**16** Work out the missing operations for these function machines so that the output is always the same as the input.

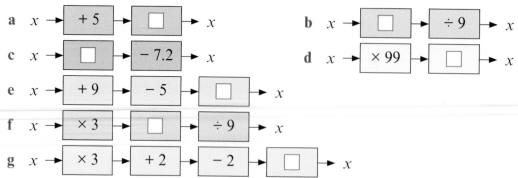

**17** Arrange the operations × 5, − 4 and + 7 in the function machine to show these outputs.

    **a**   the largest output               **b**   the smallest output

explanation 5

**18 a** Copy and complete the table of $x$ and $y$ values for this function machine.

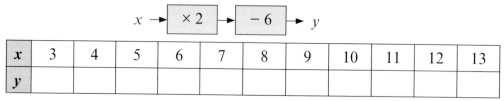

| $x$ | 3 | 4 | 5 | 6 | 7 | 8 | 9 | 10 | 11 | 12 | 13 |
|---|---|---|---|---|---|---|---|---|---|---|---|
| $y$ | | | | | | | | | | | |

   **b** Copy and complete this mapping diagram, using the values from your table.

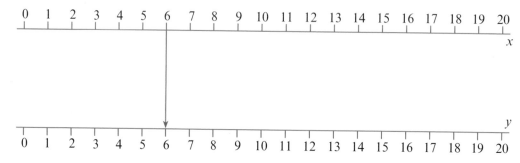

**19 a** Copy and complete the function machine and the table for
the rule $x \rightarrow \frac{x}{2} + 3$.

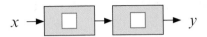

| $x$ | 0 | 1 | 2 | 3 | 4 |
|---|---|---|---|---|---|
| $y$ | | | | | |

**b** Copy and complete the mapping diagram.

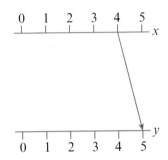

**20** Replace each function machine with a simpler version that has the same
effect. Copy and complete the corresponding rules.

**a** $x \rightarrow \boxed{+2} \rightarrow \boxed{+3} \rightarrow y$

$y = x + \square$

**b** $x \rightarrow \boxed{\times 2} \rightarrow \boxed{\times 3} \rightarrow y$

$y = \square x$

**21** The instructions below are used to convert temperatures in degrees
Fahrenheit (°F) to temperatures in degrees Celsius (°C).

Subtract 32, then divide by 9 and then multiply this by 5.

**a** Draw a function machine that will convert Fahrenheit to Celsius.

**b** On holiday the temperature was 95 °F. What is this in Celsius?

**c** At home the temperature was 20 °C. What is this in Fahrenheit?

# Decimals — ordering and rounding

- Reading decimals from a number line
- Comparing decimals
- Multiplying and dividing decimals by 10, 100 and 1000
- Rounding whole numbers and decimals

Keywords

You should know

explanation 1a  explanation 1b

**1** Write the value of each underlined digit as a fraction.

a 2.1̲65        b 0.071̲4        c 12.3̲8        d 636.9̲5

**2** Write the value of each underlined digit in words.

a 7.2̲1        b 0.208̲7        c 124.3̲8        d 0.000̲4

**3** Write these fractions in words.

a $\dfrac{3}{10}$        b $\dfrac{7}{100}$        c $\dfrac{41}{1000}$        d $\dfrac{38}{100}$

**4** Write as decimals.

a Four and seven hundredths

b Twelve and three tenths

c Sixteen and five thousandths

d Thirty-two and twenty-seven thousandths

**5** Write each of these as a decimal number.

a $5 + \dfrac{3}{10}$        b $23 + \dfrac{9}{100}$        c $2 + \dfrac{8}{10} + \dfrac{2}{100}$        d $1 + \dfrac{3}{10} + \dfrac{8}{1000}$

e $9 + \dfrac{25}{100}$        f $1 + \dfrac{73}{1000}$        g $34 + \dfrac{683}{1000}$        h $1 + \dfrac{2}{10000}$

**6** Here are some number lines. What is the number shown by each arrow?

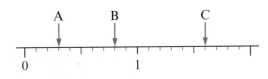 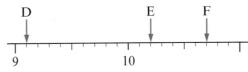

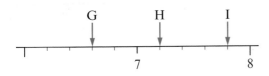 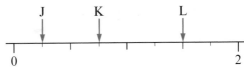

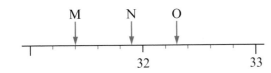 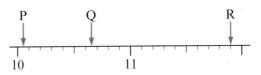

**7** Here are some number lines. What is the number shown by each arrow?

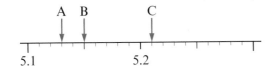 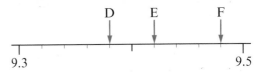

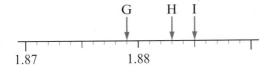 

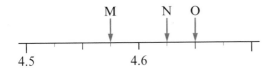 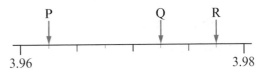

**8** Find the missing numbers. The highlighted number is halfway between the other two numbers. The first one has been done for you

   **a** 3.6 3.65 3.7    **b** 2.1 ☐ 2.2    **c** ☐ 3.95 4    **d** 0 ☐ 0.1

   **e** 7.6 7.85 ☐    **f** 5.36 ☐ 5.39    **g** 8.98 9 ☐    **h** 0 ☐ 0.01

explanation 2a    explanation 2b

**9** Work these out.

a   $2.71 \times 10$     b   $3.6 \div 10$     c   $0.209 \times 10$     d   $0.045 \times 10$

e   $0.37 \div 10$     f   $3.148 \times 10$     g   $37 \div 10$     h   $673 \div 10$

**10** Work these out.

a   $1.2 \times 100$     b   $3.42 \times 100$     c   $67 \div 100$     d   $100 \times 0.57$

e   $3.28 \div 100$     f   $0.27 \div 100$     g   $0.0286 \times 100$     h   $239 \div 100$

**11** Work these out.

a   $0.18 \times 1000$     b   $8 \div 1000$     c   $2.01 \div 1000$     d   $0.025 \times 1000$

e   $0.76 \div 1000$     f   $400 \div 1000$     g   $6781 \div 1000$     h   $1000 \times 0.006$

**12** Find the value of the missing number.

a   $\square \times 0.003 = 0.03$     b   $2.7 \div \square = 0.0027$     c   $100 \times \square = 45$

d   $\square \div 1000 = 0.653$     e   $10 \times \square = 0.09$     f   $\square \div 10 = 8.6$

g   $4.2 \times \square = 4200$     h   $\square \div 100 = 1.6$     i   $0.281 \div \square = 0.0281$

**13** a   Copy and complete this table.

| Number | Operation | | | | | | | |
|---|---|---|---|---|---|---|---|---|
| | × 10 | × 20 | × 100 | × 50 | ÷ 10 | ÷ 20 | ÷ 100 | ÷ 50 |
| 240 | | | | | | | | |
| 36 | | | | | | | | |
| 1.4 | | | | | | | | |

b   i   What is a quick way of multiplying by 50?

ii   What is a quick way of dividing by 50?

**14** A car on a motorway travels $27.8\,\text{m}$ every second. How far does it travel in each of these times?

a   10 seconds     b   50 seconds     c   1 minute

**15**   Fifty packs of CDs cost £65 and there are ten CDs in each pack.

    **a**   What is the cost of one pack?

    **b**   What is the cost of one CD in pounds?

**16**   Bob is fitting a new kitchen. He wants all of the measurements to be in millimetres..

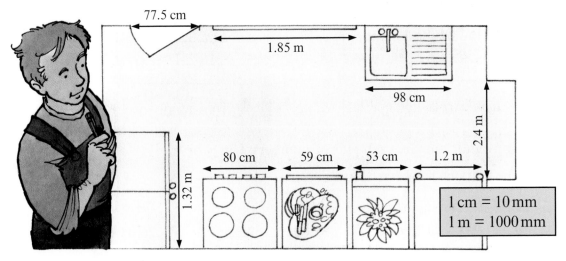

    Write each of the labelled measurements in millimetres.

**17**   Copy and complete.

    **a**  $37.5\,\text{cm} = \square\ \text{mm}$    **b**  $495\,\text{mm} = \square\ \text{cm}$    **c**  $786\,\text{cm} = \square\ \text{m}$

    **d**  $127\,\text{cm} = \square\ \text{m}$    **e**  $1230\,\text{mm} = \square\ \text{m}$    **f**  $3.2\,\text{m} = \square\ \text{mm}$

**18**   Convert each amount to the units given.

    **a**  3 litres in cl        **b**  270 cl in litres

    **c**  700 ml in cl        **d**  1200 ml in litres

    **e**  320 cl in ml         **f**  0.85 litres in cl

> 1 litre = 1000 ml
> 1 litre = 100 cl

**19**   Each 10 g serving of margarine contains 37 calories, 3.8 g of fat and 0.15 g of salt.

    **a**   How many calories are there in a 1 kg tub of margarine?

    **b**   How much fat is there in a 500 g tub of margarine?

> 1 kg = 1000 g

    **c**   How much salt is there in a 1 kg tub of margarine?

explanation 3a    explanation 3b

**20** Write these numbers in order of size, smallest first.

a   6, 5.9, 5.849, 5.85, 5.4999

b   11.3, 11.56, 11.18, 11.29, 11.06

c   0.278, 0.25, 0.3, 0.249, 0.28

d   7.127, 7.123, 7.12, 7.129, 7.192

e   0.0738, 0.0729, 0.073, 0.0732

f   19.1, 19.09, 19.18, 19.099, 19.178

**21** Write the smallest number in each set as a decimal.

a   $\dfrac{7}{10}, \dfrac{19}{100}, 0.24, \dfrac{38}{100}, 0.275$

b   $\dfrac{3}{10} + \dfrac{7}{100}, 0.41, \dfrac{3}{10} + \dfrac{9}{1000}, 0.39$

c   $\dfrac{9}{100} + \dfrac{8}{1000}, 0.092, 0.1, 0.099$

d   $\dfrac{27}{100}, \dfrac{138}{1000}, \dfrac{3}{10}, 0.14, 0.139$

**22** Copy and compare each pair of numbers. Use < or >.

The first one has been done for you.

a   2.79 < 2.8

b   0.18 ☐ 0.179

c   2.409 ☐ 2.413

d   12.23 ☐ 12.229

e   32.001 ☐ 32.01

f   26.047 ☐ 26.0467

g   $\dfrac{37}{100}$ ☐ $\dfrac{268}{1000}$

h   $\dfrac{27}{100}$ ☐ $\dfrac{89}{1000}$

i   $\dfrac{1}{10}$ ☐ $\dfrac{99}{1000}$

**23** Copy and compare each pair of quantities. Use < or >.

a   27 mm ☐ 2.5 cm

b   9.8 cm ☐ 9.7 m

c   240 cm ☐ 0.25 m

d   0.8 m ☐ 760 mm

e   −12 °C ☐ 3 °C

f   3020 g ☐ 3.1 kg

**24**

| 4.8 | 4.9 | 5.0 | 5.1 | 5.2 | 5.3 | 5.4 | 5.5 | 5.6 | 5.7 | 5.8 | 5.9 | 6.0 | 6.1 |
|-----|-----|-----|-----|-----|-----|-----|-----|-----|-----|-----|-----|-----|-----|

Which the numbers above could be possible values of $x$?

a   $x > 5.6$

b   $x \le 5.3$

c   $x \ge 5.8$

d   $x > 5.8$

e   $x \le 5.0$

f   $4.8 < x < 5.2$

g   $4.95 < x \le 5.1$

h   $x > 5.95$

i   $5.6 \le x \le 5.8$

j   $5.4 \le x \le 5.55$

**25** The number 3.7 has only one digit after the decimal point. The numbers 3.70 and 3.71 have two digits after the decimal point. List all the possible values of $x$ for these statements.

a   $32.7 \le x < 32.9$ and $x$ has one digit after the decimal point.

b   $0.65 < x < 0.7$ and $x$ has two digits after the decimal point.

**26**  The four cards $\boxed{3}\ \boxed{0}\ \boxed{.}\ \boxed{5}$ show the number 30.5. Use all the cards to make as many different numbers as possible. Write them in order of size, smallest first.

**27**  The five cards $\boxed{6}\ \boxed{.}\ \boxed{7}\ \boxed{0}\ \boxed{5}$ show the number 6.705. Use all the cards to find these numbers.

    **a**  the smallest number

    **b**  the largest number

    **c**  all the possible values of $x$ if $5 < x < 5.5$

    **d**  all the possible values of $x$ if $6.5 < x < 6.75$

**28**  Each clue refers to a number shown by an arrow on the number line. Find the value of each letter.

$a > 5.03$     $b > 5$ and $b < 5.005$     $c < 5$

$5.01 < d < 5.02$     $5.002 < e < 5.015$

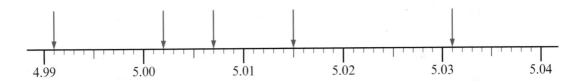

**29**  Trace the diagram.

  Join the four smallest values in order.

  Make a closed shape by joining to the smallest value again.

  If you are right, the diagram should let you know! Explain.

    8.71

    8.713

    8.714

    8.703

    8.711

    8.72

    8.709

explanation 4a　　explanation 4b　　explanation 4c

**30　a**　Use the diagram to help you write each of these numbers to the nearest 10.

　　**i**　1623　　　　**ii**　1639　　　　**iii**　1644　　　　**iv**　1602

　　**v**　1654　　　　**vi**　1605　　　　**vii**　1597　　　　**viii**　1635

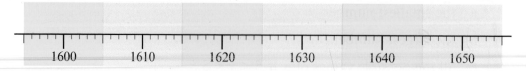

**b**　Write the numbers where each of the yellow and blue regions meet.

| ≤ means 'is less than or equal to'. |
| --- |

**c**　The number $x$ is 1620 to the nearest 10. What colour is the region containing $x$?

**d**　Copy and complete. $\square \leq x < \square$

**e**　The number $y$ is 1650 to the nearest 10. Copy and complete. $\square \leq y < \square$

**31　a**　Use the diagram to help you write each of these numbers to the nearest 10.

　　**i**　1014　　　　**ii**　986　　　　**iii**　975　　　　**iv**　992

　　**v**　998　　　　**vi**　1005　　　　**vii**　1024　　　　**viii**　969

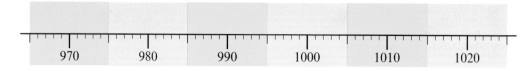

**b**　The number $x$ is 1010 to the nearest 10. Copy and complete. $\square \leq x < \square$

**c**　The number $y$ is 980 to the nearest 10. Copy and complete. $\square \leq y < \square$

**32**　Round each number to the nearest 100.

　　**a**　479　　　　**b**　548　　　　**c**　839.2　　　　**d**　451.8

　　**e**　67.5　　　　**f**　41　　　　**g**　80.27　　　　**h**　149.3

　　**i**　1783　　　　**j**　4709　　　　**k**　21386　　　　**l**　17449

**33** Here are the attendance figures for the first game in one football season.

Round each figure to the nearest thousand.

  **a**  Real Madrid 64867     **b**  Le Mans 32131     **c**  Hamburg 49713

  **d**  Millwall 10012        **e**  Luton Town 8131   **e**  Stoke City 8971

**34** Strawberry pickers are paid at the end of each day. Sam likes to keep his accounts simple, so he pays everyone to the nearest £10 on what they earn.

  **a**  Work out how much Sam pays to each picker.

   **i**  Rob earns £37        **ii**  Nadia earns £63      **iii**  Sacha earns £54

   **iv**  Aziz earns £78       **v**  Emma earns £74.50    **vi**  Leela earns £65

   **vii**  Jack earns £57.41   **viii**  Winston earns £82.29   **ix**  Raj earns £59.78

  **b**  How much more did Emma need to earn to be paid an extra £10?

  **c**  Sam pays Maria £60.

   **i**  What is the least amount that Maria might have earned?

   **ii**  What is the greatest amount that Maria might have earned?

explanation 5a     explanation 5b

**35** Use the diagram to help you round these decimals to the nearest whole number.

  **a**  9.4        **b**  7.7        **c**  5.5        **d**  7.48

  **e**  9.75       **f**  8.51       **g**  10.47      **h**  6.6002

**36** Use the diagram to help you round these decimals to 1 d.p.

  **a**  8.93       **b**  8.66       **c**  9.04       **d**  8.74

  **e**  8.75       **f**  9.048      **g**  8.863      **h**  9.119

**37** **a**   What is the least amount that would round to £20 to the nearest £1?

**b**   What is the greatest amount that would round to £20 to the nearest £1?

**c**   What is the least amount that would round to £20 to the nearest £10?

**d**   What is the greatest amount that would round to £20 to the nearest £10?

**38** Copy and complete the table.

| Number | Nearest whole number | To 1 d.p. | To 2 d.p. | To 3 d.p. | To 4 d.p. |
|---|---|---|---|---|---|
| 9.304561 | | | | | |
| 0.57086 | | | | | |
| 1.39942 | | | | | |
| 41.073693 | | | | | |
| 107.35952 | | | | | |
| 10.94761 | | | | | |
| 17.00455 | | | | | |
| 59.54458 | | | | | |
| 74.99501 | | | | | |
| 8.99835 | | | | | |

**39** The width of a filing cabinet is 46 cm correct to the nearest centimetre. Explain why it is possible for two of these cabinets to fit in a space that is only 91.4 cm wide.

**40** A certain type of brick is 21 cm long correct to the nearest centimetre. Three of these bricks are placed end-to-end. Peter wants to know what the shortest possible length would be.

# Number N1.2

## Negative numbers

- Using a number line for positive and negative numbers
- Adding and subtracting using negative numbers
- Multiplying and dividing negative numbers

Keywords

You should know

explanation 1

1  Use the number line to help you find the missing terms in these sequences.

  a   $-3, -1, 1, \square, \square, \square$    b   $-4, -2, 0, \square, \square, \square$    c   $8, 5, \square, \square, -4, \square$

  d   $10, \square, 4, \square, -2, \square$    e   $-9, \square, -1, \square, 7, \square$    f   $-5, \square, 0, \square, \square, 7.5$

2  Describe each of the sequences in question **1** as increasing or decreasing.

3  Use the symbols < and > to compare each pair of numbers.

  a   $-6 \square -3$      b   $0 \square -2$      c   $-7 \square -10$

  d   $-1 \square 8$      e   $-31 \square -20$      f   $-15 \square -19$

  g   $-5.2 \square -5$      h   $-4.9 \square -5$

> < means 'is less than'
> > means 'is greater than'

4  $x$ is an integer. What are the possible numbers for $x$ if:

  a   $-2 < x < 1$    b   $-3 \le x \le 0$    c   $-8 < x < -4$    d   $-5 < x < 3$

5  Write these numbers in order of size, smallest first.

  a   $2, -1, -3, -4, 3$          b   $-1.2, -0.7, 0.1, 7.2, -2$

  c   $1, -7.2, -1.8, -3, -1.75$

**6** The highlighted number is halfway between the other two numbers.
Find each missing number.

a  −1 ☐ 1     b  −8 ☐ −2     c  −5 ☐ 2     d  ☐ 1 6     e  ☐ −4 1

explanation 2

**7** Increase each number by 5.

a  7        b  −2        c  −8        d  −5        e  −1        f  −100

**8** Decrease each of these numbers by 7.

a  11       b  3         c  0         d  2         e  −1        f  −5

**9** One morning in March the outside temperature was −3 °C. By midday this
had risen to 12 °C. By how much had the temperature increased?

**10** On a cold day, wind chill can make it
feel even colder. If the wind chill
is −10 °C, then a temperature of 4 °C
will feel like −6 °C. What does the
temperature feel like for each of these
actual values?

a  1 °C         b  3 °C

c  −2 °C        d  −15 °C

**11** What calculations are represented by these diagrams?

a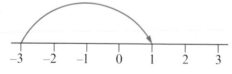

b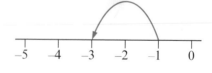

c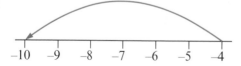

d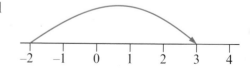

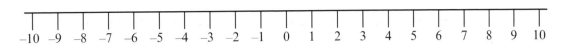

**12** Work these out.

    **a** $3 - 8$         **b** $-9 + 7$         **c** $-3 - 6$         **d** $-8 + 1$

    **e** $-10 + 10$       **f** $-5 - 15$       **g** $-3 + 11$       **h** $-6 - 20$

    **i** $-7 + 3 + 1$     **j** $-9 + 5 + 7$     **k** $2 - 6 - 4$     **l** $-11 + 6 + 9$

**13** Work these out.

    **a** $-1 - 1$        **b** $-4 - 11 + 3$     **c** $-12 + 30$       **d** $3 - 16 - 4$

    **e** $-19 - 31$     **f** $12 - 16 - 7$     **g** $-1 - 14 - 20$     **h** $-57 - 3 + 14$

**14** Copy and complete.

    **a** $-6 + \square = 3$       **b** $2 - \square = -8$       **c** $-1 + \square = 6$

    **d** $-3 \square \square = -7$     **e** $-5 \square \square = 3$      **f** $-7 \square \square = -10$

    **g** $-3 \square \square = +7$     **h** $-4 \square \square = 1$       **i** $\square + 8 = 7$

    **j** $\square - 6 = -4$       **k** $\square + 5 = -4$      **l** $\square - 9 = -10$

**15** Subtract 4 from each number.

    **a** $3$             **b** $1$             **c** $-2.5$         **d** $-5.5$

**16** Add 7.5 to each number.

    **a** $-3$           **b** $-1$          **c** $-7.5$         **d** $-10$

**17** Copy and complete.

    **a** $2 - 10 = \square$                  **b** $-0.5 - 0.5 = \square$

    **c** $-3.5 + \square = 7$             **d** $-7.5 - \square = -18.5$

**18** Find the value when:

    **a** $-2$ is decreased by 0.4        **b** $-3$ is increased by 0.2

    **c** $-1$ is decreased by 0.9        **d** $0.3$ is added to $-1$

    **e** $1.1$ is subtracted from $-2$     **f** $2$ is added to $-0.4$

explanation 3

**19** The table shows two sets of equivalent instructions. Copy and complete.

| Instruction using positive numbers | Instruction using negative numbers |
|---|---|
| Move 3 places to the left | |
| | Move −5 places up |
| | Increase by −3 |
| | Move −8 places to the right |
| Decrease by 4 | |

**20** Rewrite the following statements without using negative numbers.

a  The ship travelled −50 miles north.

b  In the evening, the temperature rose by −8 °C.

c  As the plane approached the airport, it gained −5000 ft in height.

d  The car that Peter bought last year is now worth −£3200 more.

e  The population of the UK has fallen by −10 million since 1950.

explanation 4a    explanation 4b    explanation 4c

**21** Copy and complete.

a  Adding −4 is equivalent to ...

b  Subtracting −10 is equivalent to ...

c  $1 + -4 = 1 \square 4 = \square$

d  $16 - -10 = 16 \square 10 = \square$

e  ... is the same as adding 9

f  ... is the same as subtracting 5

g  $-3 - \square = -3 + 9 = \square$

h  $2 + \square = 2 - 5 = \square$

**22** Work these out.

a  $-2 + -6$    b  $4 - -5$    c  $-3 - -3$    d  $-4 - -7$

e  $8 + -9$    f  $0 - -4$    g  $-10 + -1$    h  $-12 - -13$

i  $-3 - -2$    j  $5 + -6$    k  $10 + -0.5$    l  $3.5 - -0.5$

**23** Copy and complete.

a   $-5 - -7 = -5 \,\square\, 7 = \square$

b   $3 + -10 = 3 \,\square\, 10 = \square$

c   $-8 \,\square\, -9 = -8 \,\square\, 9 = 1$

d   $5 + \square = 5 - \square = -6$

e   $-4 \,\square\, -3 = -4 \,\square\, 3 = -7$

f   $\square + -8 = -10$

g   $\square - -9 = -1$

h   $-6 + \square = -11$

**24** Copy and complete. The first one has been done for you.

a   $-7 + (-3) = -7 - 3 = -10$

b   $8 + (-6)$

c   $-8 - (+5)$

d   $-8 - (-5)$

e   $-8 + (+5)$

f   $-12 - (-4)$

g   $9 + (-11)$

**25** Copy and complete these addition and subtraction grids.

a

| + | −7 | 3 | 0 | |
|---|---|---|---|---|
| | −11 | | | |
| −2 | | | | −6 |
| 0 | | | | |
| | | −2 | | |

b

| − | −1 | −3 | | 6 |
|---|---|---|---|---|
| 5 | 6 | | | |
| −3 | | | −8 | |
| | 0 | | | |
| −7 | | | | |

**26** Copy and complete these addition and subtraction grids.

a

| − | | 4 | −6 | |
|---|---|---|---|---|
| −3 | −5 | | | |
| 2 | | | | |
| | −3 | | | |
| −5 | | | −4 | |

b

| + | 1 | −4 | −1 | |
|---|---|---|---|---|
| | −3 | | | −7 |
| −5 | | | | |
| −2 | | | | |
| | | | | −9 |

**27** Here are some magic squares. Complete them so that each row, column and diagonal has the same total.

| 2 | 0 | −7 | 9 |
|---|---|---|---|
| | 5 | | −2 |
| | −6 | | |
| −3 | | 6 | |

| 7 | | | −6 |
|---|---|---|---|
| | | −1 | 4 |
| −2 | 3 | | |
| 0 | | 6 | −5 |

**28** Copy and complete these addition pyramids.

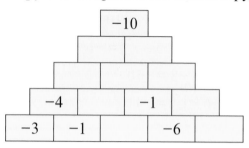
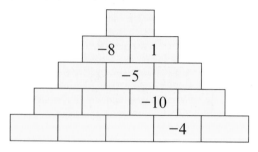

**29 a**  Two numbers have a sum of 4 and a difference of 10.
What are the numbers?

 **b**  Find three consecutive numbers that total −12.

 **c**  20 + $x$ < 20. What can you say about $x$?

---

explanation 5

**30** Copy and complete this
multiplication table and then
work out the answers **a** to **l**.

| | | | | 4 | | | | |
|---|---|---|---|---|---|---|---|---|
| | | −6 | −3 | 3 | 3 | 6 | 9 | |
| | | | −2 | 2 | 2 | 4 | 6 | |
| | −3 | −2 | −1 | 1 | 1 | 2 | 3 | |
| −4 | −3 | −2 | −1 | × | 1 | 2 | 3 | 4 |
| | 3 | 2 | 1 | −1 | −1 | −2 | −3 | |
| | | 4 | | −2 | | −4 | | |
| | | 6 | | −3 | | −6 | | |
| | | | | −4 | | | | |

**a**  −4 × −3      **b**  +4 × −3

**c**  −4 × +2      **d**  +4 × +3

**e**  −6 × +5      **f**  8 × −2

**g**  −8 × −3      **h**  −5 × −7

**i**  −1 × −1      **j**  9 × −4

**k**  −2 × 100     **l**  −50 × −2

**31** Add, subtract and multiply each pair of numbers.
The first one has been done for you.

 **a**  −9  −2

 −9 + −2 = −9 − 2 = −11,  −9 − −2 = −9 + 2 = −7,  −9 × −2 = 18

 **b**  −3  +5        **c**  +7  −10        **d**  −5  −4        **e**  −8  +1

**32** Two numbers have a product of 30 and a total of −11. What are the numbers?

**33** Copy and complete this multiplication pyramid.

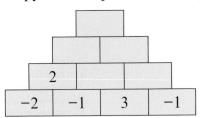

explanation 6

**34** Work out.

| | | | | | | | |
|---|---|---|---|---|---|---|---|
| a | $-15 \div +3$ | b | $+20 \div -5$ | c | $20 \div -10$ | d | $-100 \div -25$ |
| e | $-18 \div -3$ | f | $+12 \div +6$ | g | $-14 \div +2$ | h | $-15 \div -5$ |
| i | $+27 \div +3$ | j | $-8 \div -2$ | k | $+15 \div -15$ | l | $-9 \div +2$ |

**35 a** If $216 \div 12 = 18$ write down the answer to:

   **i** $+216 \div +12$   **ii** $-216 \div -12$   **iii** $+216 \div -12$   **iv** $-216 \div +12$

   **b** Copy and complete these division pyramids. Each number is divided by the number to its right.

   **i** 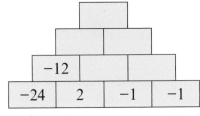   **ii**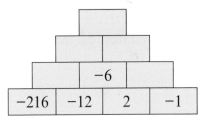

**36** For each pair of numbers below work out the answers when you add, subtract, multiply and divide them. The first one has been done for you.

**a**   +14   −2

   $+14 + -2 = +14 - 2 = 12$,   $+14 - -2 = +14 + 2 = 16$,

   $+14 \times -2 = -28$,   $+14 \div -2 = -7$

| | | | | | | | | | |
|---|---|---|---|---|---|---|---|---|---|
| b | −8 | −4 | c | +10 | +2 | d | +2 | −2 | e | +30 | −6 |
| f | −10 | −20 | g | −1 | −1 | h | −30 | +2 | i | +8 | −8 |

# Multiples, factors and primes

- Finding multiples of a number
- Finding all of the factors of a number
- Exploring the connection between multiples and factors
- Working with prime numbers

Keywords

You should know

explanation 1

1 The red dots on the number line show the first six multiples of 3.

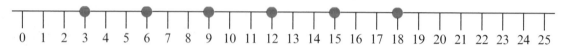

    **a**  What is the difference between any multiple of 3 and the next?

    **b**  What are the next two multiples of 3 after 18?

    **c**  What is the tenth multiple of 3?

    **d**  What is the hundredth multiple of 3?

2 The red dots on the number line show multiples of a number that is greater than 1.

    **a**  What is the number?

    **b**  What are the next two multiples of this number after 196?

3 The multiples of 5 make a sequence.

    **a**  Write the first six terms.        **b**  What is the tenth term?

    **c**  What is the twentieth term?     **d**  How many terms are less than 60?

    **e**  What is the largest term less than 200?

**4** The multiples of 17 make a sequence. One term in the sequence is 323.

   **a** What is the next term in the sequence?

   **b** What is the previous term?

**5** The square contains all the numbers from 1 to 49. Some of the numbers are hidden.

   **a** Describe the numbers highlighted in yellow.

   **b** How many multiples of 9 are shown?

   **c** What is the largest multiple of 11 shown?

   **d** The hidden numbers are multiples of the same number. What are the hidden numbers?

| 43 | | 25 | 1 | | 11 | 7 |
|---|---|---|---|---|---|---|
| 35 | 29 | 37 | | 20 | 15 | 49 |
| 5 | 22 | 21 | 12 | 41 | 38 | 9 |
| 39 | 45 | 2 | 6 | 27 | 33 | 13 |
| | 30 | 18 | 26 | 36 | 4 | 31 |
| 44 | 28 | 42 | 34 | 3 | 47 | 17 |
| | 14 | 46 | 19 | 10 | | 23 |

**6 a** Copy the diagram. Write down the first nine multiples of 8 in line 1 and the first nine multiples of 5 in line 2.

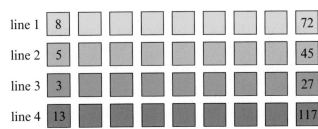

line 1   8   ...   72

line 2   5   ...   45

line 3   3   ...   27

line 4   13   ...   117

   **b** Line 3 is the difference between each term in lines 1 and 2, and line 4 is the sum. Complete lines 3 and 4 and describe them in words.

   **c** Line 5 is the difference between line 4 and line 3. Describe line 5.

explanation 2a    explanation 2b

**7** Describe each of the following statements as *true* or *false*.

   If the statement is false, give a counter example.

   **a** Any multiple of 8 is also a multiple of 4.

   **b** Any multiple of 3 is also a multiple of 6.

   **c** A common multiple of 6 and 4 is 24.

   **d** You can always find a common multiple of a pair of numbers by multiplying them together.

   **e** Multiplying a pair of numbers never gives their lowest common multiple (LCM).

**8** The function machine accepts two
   different inputs. It compares the
   multiples of each number and outputs
   the LCM.

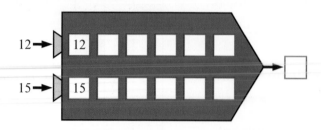

a  Copy and complete the machine
   below with inputs 12 and 15.

b  What are the possible inputs if the output is 8?

c  What are the possible inputs if the output is 18?

**9** Find the LCM of each set of numbers.

| | | | |
|---|---|---|---|
| a  5, 3 | b  8, 6 | c  10, 15 | d  4, 7 |
| e  3, 9 | f  12, 10 | g  7, 8 | h  9, 15 |
| i  2, 4, 8 | j  5, 10, 15 | k  6, 8, 12 | l  3, 4, 5 |

**10** At a recycling point paper is collected every four working days and aluminium
   cans every six working days. Emma noticed that on Monday both paper and
   cans were collected.

a  Write the first seven multiples of 4 and 6.

b  How long before the collection will take place on the same day again?

c  What day will this be?

**11** Jenny is buying food for a barbecue. Burgers are sold in packs of 6 and buns
   are sold in packs of 8. What is the least number of packs of burgers and buns
   Jenny should buy so that there is one bun for each burger?

explanation 3

**12** Describe each of the following statements as *true* or *false*.

If the statement is true, write the result as a multiplication.

The first one has been done for you.

a   3 is a factor of 15     True, 3 × 5 = 15     b   8 is a factor of 32

c   9 is a factor of 27     d   6 is a factor of 14

e   11 is a factor of 32     f   16 is a factor of 48

g   25 is a factor of 100     h   12 is a factor of 72

i   7 is a factor of 45     j   21 is a factor of 105

**13** Copy and complete this diagram to show the factor pairs of 12.

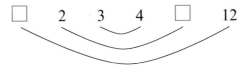

**14**  Draw a diagram showing the factor pairs for each number.

a   24          b   32          c   27          d   56

**15** List all of the factors of each of these numbers.

a   30          b   28          c   60          d   108

e   125         f   72          g   84          h   64

**16** A number is perfect if the sum of its factors is equal to twice the number. The number 6 is a perfect number. The factors of 6 are 1, 2, 3 and 6. The sum of the factors is 1 + 2 + 3 + 6 = 12. Find the sum of the factors of each of the following numbers. Are any of these a perfect number?

a   7          b   12          c   28          d   40

**17** 3384 is a multiple of 72 and 36 is a factor of 72.

Use this information to write two statements connecting 36 and 3384.

**18** Machine A takes two input numbers and gives
their common factors as the output numbers.

Find the output for each input.

| | | |
|---|---|---|
| a   8, 12 | b   15, 30 | c   18, 24 |
| d   24, 40 | e   32, 128 | f   27, 29 |
| g   36, 45 | h   27, 81 | i   84, 144 |

Machine A

**19** Machine B takes any number of input numbers. The
highest input number is given as the output number.

a   Put 36 and 45 into Machine A and then put
the output values into Machine B. What is
the output from Machine B?

b   What is the connection between your answer
to part **a** and the numbers 36 and 45?

Machine B

**20** Find the highest common factor (HCF) of each set of numbers.

| | | | |
|---|---|---|---|
| a   12, 18 | b   21, 42 | c   33, 77 | d   44, 88 |
| e   35, 49 | f   4000, 4500 | g   26, 78 | h   260, 780 |
| i   8, 12, 24 | j   30, 60, 75 | k   44, 88, 121 | l   36, 90, 180 |

**21** 104 has eight factors and $4 \times 26 = 104$. Explain how to find all the factors.
Write the factors of 64, and find the HCF of 104 and 64.

**22** a   Write down all of the factors of each number.

   i  2       ii  1       iii  7       iv  22

b   Which of the numbers in part **a** are prime numbers?

**23 a** Find a pair of prime numbers that total each of these numbers.

  **i** 12      **ii** 16      **iii** 24      **iv** 32

**b** Which number can be written as the sum of two primes in only one way?

**24** These numbers are products of prime numbers. Find a pair of prime numbers for each product.

  **a** 21          **b** 55          **c** 26          **d** 51

**25** The prime number 13 is an emirp (prime written in reverse) because reversing the digits gives 31, which is another prime number. Find two more emirps.

**26** Twin primes are prime numbers with a difference of 2. The first pair of twin primes is 3 and 5. What are the next three pairs of twin primes?

**27** The factors of 6 are 1, 2, 3 and 6. The prime factors of 6 are 2 and 3.

In a similar way find the prime factors of the following numbers.

  **a** 12          **b** 20          **c** 36

  **d** 35          **e** 66          **f** 130

> 2 and 3 are the only prime numbers in the list of factors.

---

explanation 6

**28** Riaz is writing the number 180 as a product of its prime factors. Use this method to write each of these numbers as a product of prime factors.

  **a** 10          **b** 18          **c** 8

  **d** 30          **e** 36          **f** 100

  **g** 24          **h** 168          **i** 196

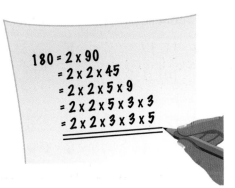

$$180 = 2 \times 90$$
$$= 2 \times 2 \times 45$$
$$= 2 \times 2 \times 5 \times 9$$
$$= 2 \times 2 \times 5 \times 3 \times 3$$
$$= 2 \times 2 \times 3 \times 3 \times 5$$

**29** 61, 71, 83, 89, 97, 101, 105, 109, 113, 127, 131, 139, 151, 163, 173, 197, 199

**a** Only one of these numbers is *not* prime. Explain which number it is.

**b** Think of a number between 1 and 14. Multiply it by one less than the number you chose and then add 41.
Do this a few times and comment on your answers.

# Patterns, squares and roots

- Working out square numbers and square roots
- Exploring the connection between odd numbers and square numbers

Keywords

You should know

explanation 1a    explanation 1b

**1** Here is a sequence of diagrams showing the square numbers 1, 4 and 9.

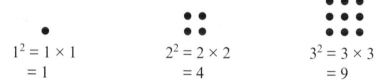

$1^2 = 1 \times 1$         $2^2 = 2 \times 2$         $3^2 = 3 \times 3$
$\quad = 1$                $\quad = 4$                $\quad = 9$

**a** Copy and continue the pattern to show the next two square numbers in the same way.

You should learn the square numbers.

**b** Copy and complete the table below.

| $n$ | 1 | 2 | 3 | 4 | 5 | 6 | 7 | 8 | 9 | 10 | 11 | 12 | 13 | 14 | 15 |
|---|---|---|---|---|---|---|---|---|---|---|---|---|---|---|---|
| $n^2$ | | | | | | | | | | | | | | | |

**2** Find a square number between the numbers in each pair.

   **a** 11, 17       **b** 23, 31       **c** 57, 66       **d** 70, 82

   **e** 101, 130      **f** 200, 250      **g** 180, 200      **h** 59.8, 72.6

**3** Work these out.

   **a** $7^2 + 1^2$      **b** $3^2 + 4^2$      **c** $4^2 + 8^2$      **d** $10^2 - 7^2$

   **e** $6^2 - 5^2$      **f** Twice $3^2$      **g** Half of $8^2$      **h** $6^2 \div 4$

**4 a** Write two consecutive odd numbers, multiply them together, then add 1.

Repeat the process several times. What do you notice about your final answers?

**b** What happens if you start with even numbers instead?

**5** Copy and complete.

**a** $3^2 + 4^2 = \square^2$ **b** $13^2 - 12^2 = \square^2$ **c** $10^2 - \square^2 = 6^2$

**6** Peter and Katie were given these instructions. Choose a number, then square the digits and add them. Repeat this process.

Peter chose 7 and Katie chose 12. Look at their working.

7 is a happy number because the process eventually ends at 1. Katie's working keeps on going on and on, so 12 is an unhappy number.

```
Peter number 7

7² = 49
4² + 9² = 16 + 81 = 97
9² + 7² = 81 + 49 = 130
1² + 3² + 0² = 1 + 9 + 0 = 10
1² + 0² = 1 + 0 = 1  ☺
```

```
Katie number 12

1² + 2² = 1 + 4 = 5
5² = 25
2² + 5² = 4 + 25 = 29
2² + 9² = 4 + 81 = 85
8² + 5² = 64 + 25 = 89
8² + 9² = 64 + 81 = 145
1² + 4² + 5² = 1 + 16 + 25 = 42  ☹
```

Which of these numbers are happy numbers? Show your working.

**a** 19 **b** 44 **c** 9 **d** 82

explanation 2a   explanation 2b

**7** Find the value of these.

**a** $\sqrt{16}$ **b** $\sqrt{100}$ **c** $\sqrt{36}$ **d** $\sqrt{144}$

**e** $\sqrt{49}$ **f** $\sqrt{25}$ **g** $\sqrt{64}$ **h** $\sqrt{169}$

**i** $\sqrt{121}$ **j** $\sqrt{225}$ **k** $\sqrt{1}$ **l** $\sqrt{0}$

**m** $\sqrt{900}$ **n** $\sqrt{2500}$ **o** $\sqrt{1600}$ **p** $\sqrt{3600}$

**q** $2 \times \sqrt{64}$ **r** $5 \times \sqrt{9}$ **s** $\sqrt{4} \times \sqrt{196}$ **t** $32 \div \sqrt{16}$

**8** $\sqrt{10}$ is not a whole number.

$\sqrt{10}$ lies between 3 and 4 because $3 \times 3 = 9$ and $4 \times 4 = 16$ and 10 is between 9 and 16.

Copy and complete these statements using two consecutive numbers.

**a** $\sqrt{3}$ lies between ☐ and ☐ because ...

**b** $\sqrt{20}$ lies between ☐ and ☐ because ...

**9** Here is another diagram showing square numbers. This one shows the connection between square numbers and odd numbers.

$1^2 = 1$      $2^2 = 1 + 3$      $3^2 = 1 + 3 + 5$

**a** Copy and continue the pattern for the next three square numbers.

**b** Copy and complete the statements.

  **i** The sum of the first 5 odd numbers is ☐$^2$

  **ii** The sum of the first 10 odd numbers is ☐$^2$

         Don't do it by adding up all of the values.

**c** Work out the sum of the first 100 odd numbers. ◄

**10 a** Copy and complete all the sections of the dragons. Use whole numbers.

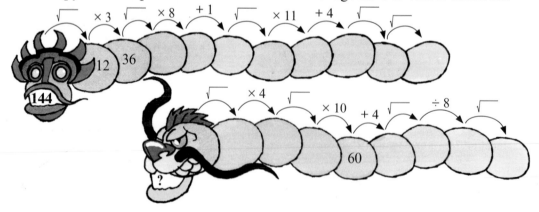

**b** Show that the last dragon can be completed in two different ways by using whole numbers.

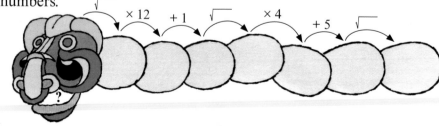

# Adding and subtracting

- Adding and subtracting decimals
- Using addition and subtraction of decimals to solve problems

Keywords

You should know

explanation 1

**1** Work these out.

a   16.3 + 7.25

b   0.146 + 2.59

c   5.23 + 11.9 + 6

d   2.31 + 17.5 + 1.47

e   32 + 4.76 + 12.38

f   0.076 + 0.14 + 2.83

**2** Copy and complete these calculations.

a
```
   2.■8
 +1■.37
  ■2.8■
```

b
```
  17.■9
 +2■.3■
  ■2.04
```

c
```
  ■8.■2
 +23.7■
  4■.21
```

d
```
  48.■3
 +1■.7■
  ■4.81
```

**3** Copy and complete these addition pyramids.

a

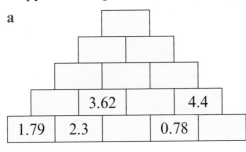

b

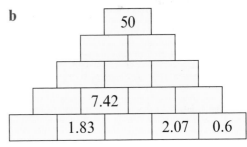

**4** Explain how to use addition to double or triple a number.

a   Double 1703.683 by using addition.

b   Triple 94.082 by using addition.

**5** Pupils sold fruit at break and lunch time for one week and donated the proceeds to charity. The table below shows the amount of money raised each day.

| Group | Monday | Tuesday | Wednesday | Thursday | Friday |
|-------|--------|---------|-----------|----------|--------|
| 1 | £5.98 | £3.07 | £6.37 | £4.88 | £6.39 |
| 2 | £6.02 | £2.98 | £5.90 | £5.11 | £4.77 |
| 3 | £4.73 | £3.50 | £4.44 | £6.01 | £5.58 |

**a**   One day during the week many pupils were out of school on a trip.
Which day was the trip? Explain your answer.

**b**   On which day did the pupils raise the most money?

**c**   Which group raised the most money?

**d**   What was the total amount of money raised?

**e**   The school agreed to double the amount of money raised by the pupils.
How much money was given to charity?

> explanation 2

**6** Work these out.

**a**   $39.4 - 8.7$

**b**   $9.45 - 1.637$

**c**   $76.8 - 9.651$

**d**   $456 - 67.83$

**e**   $1.78 - 0.3486$

**f**   $234.68 - 97$

**7** You will need to do two calculations for each of these.

**a**   $5.37 + 6.28 - 7.9$

**b**   $12.3 - 6.74 + 8.6$

**c**   $82.6 - 19.8 - 7.53$

**d**   $500 - 123.78 - 237.6$

**e**   $0.79 + 0.0286 - 0.0179$

**f**   $27 - 3.14 + 0.486$

**8** Copy and complete these calculations.

**a**
$$
\begin{array}{r}
9.7\,\blacksquare\,3 \\
-\ 4.\blacksquare\,7\,\blacksquare \\
\hline
\blacksquare.392 \\
\end{array}
$$

**b**
$$
\begin{array}{r}
\blacksquare\,5.\blacksquare\,9 \\
-\ 27.1\,\blacksquare \\
\hline
3\,\blacksquare.89 \\
\end{array}
$$

**c**
$$
\begin{array}{r}
8.1\,\blacksquare\,0 \\
-\ \blacksquare.\blacksquare\,3\,\blacksquare \\
\hline
3.154 \\
\end{array}
$$

**9** The diagrams below show some scales with weights given in grams.

Find the value of the missing weights to make the scales balance.

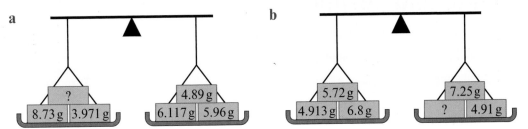

a

b

**10** Priya wrote down six numbers.

4.1    6.78    4.84    12    7.89    4.4

**a** Work out the sum of these numbers.

**b** She added up five of these numbers and her total came to 35.17. Which five numbers did she add up?

**11** David delivers leaflets each week with his paper round and gets paid every Thursday. His wage slip for June is

| week 1 | week 2 | week 3 | week 4 | total |
|--------|--------|--------|--------|-------|
| £19.78 | £ ?    | £20.40 | £19.25 | £81.15 |

His wage for week 2 has not printed properly. How much did he make that week?

**12** Find the length of the blade of this saw.

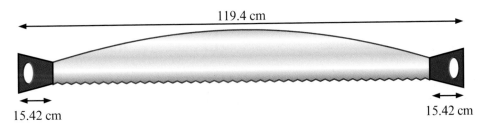

119.4 cm

15.42 cm                                        15.42 cm

# Length and perimeter

- Measuring to the nearest millimetre.
- Estimating distances using appropriate units.
- Calculating the perimeter of a figure.

Keywords

You should know

explanation 1

**1** Measure the length of each line. Give your answers to the nearest millimetre.

a _____

b _____

c _____

d _____

e _____

**2 a** Draw each of the diagrams below as accurately as you can, using the measurements shown.

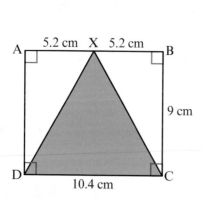

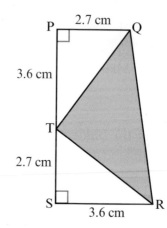

**b** Measure these distances to the nearest 0.1 cm.

   i  CX        ii  DX        iii  QT        iv  RT        v  QR

**c** What type of triangle is

   i  triangle CDX           ii  triangle QRT

**3** Here are some pictures of computer monitors. Screen sizes are measured along a diagonal of the rectangle containing the picture. The screen size is the length of the red line.

  **a** Measure each screen size as shown to the nearest millimetre.

  **b** The real screen sizes are ten times the sizes shown here.
    Write down the three real screen sizes.

  **i**

  **ii**

  **iii**

---

explanation 2

---

**4** Choose from the numbers and units given in the table to estimate the measurements shown below.

> Choose the most sensible units first, then look for a suitable number.

| Numbers | Units |
|---------|-------|
| 105 | mm |
| 0.05 | |
| 5.4 | cm |
| 27 | |
| 68 | m |
| 11 | |

Wingspan of a bumblebee

Height of a giraffe

Height of a table

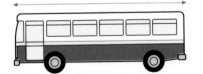

Length of a bus

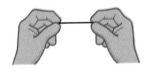

Thickness of a human hair

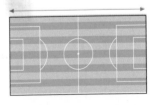

Length of Wembley pitch

explanation 3

**5 a** Here are three rectangles and one square. Find the perimeter of each shape.

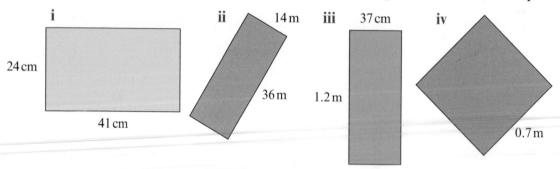

i  24 cm  41 cm

ii  14 m  36 m

iii  37 cm  1.2 m

iv  0.7 m

**b** The perimeter of a square is 84 cm. What is the length of each side?

**6 a** The perimeter of the blue rectangle is 21 cm and its base measures 3.5 cm. Find the height of the rectangle.

**b** Four of these rectangles are used to make the grey logo. Find the perimeter of this logo.

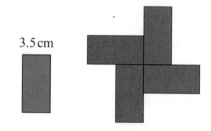

3.5 cm

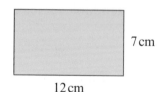

explanation 4a   explanation 4b

**7 a** Which of the shapes below must have the same perimeter as this green rectangle?

7 cm

12 cm

**b** Find the perimeter of each shape.

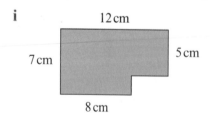

i  12 cm  7 cm  5 cm  8 cm

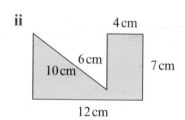

ii  4 cm  6 cm  10 cm  7 cm  12 cm

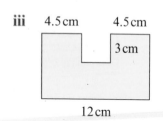

iii  4.5 cm  4.5 cm  3 cm  12 cm

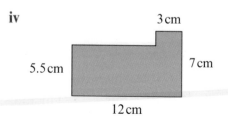

iv  3 cm  5.5 cm  7 cm  12 cm

**8** Peter is struggling to work out the perimeter of each shape. He thinks there are some lengths missing but Sally has already worked out the perimeters correctly. What answers did she get?

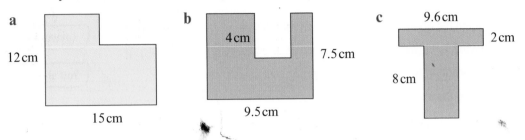

**a**  12 cm  15 cm

**b**  4 cm  7.5 cm  9.5 cm

**c**  9.6 cm  2 cm  8 cm

**9** The perimeter of each figure is 30 m. Calculate the values of *a*, *b* and *c*.

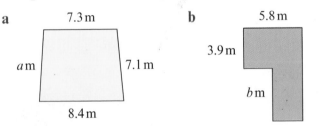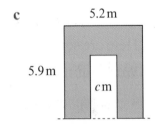

**a**  7.3 m  *a* m  7.1 m  8.4 m

**b**  5.8 m  3.9 m  *b* m

**c**  5.2 m  5.9 m  *c* m

**10** A logo is made from four grey triangles, two orange squares, two yellow squares and one blue rectangle. The perimeter of the logo is 51 cm. What is the length of the longest side of each triangle?

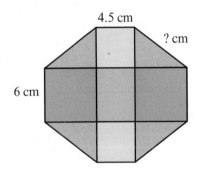

4.5 cm  ? cm  6 cm

**11** **a** Find the perimeter of the yellow triangle.

**b** Pupils design a badge using four of these triangles. Find the perimeter of the badge.

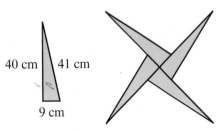

40 cm  41 cm  9 cm

**12** Find the perimeter of each shape. Explain your method.

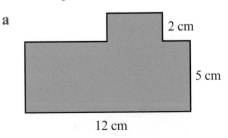

**a**  2 cm  5 cm  12 cm

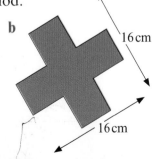

**b**  16 cm  16 cm

43

## Area

- Finding the areas of shapes based on rectangles
- Converting between square centimetres and square millimetres
- Converting between square centimetres and square metres
- Finding the area of a triangle
- Estimating the area of complex shapes

Keywords

You should know

explanation 1

**1** Here are some tile patterns. All of the tiles are squares of the same size.

Work out the number of tiles needed for each one.

a
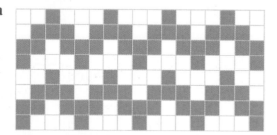

b
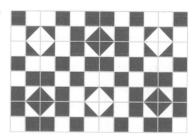

c
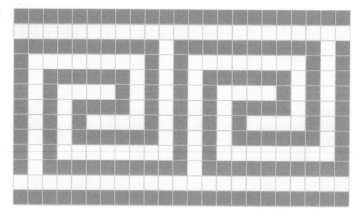

d
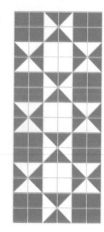

2 How many one centimetre square tiles would fit inside this rectangle?

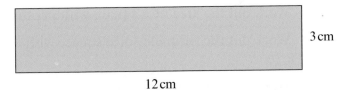

3 cm

12 cm

explanation 2

3 Work out the area of each of these rectangles.

a

3 cm

8 cm

b

14 m

10 m

c

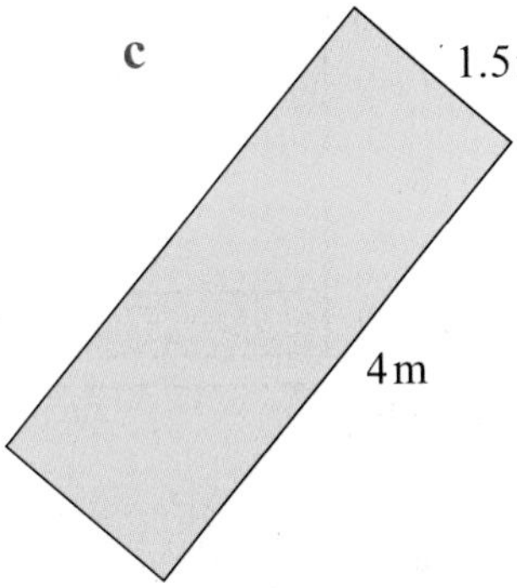

1.5 m

4 m

4 Find the area of each rectangle and explain what units you have used in each case.

Remember: 1 m = 100 cm
1 cm = 10 mm

a

10 cm

14.8 cm

b

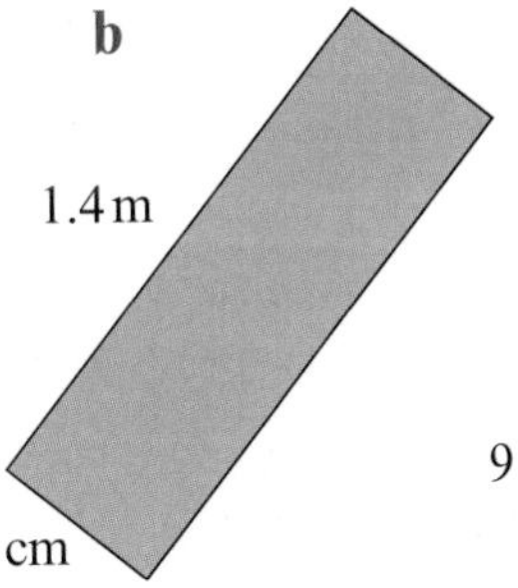

1.4 m

37.4 cm

c

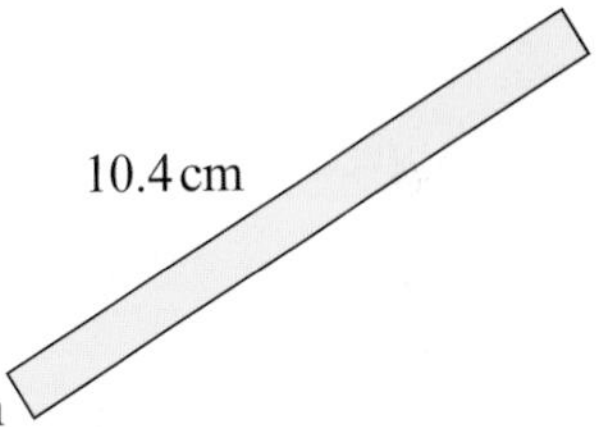

10.4 cm

9 mm

5 Work out the height of a rectangle which has a base of length 15 cm and an area of 120 cm².

6 Find the area of each of these squares.

a

17 mm

b

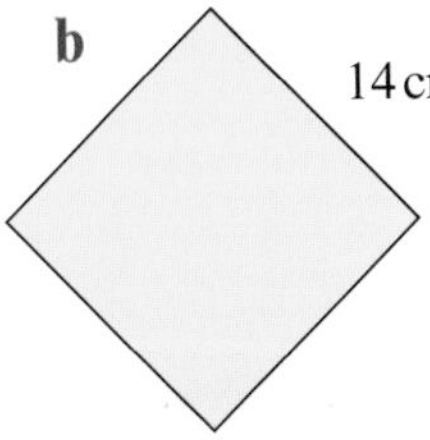

14 cm

c

8 m

**7 a** Work out the area of a square with perimeter 36 cm.

**b** Work out the perimeter of a square with area 121 m².

**8** Two flags are shown below. Find the area of the yellow rectangle and explain how this can help you find the area of the blue region on the second flag.

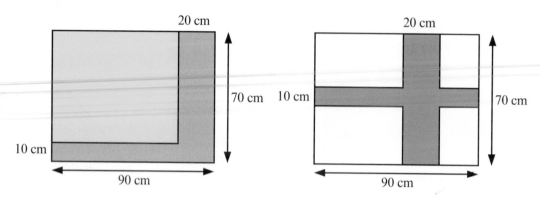

**9 a** Copy and complete the table showing how the area of a rectangle can change, even though its perimeter is fixed at 24 cm.

**b** What can you say about the shape when it has the largest area?

| Base (cm) | Height (cm) | Area (cm²) |
|-----------|-------------|------------|
| 11 | 1 | |
| 10 | | |
| 9 | | |
| 8 | | |
| 7 | | |
| 6 | | |

**c** A farmer has 80 m of fencing. What is the size and area of the largest pen she can make?

explanation 3

10  a  Use these diagrams to work out how many square millimetres make 1 cm$^2$.

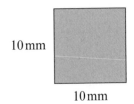

b  Copy and complete.

i  $200 \, mm^2 = \square \, cm^2$      ii  $50 \, mm^2 = \square \, cm^2$      iii  $146 \, mm^2 = \square \, cm^2$

iv  $0.8 \, cm^2 = \square \, mm^2$      v  $0.03 \, cm^2 = \square \, mm^2$      vi  $2.4 \, cm^2 = \square \, mm^2$

c  Use these diagrams to work out how many square centimetres make one square metre.

explanation 4

11  Copy and complete these area calculations.

a

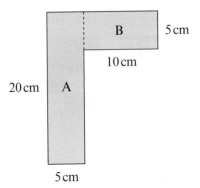

b

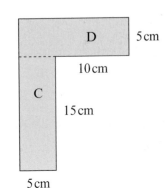

Area A = 5 cm  × 20 cm = $\square$ cm$^2$      Area C = 5 cm  × 15 cm = $\square$ cm$^2$

Area B = $\square$ cm × $\square$ cm = $\square$ cm$^2$      Area D = $\square$ cm × $\square$ cm = $\square$ cm$^2$

      Total area = $\square$ cm$^2$                      Total area = $\square$ cm$^2$

c  What does this question show about calculating the total area of a shape?

**12** Work out the area of each of these shapes.

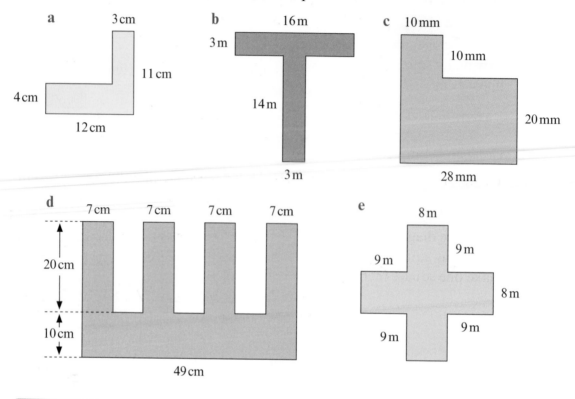

a   3 cm  11 cm  4 cm  12 cm

b   16 m  3 m  14 m  3 m

c   10 mm  10 mm  20 mm  28 mm

d   7 cm  7 cm  7 cm  7 cm  20 cm  10 cm  49 cm

e   8 m  9 m  9 m  8 m  9 m  9 m

explanation 5

**13** This tile pattern includes an area where there are no tiles.

How many tiles are used in the pattern?

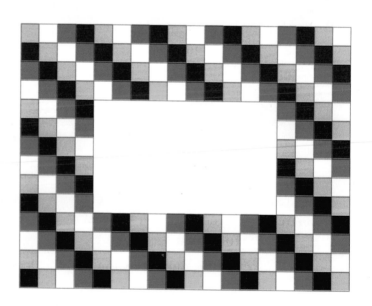

**14** Work out the coloured areas of these diagrams.

a

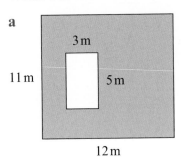

b

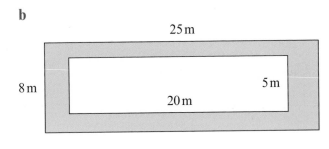

**15** Calculate the coloured areas of these diagrams in square millimetres.

a

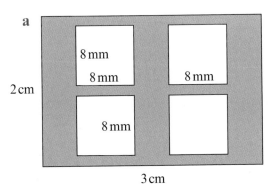

b

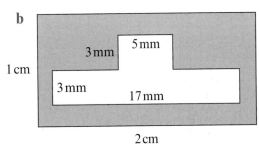

explanation 6a    explanation 6b    explanation 6c

**16** Find the area of each of these triangles.

a

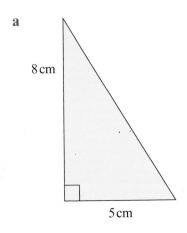

b

c

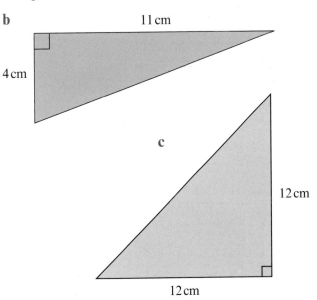

**17** Miguel is working out the area of the green shape by dividing it into rectangles and triangles.

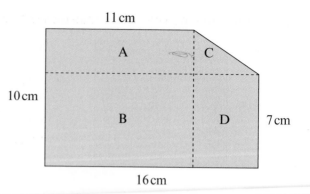

Area of rectangle A  = base × height
= 11 × 3
= 33 cm²

**a**  Use Miguel's method to work out the area of the shape.

**b**  Debbie draws a similar shape with every side twice as long as Miguel's. She uses red dotted lines to draw a rectangle 32 cm by 20 cm and then took the area of the corner triangle from the area of the rectangle. Use this method to find the area of the blue shape.

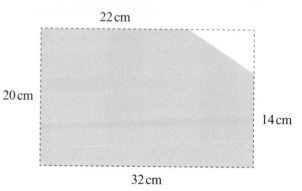

**c**  Is the area of Debbie's shape twice the area of Miguel's shape?

**18** Find the area of each of these shapes

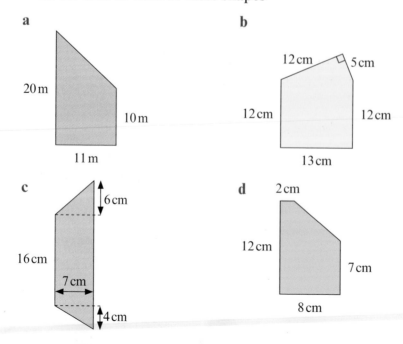

**19** Find the area of each of these triangles.

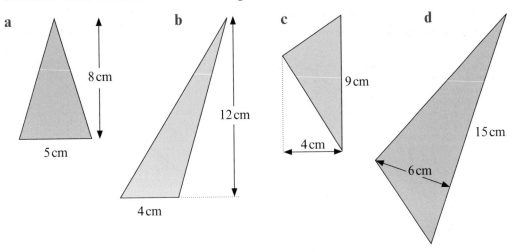

a

8 cm

5 cm

b

12 cm

4 cm

c

9 cm

4 cm

d

15 cm

6 cm

**20** Find the area of each of these shapes.

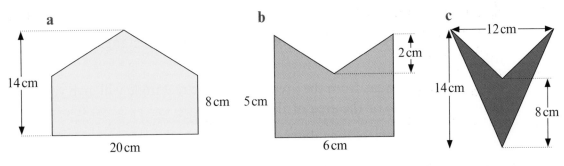

a

14 cm

20 cm

8 cm

b

5 cm

2 cm

6 cm

c

12 cm

14 cm

8 cm

explanation 7

**21** The diagram shows an outline map of the Isle of Man on a square grid. Each square of the grid has an area of 25 km².

Use the grid to estimate the area of the Isle of Man.

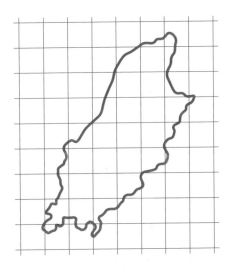

**22** Diagram 1 shows a map of Loch Ness with a rectangle drawn around it.

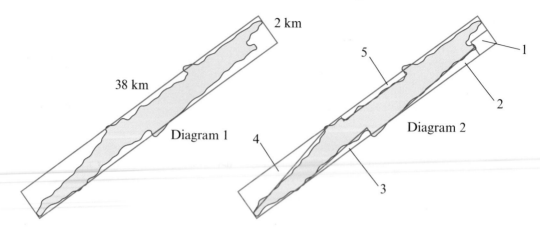

2 km

38 km

Diagram 1

Diagram 2

5

1

2

4

3

**a** Use diagram 1 to estimate the area of the loch.

**b** Do you think that your estimate is more or less than the true area? Explain.

**c** Diagram 2 shows the loch again, but with some extra rectangles and triangles marked.

Removing these areas from the area of the large rectangle will give you an improved estimate of the area of the loch.

**i** Copy and complete the table.

| Number | Shape | Base (km) | Height (km) | Area (km²) |
|--------|-------|-----------|-------------|------------|
| 1 | rectangle | 1.5 | 2 | |
| 2 | triangle | 0.4 | 10 | |
| 3 | triangle | 0.8 | 7.5 | |
| 4 | triangle | 1.5 | 12 | |
| 5 | rectangle | 10 | 0.4 | |
| | | | Total | |

**ii** What is your improved estimate of the area of Loch Ness?

# Order of operations

- Working out calculations involving more than one operation
- Working out calculations involving squares and square roots
- Working out calculations involving brackets

Keywords

You should know

explanation 1a    explanation 1b

**1** Work these out.

a  $50 \div 5 \div 5$

b  $200 \div 2 \times 10$

c  $3 \times 10 \div 10$

d  $16 \times 2 \div 4$

e  $40 \div 4 \times 7$

f  $27 - 11 + 30$

**2** Copy and complete these calculations.

a  $\square \times 3 \times 2 = 24$

b  $\square \div 2 \div 5 = 12$

c  $\square \times 100 \div 20 = 35$

d  $48 \div \square \times 3 = 36$

e  $427 - \square - 99 = 327$

f  $1000 \div \square \div 5 = 8$

explanation 2

**3** Work out these calculations.

a  $4 + 6 \times 3$

b  $24 - 3 \times 7$

c  $20 - 7 + 3 \times 4$

d  $11 - 21 \div 3$

e  $12 \div 4 + 36 \div 9$

f  $6 \times 8 - 4 \times 12$

g  $3 + 11 \times 2 - 9$

h  $5 \times 4 - 18 \div 6$

i  $4 + 7 \times 2 - 40 \div 5$

j  $1 + 5 \times 6 + 8$

k  $6 \times 4 + 3 \times 5$

l  $8 - 3 \div 2 + 5 \times 4$

**4** Copy and complete these calculations using the correct operations.

a  $5 \square 7 \times 2 = 19$

b  $21 \square 3 + 11 = 18$

c  $18 + 6 \square 2 = 21$

d  $12 \square 2 \square 4 \times 5 = 26$

e  $45 \square 15 \square 2 - 11 = 4$

f  $24 \square 8 \square 5 = 15$

explanation 3

**5** Work out these calculations.

a   $3 + 5^2$

b   $2 \times 3^2$

c   $4^2 + 5^2$

d   $100 - 7^2$

e   $12 - \sqrt{16}$

f   $\sqrt{25} + \sqrt{100}$

g   $26 - 2 \times \sqrt{81}$

h   $6^2 - 5 \times \sqrt{49}$

i   $8^2 + 3 \times 10^2$

**6** Work out these calculations.

a   $1 + 4 \times 3^2$

b   $2 \times 5^2 \div 10$

c   $7 \times 3 - 2 \times 4^2$

d   $5 \times 3^2 \times 2$

e   $2 + 20 \div 2^2$

f   $14 \div 2 + 6^2 \div 4$

**7** The six cards can be used to make many different calculations.

One calculation is $2^2 \times 4 - 10$. The answer is 6.

Use all six cards to make calculations with these answers.

a   an answer of 22

b   the lowest answer

c   the smallest positive answer

d   the highest answer

explanation 4

**8** Work out these calculations.

a   $17 - (21 - 10)$

b   $3 \times (6 + 5)$

c   $(10 - 3)^2$

d   $4 \times (2 + 6)^2$

e   $\sqrt{(9 + 5 \times 8)}$

f   $16 - 5 \times (31 - 28)$

g   $\sqrt{(3^2 + 4^2)}$

h   $42 \div (5^2 - 6 \times 3)$

i   $(9 + 11) \times (50 - 9 \times 5)$

**9** Rewrite these statements to make them correct. Use brackets.

a   $5 \times 4 + 3 = 35$

b   $44 - 26 - 3 + 8 = 7$

c   $98 + 10 \div 12 = 9$

d   $48 \div 16 - 4 = 4$

e   $7 + 24 \div 3 + 5 = 10$

f   $11 + 21 \div 7 + 9 = 2$

**10** The seven green cards can be used to make different calculations.

You can make (4 ÷ 2) + 18. The answer is 20.

Use all seven cards to make calculation
with these answers.

**a**  11                    **b**  5                    **c**  13

**d**  3                    **e**  6.5

**11** Copy these calculations and find the missing numbers.

**a**  (☐ + 4) ÷ 8 = 2        **b**  4 + (☐ − 8)² = 13        **c**  (☐ + 3) × 7 = 70

explanation 5a    explanation 5b

**12** Find the value of these calculations.

**a**  $\sqrt{5^2 + 24}$                    **b**  $5 \times \sqrt{36} - 10$                    **c**  $\dfrac{48}{1 + 3 \times 5}$

**d**  $\dfrac{21 + 14}{7}$                    **e**  $23 - \dfrac{15}{3}$                    **f**  $\dfrac{45}{\sqrt{21 + 3 \times 20}}$

**g**  $\dfrac{8^2 - 20}{11}$                    **h**  $\dfrac{72}{3 \times (21 - 3^2)}$                    **i**  $45 - \dfrac{10^2 - 8^2}{9}$

**13** Write each set of instructions as a calculation. You don't have to work it out.
The first one is done for you.

**a**  Subtract the value of 17 squared from 400 and find the positive square
root.

Answer: $\sqrt{400 - 17^2}$

**b**  Divide the sum of 57 and 96 by the sum of 38 and 53.

**c**  Add 67.2 to 19.9, multiply the answer by 8 and subtract from 1000.

**d**  Divide the positive square root of the sum of the squares of 11 and 15 by 28.

**e**  Square the sum of 4.9 and 7.38 and divide the answer by 9.

**f**  Subtract the difference between 17.9 and 83 from 100.

# Using a calculator (1)

- Using your calculator for complex calculations
- Using the calculator memory
- Checking calculator answers by estimation

Keywords

You should know

explanation 1

**1** Work these out without a calculator. Then check that you get the same answers when a calculator is used.

 a $7 + 5 \times 2$   b $25 - 3 \times 8$   c $14 + 7 - 3 \times 5$

**2** Use a calculator to work out these calculations.

 a $37.2 - 7 \times 4.9$   b $12.8 + 9.4 \times 8$   c $11.3 - 9.8 + 7.2 \times 6$

 d $67.8 - 35.7 \div 7$   e $46.2 \div 3 + 71.1 \div 9$   f $18.6 + 11 \times 9.2 - 45.3$

**3** Use the $x^2$ key on your calculator to find these values.

 a $3.9^2$   b $12.8^2$   c $6.72^2$

 d $50 - 6.8^2$   e $8.4^2 + 6.5^2$   f $21.6^2 - 19.9^2$

**4** Use the $x^2$ key on your calculator to find these values.

 a $3 \times 2.5^2 - 2.5 + 1$   b $3 + 2 \times 5 - 5^2$   c $2 \times 0.5^2 - 7 \times 0.5 - 1$

**5** Use the $\sqrt{\ }$ key on your calculator to find these values.

 a $\sqrt{70.56}$   b $\sqrt{151.29}$   c $\sqrt{376.36}$

 d $11.7 + \sqrt{210.25}$   e $\sqrt{353.44} - 7.69$   f $10 \times \sqrt{34.4569}$

explanation 2

**6** Use the bracket keys on your calculator to find these values.

 a $6.4 \times (12.8 - 7.95)$   b $(3.7 + 5.4)^2$   c $32 - 4.8 \times (7.6 - 1.9)$

 d $(18.6 + 19.7) \div 5$   e $29 \div (6.72 + 3.28)$   f $(2.3 + 6.9) \times (3.8 + 4.7)$

**7** Peter lists the keys that he presses to work out

$\dfrac{5.7 + 3.9}{5.7 - 3.9}$.

(5.7 + 3.9) ÷ (5.7 - 3.9)

a What answer did he get?

b List the keys you have to press and the answers for these.

i $\dfrac{6.3 - 4.8}{6.3 + 4.8}$   ii $\dfrac{8.4}{2.6 - 1.35}$   iii $\dfrac{2.1 + 3.2}{1 - 0.6 \times 0.4}$   iv $\dfrac{3.1^2 - 1.91^2}{0.005}$

c What should you do when the calculator answer contains many digits?

**8** Use your calculator and insert brackets where necessary to work these out.

a $\sqrt{73.95 + 4.7^2}$

b $\dfrac{83.2}{4.7 + 3 \times 2.7}$

c $\dfrac{\sqrt{300} - 4 \times 4.44}{7}$

d $\dfrac{89.94 + 41.92}{12.7 - 8.9}$

e $25.8 + \dfrac{179.01}{2.6 \times 4.5}$

f $11 \times \sqrt{1.5^2 + 3.6^2}$

g $\dfrac{44.5 + \sqrt{20.25}}{9.8}$

h $\dfrac{8.7^2 - 5.3^2}{8.7 - 5.3}$

i $\dfrac{16^2 + 9.409}{4.63 + 7.2^2}$

**9** Work these out and round your answers to the nearest whole number.

a $5.87 + 7.9 \times 6.3$

b $4.87^2$

c $\sqrt{11.92}$

d $450 - 9 \times (2.7 + 11.8)$

e $\sqrt{11^2 + 12^2}$

f $4 \times 2.35^2$

explanation 3

**10** Use the (−) or +/− key on your calculator to work out these calculations.

a $-3 + -10$

b $-7 - -6 + -19$

c $-8 \div -5$

d $20 - 2 \times -7.5$

e $(-6.2)^2$

f $(-8.8)^2 - (-2.1)^2$

**11** a Choose two negative numbers and use a calculator to multiply them together. Do this a few times and write down your answers. What do you notice?

b Find the square of a few negative numbers by using a calculator. Remember to use brackets. What do you notice?

c Why are brackets needed to square a negative number on a calculator?

explanation 4

**12**  A group of students returns from holiday with some American dollars. The bank will pay them £0.503 for each dollar. Put 0.503 into the calculator memory and use it to work out how much the students receive to the nearest penny for these amounts.

    **a**  $147          **b**  $28          **c**  $89

    **d**  $63          **e**  $185        **f**  $96

**13**  The price of petrol at a garage is 96.431p per litre. Put 96.431 in the calculator memory.

    **a**  Find the cost, to the nearest penny, of filling a car with these amounts.

        **i**  29.5 litres    **ii**  35.8 litres    **iii**  13.8 litres

    **b**  A man paid £33.75 for his petrol. How many litres of petrol did he buy?

explanation 5

**14**  Copy and complete the following statements to estimate the answers.

In each case, state whether the actual value is more or less than your estimate.

    **a**  $20.657 + 3.869 \approx 21 + \square = \square$        **b**  $9.8734 \times 14.91079 \approx 10 \times \square = \square$

    **c**  $8.19243^2 \approx \square^2 = \square$              **d**  $\sqrt{84.34821} \approx \sqrt{\square} = \square$

**15**  Some of these calculations have incorrect answers. Use estimation to find which are incorrect and work out the correct values with a calculator.

    **a**  $4.768 \times 9.976 = 87.565568$        **b**  $7.1489^2 = 51.10677121$

    **c**  $3127 + 4865 + 8076 + 2998 = 17\,366$    **d**  $\sqrt{47.987} = 7.1365874$

    **e**  $(5.738 + 10.279)^2 = 256.544289$    **f**  $129.7836 \div 25 = 5.191344$

    **g**  $\dfrac{96.8}{14.723 - 5.186} = 24.3734458$    **h**  $\sqrt{8.27^2 + 3.99^2} = 10.1743892$

# Fractions and decimals

- Expressing one quantity as a fraction of another
- Using equivalent fractions
- Changing between improper fractions and mixed numbers
- Writing fractions as decimals

Keywords

You should know

explanation 1

**1** Each of these shapes is divided into smaller parts of equal size.

**a** What fraction of each shape is coloured green?

i 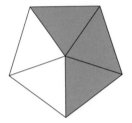  ii 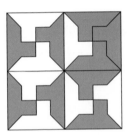  iii

**b** What fraction of each shape is not coloured green?

**2** Three triangles are shown below. Each triangle has one part out of three coloured red.
Does any shape have $\frac{1}{3}$ coloured red? Explain your answer in each case.

Triangle A  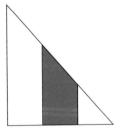  Triangle B  Triangle C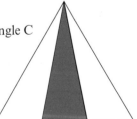

**3** Draw the diagram and shade in $\frac{3}{10}$ of it.

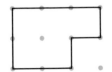

**4** For each of these pairs write the first quantity as a fraction of the second quantity.

    **a**   73 cm, 90 cm          **b**   17 mm, 30 mm          **c**   24 mm, 49 mm

    **d**   873 m, 2000 m        **e**   290 mm, 700 mm      **f**   0.3 cm, 100 cm

> **explanation 2**

**5** Find a pair of equivalent fractions to represent the coloured part of each diagram.

    **a**       **b**       **c**

**6** Copy and complete these equivalent fractions.

    **a** $\dfrac{2}{3} = \dfrac{10}{\square}$          **b** $\dfrac{4}{7} = \dfrac{\square}{21}$          **c** $\dfrac{3}{8} = \dfrac{12}{\square}$

    **d** $\dfrac{5}{6} = \dfrac{20}{\square}$          **e** $\dfrac{7}{10} = \dfrac{\square}{60}$          **f** $\dfrac{4}{9} = \dfrac{\square}{81}$

    **g** $\dfrac{4}{5} = \dfrac{8}{\square} = \dfrac{\square}{25}$      **h** $\dfrac{3}{10} = \dfrac{\square}{30} = \dfrac{27}{\square}$      **i** $\dfrac{5}{6} = \dfrac{35}{\square} = \dfrac{\square}{54}$

**7** A tube of sweets contains 50 sweets and 8 of them are coloured red.
What fraction are red? Gordon says $\dfrac{8}{50}$ and Susan says $\dfrac{4}{25}$ are red.
Who is right? Why?

**8** Copy and complete these equivalent fractions.

    **a** $\dfrac{21}{28} = \dfrac{3}{\square}$          **b** $\dfrac{35}{45} = \dfrac{\square}{9}$          **c** $\dfrac{50}{75} = \dfrac{2}{\square}$

    **d** $\dfrac{12}{30} = \dfrac{\square}{5}$          **e** $\dfrac{40}{48} = \dfrac{5}{\square}$          **f** $\dfrac{16}{36} = \dfrac{\square}{9}$

    **g** $\dfrac{44}{88} = \dfrac{22}{\square} = \dfrac{\square}{2}$      **h** $\dfrac{36}{48} = \dfrac{9}{\square} = \dfrac{\square}{4}$      **i** $\dfrac{60}{\square} = \dfrac{20}{30} = \dfrac{2}{\square}$

**9** For each diagram use the scale to write down what fraction of the bar is coloured green and what fraction is coloured yellow. Cancel each fraction to give the simplest answer.

a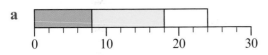

b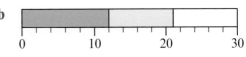

c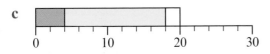

d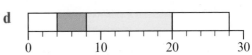

**10** The table shows how a class of pupils get to school.

|  | Walk | Bus | Car | Total |
|---|---|---|---|---|
| **Boys** | 6 | 8 | 4 | 18 |
| **Girls** | 4 | 6 | 2 | |
| **Total** | 10 | | | |

a   Copy and complete the table.

b   What fraction of boys travel by bus?

c   What fraction of pupils who walk are girls?

d   What fraction of the class travel by car?

**11** Write each of these fractions in their lowest terms.

a   $\dfrac{45}{90}$    b   $\dfrac{55}{77}$    c   $\dfrac{54}{72}$

d   $\dfrac{48}{60}$    e   $\dfrac{14}{112}$    f   $\dfrac{110}{132}$

g   $\dfrac{72}{240}$    h   $\dfrac{225}{250}$    i   $\dfrac{324}{396}$

j   $\dfrac{66}{72}$    k   $\dfrac{200}{560}$    l   $\dfrac{108}{396}$

**12** Write 108 as a fraction of 144 and cancel your answer as far as possible.

explanation 3a   explanation 3b

**13**  Use this fraction wall to compare fractions using  < or >.

a  $\dfrac{2}{7} \square \dfrac{1}{3}$     b  $\dfrac{3}{5} \square \dfrac{4}{7}$     c  $\dfrac{2}{3} \square \dfrac{7}{8}$

d  $\dfrac{3}{8} \square \dfrac{2}{5}$     e  $\dfrac{4}{5} \square \dfrac{6}{7}$     f  $\dfrac{5}{6} \square \dfrac{2}{3}$

**14**  Use the fraction wall to write these groups of fractions in order of size, smallest first.

a  $\dfrac{1}{2} \quad \dfrac{1}{3} \quad \dfrac{2}{5}$     b  $\dfrac{3}{5} \quad \dfrac{4}{7} \quad \dfrac{5}{8}$     c  $\dfrac{3}{4} \quad \dfrac{5}{6} \quad \dfrac{5}{7}$

d  $\dfrac{7}{8} \quad \dfrac{6}{7} \quad \dfrac{3}{4} \quad \dfrac{5}{6}$     e  $\dfrac{1}{2} \quad \dfrac{4}{7} \quad \dfrac{3}{8} \quad \dfrac{2}{5}$     f  $\dfrac{2}{3} \quad \dfrac{4}{7} \quad \dfrac{3}{5} \quad \dfrac{5}{8}$

**15**  Write the fractions in each group with common denominators. Then put the original fractions in order of size, starting with the smallest.

a  $\dfrac{5}{12} \quad \dfrac{9}{20}$     b  $\dfrac{7}{10} \quad \dfrac{11}{15} \quad \dfrac{2}{3}$     c  $\dfrac{3}{8} \quad \dfrac{1}{3} \quad \dfrac{5}{12}$

d  $\dfrac{9}{16} \quad \dfrac{13}{24} \quad \dfrac{5}{12}$     e  $\dfrac{8}{15} \quad \dfrac{1}{2} \quad \dfrac{2}{3} \quad \dfrac{3}{5}$     f  $\dfrac{25}{27} \quad \dfrac{17}{18} \quad \dfrac{8}{9}$

explanation 4

**16** Write these improper fractions as mixed numbers.

a $\dfrac{7}{3}$        b $\dfrac{11}{4}$        c $\dfrac{24}{5}$

d $\dfrac{31}{8}$        e $\dfrac{45}{11}$        f $\dfrac{99}{10}$

g $\dfrac{3}{2}$        h $\dfrac{8}{3}$        i $\dfrac{29}{8}$

j $\dfrac{11}{3}$        k $\dfrac{35}{12}$        l $\dfrac{93}{16}$

m $\dfrac{23}{4}$        n $\dfrac{65}{6}$        o $\dfrac{50}{7}$

p $\dfrac{43}{9}$        q $\dfrac{113}{10}$        r $\dfrac{127}{5}$

**17** Write these mixed numbers as improper fractions.

a $4\dfrac{2}{3}$        b $2\dfrac{1}{5}$        c $6\dfrac{3}{4}$

d $9\dfrac{1}{2}$        e $7\dfrac{4}{5}$        f $5\dfrac{8}{9}$

g $2\dfrac{3}{5}$        h $7\dfrac{1}{2}$        i $1\dfrac{2}{3}$

j $3\dfrac{4}{7}$        k $10\dfrac{4}{9}$        l $2\dfrac{3}{16}$

m $4\dfrac{3}{8}$        n $3\dfrac{2}{5}$        o $4\dfrac{1}{6}$

p $2\dfrac{6}{11}$        q $8\dfrac{3}{4}$        r $2\dfrac{5}{18}$

**18** Give your answers to these divisions as proper fractions in their lowest terms.

a $4 \div 6$        b $9 \div 12$        c $14 \div 20$

d $15 \div 18$        e $24 \div 30$        f $25 \div 75$

g $50 \div 75$        h $48 \div 60$        i $30 \div 42$

**19** Give your answers to these divisions as mixed numbers.

a $18 \div 5$        b $30 \div 4$        c $24 \div 10$

d $21 \div 14$        e $50 \div 8$        f $11 \div 6$

g $40 \div 32$        h $250 \div 150$        i $140 \div 60$

explanation 5

**20**  Write these decimals as fractions in their lowest terms.

    **a**  0.7             **b**  0.3             **c**  0.29

    **d**  0.97           **e**  0.5             **f**  0.25

    **g**  0.75           **h**  0.8             **i**  0.24

    **j**  0.35            **k**  0.6             **l**  0.55

    **m**  0.08          **n**  0.65          **o**  0.024

    **p**  0.145         **q**  0.336         **r**  0.070

**21 a**  Copy and complete.

      **i**  $\dfrac{1}{5}=\dfrac{\square}{10}$          **ii**  $\dfrac{2}{5}=\dfrac{\square}{10}$          **iii**  $\dfrac{7}{20}=\dfrac{\square}{100}$

      **iv**  $\dfrac{11}{25}=\dfrac{\square}{100}$      **v**  $\dfrac{9}{20}=\dfrac{\square}{100}$       **vi**  $\dfrac{3}{50}=\dfrac{\square}{100}$

      **vii**  $\dfrac{49}{50}=\dfrac{\square}{100}$      **viii**  $\dfrac{18}{75}=\dfrac{\square}{25}=\dfrac{\square}{100}$      **ix**  $\dfrac{24}{80}=\dfrac{\square}{20}=\dfrac{\square}{100}$

    **b**  Write each of the fractions in part **a** as a decimal.

**22**  Write each of these fractions as a decimal.

    **a**  $\dfrac{19}{20}$            **b**  $\dfrac{7}{25}$            **c**  $\dfrac{27}{60}$

    **d**  $\dfrac{126}{200}$          **e**  $\dfrac{29}{50}$           **f**  $\dfrac{3}{10}$

    **g**  $\dfrac{7}{20}$            **h**  $\dfrac{22}{40}$           **i**  $\dfrac{28}{80}$

**23**  Write these groups of numbers in order of size, smallest first.

    **a**  $\dfrac{3}{4}$     0.7      0.59      $\dfrac{1}{2}$

    **b**  $\dfrac{2}{3}$     0.62     0.575     $\dfrac{3}{5}$

    **c**  0.8    0.72     $\dfrac{7}{10}$      $\dfrac{15}{20}$

# Number N2.4

## Percentages

- Representing a percentage on a diagram
- Changing between fractions, decimals and percentages

Keywords

You should know

explanation 1a   explanation 1b   explanation 1c

**1** Answer the questions about each of the 100 squares shown below.

   **i**   What fraction of squares are coloured yellow?

   **ii**   What percentage of squares are coloured yellow?

   **iii**   What fraction of squares are not coloured yellow?

   **iv**   What percentage of squares are not coloured yellow?

**a** 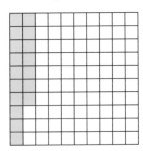  **b** 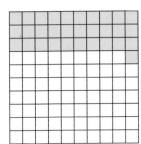  **c**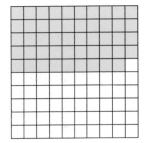

**2** Copy and complete.

   **a** $\dfrac{32}{100} = \square\%$

   **b** $\dfrac{44}{100} = \square\%$

   **c** $\dfrac{\square}{100} = 9\%$

   **d** $\dfrac{8}{10} = \dfrac{\square}{100} = \square\%$

   **e** $\dfrac{7}{20} = \dfrac{\square}{100} = \square\%$

   **f** $\dfrac{11}{25} = \dfrac{\square}{100} = \square\%$

   **g** $\dfrac{19}{50} = \dfrac{\square}{100} = \square\%$

   **h** $\dfrac{124}{200} = \dfrac{\square}{100} = \square\%$

   **i** $\dfrac{24}{300} = \dfrac{\square}{100} = \square\%$

   **j** $\dfrac{97}{100} = \square\%$

   **k** $\dfrac{8.4}{100} = \square\%$

   **l** $\dfrac{109}{100} = \square\%$

**3** What percentage of each diagram is not white?

a

b

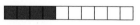

c

d

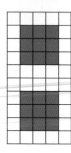

e

f

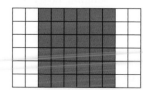

**4** Compare your answers for question **3 a**, **b** and **c** with those for **3 d**, **e** and **f**.

Explain any connection that you find.

**5 a** Here are two tiling patterns. What percentage of each pattern is coloured grey?

i

ii

**b** The two tiling patterns from part **a** are combined to make this pattern.

What percentage of this pattern is coloured grey?

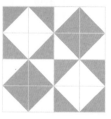

**6** If the percentage of boys in a school is 43%, what is the percentage of girls?

**7 a** What is $3 \times 33\frac{1}{3}$?

**b** Copy and complete.

$$\frac{1}{3} = \frac{\square}{100} = \square\%$$

**c** What is $\frac{2}{3}$ as a percentage?

**8 a** Copy and complete this table showing the results of a survey on hair colour.

| | Blonde | Black | Brown | Red | total |
|---|---|---|---|---|---|
| **Male** | 6 | 5 | 3 | 1 | 15 |
| **Female** | 8 | 3 | 10 | 4 | |
| **Total** | 14 | | | | |

**b** Isaac is working out what percentage of males do not have blonde hair. Is his answer right?

**c** What percentage of females have blonde hair?

**d** What percentage of people have blonde hair?

**e** What percentage of people with red hair are female?

**f** What percentage of males have black hair?

$$\text{NOT BLONDE} = \overset{\div 3}{\overbrace{\frac{9}{15}}} = \underset{\div 3}{\underbrace{\frac{3}{5}}} \overset{\times 20}{\overbrace{= \frac{60}{100}}} = 60\%$$

**9** Use equivalent fractions to write each of these fractions as a percentage.

  **a** $\frac{1}{2}$   **b** $\frac{1}{4}$   **c** $\frac{1}{5}$   **d** $\frac{1}{10}$   **e** $\frac{3}{4}$   **f** $\frac{4}{5}$

**10** Use equivalent fractions to write each of these fractions as a percentage.

  **a** $\frac{7}{25}$   **b** $\frac{11}{20}$   **c** $\frac{27}{50}$

  **d** $\frac{7}{10}$   **e** $\frac{162}{200}$   **f** $\frac{240}{400}$

  **g** $\frac{63}{75}$   **h** $\frac{45}{60}$   **i** $\frac{30}{125}$

**11** Write each of these percentages as a fraction and simplify where possible.

    **a** 60%          **b** 29%          **c** 80%

    **d** 45%          **e** 32%          **f** 70%

    **g** 7%           **h** 84%         **i** 12.5%

    **j** $33\frac{1}{3}$%       **k** 5%           **l** 2.5%

**12** Copy this diagram and shade 35% of it.

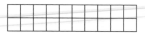

**13** Copy these diagrams and shade the percentage shown.

    **a**     **b** 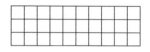    **c**

        36%                  40%                65%

    **d** 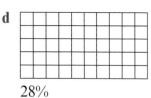    **e** 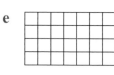    **f**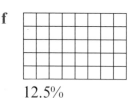

        28%                  75%               12.5%

explanation 2

**14** Bart is converting percentages directly to decimals. Write the following percentages as decimals.

    **a** 7%          **b** 6%

    **c** 7.2%        **d** 15%

    **e** 10%        **f** 51.4%

    **g** 96%        **h** 64.1%

    **i** 120%       **j** 139%

| | |
|---|---|
| 1% | = 0.01 |
| 2% | = 0.02 |
| ⋮ | |
| 8% | = 0.08 |
| 8.5% | = 0.085 |
| 9% | = 0.09 |
| ⋮ | |
| 29% | = 0.29 |
| ⋮ | |
| 83% | = 0.83 |

**15** Write these fractions and percentages as decimals.

a   $\dfrac{23}{100}$          b   $\dfrac{9}{100}$          c   47%

d   8%          e   50%          f   25%

g   86%          h   12.5%          i   17.5%

j   14.8%          k   3.5%          l   6.3%

**16** Write these decimals as percentages.

a   0.39          b   0.75          c   0.06

d   0.01          e   0.275          f   0.375

g   0.764          h   0.083          i   0.108

**17** Copy and complete this table.

|   | Fraction | Fraction with denominator 100 | Decimal | Percentage |
|---|---|---|---|---|
| a |  | $\dfrac{40}{100}$ | 0.4 |  |
| b | $\dfrac{7}{20}$ |  |  |  |
| c |  |  | 0.95 |  |
| d |  |  |  | 65% |
| e | $\dfrac{12}{25}$ |  |  |  |
| f |  |  |  | 72% |
| g | $\dfrac{11}{50}$ |  |  |  |
| h |  |  |  | 2% |

**18** Write these numbers in order of size, with the smallest number first.

66%          0.085          $\dfrac{7}{10}$          57.9%          $\dfrac{17}{20}$

# Working with data

- Finding the mean, median and mode of some data
- Choosing the best average to fit the data
- Finding the range of some data

Keywords

You should know

explanation 1

**1** Find the mode of each set of data.

**a** 7, 11, 10, 7, 9, 10, 7, 12, 9

**b** 18, 24, 21, 20, 23, 21, 18, 21, 22

**c** 5 m, 3 m, 4 m, 6 m, 3 m, 6 m, 8 m, 6 m, 5 m, 6 m, 8 m, 3 m, 5 m, 6 m, 7 m

**d** red, blue, yellow, blue, yellow, green, blue, red, blue, yellow, red, blue, white

**e** bus, car, car, walk, bus, car, bus, walk, walk, bus, car, cycle, car, walk, cycle

**2 a** The prices, in pence, of a litre of unleaded petrol at nine petrol stations are shown below. Find the modal price.

96.8     97.9     95.8     97.7     97.9     98.0     99.9     97.9     95.9

**b** The data below show the colour of each car waiting at one of the petrol stations. What is the modal colour?

Silver   Black   Silver   Red   Blue   Red   Silver   Green   Silver   Red   Blue

**3** There are 31 pupils in class 7N. The table shows the number of absences recorded for the class in one week.

| Number of absences | 0 | 1 | 2 | 3 | More than 3 |
|---|---|---|---|---|---|
| Number of pupils | 24 | 3 | 2 | 0 | |

   **a** How many pupils were absent on more than 3 occasions?

   **b** What is the modal number of absences?

**4** The results of two traffic surveys of 100 vehicles are shown in the tables below.

One survey involved early morning motorway traffic on a weekday.

The other survey involved vehicles approaching the Dover ferry on a Saturday.

**Table 1**

| Number of people in vehicle | 1 | 2 | 3 | 4 | More than 4 |
|---|---|---|---|---|---|
| Number of vehicles | 12 | 28 | 35 | | 11 |

**Table 2**

| Number of people in vehicle | 1 | 2 | 3 | 4 | More than 4 |
|---|---|---|---|---|---|
| Number of vehicles | | 21 | 15 | 5 | 3 |

   **a** Find the missing value in each table.

   **b** What is the mode for each survey?

   **c** Which survey do you think Table 1 represents? Explain how you made your decision.

**5** The data shows the mark out of 60 that pupils got in a French test.

52   49   57   51   52   51   49   55   57   53

55   52   49   57   56   49   54   57   51   56

   **a** This data has two modal values. Find them.

   **b** Is the mode a good measure of the average mark in this test?

> explanation 2

**6** The pulse rates of 60 pupils are shown below.

| | | | | | | | | | | | |
|---|---|---|---|---|---|---|---|---|---|---|---|
| 65 | 48 | 79 | 76 | 53 | 91 | 64 | 93 | 87 | 89 | 74 | 58 |
| 69 | 83 | 75 | 59 | 48 | 76 | 78 | 69 | 82 | 93 | 68 | 57 |
| 49 | 62 | 70 | 75 | 74 | 92 | 65 | 79 | 84 | 77 | 92 | 75 |
| 54 | 71 | 68 | 73 | 58 | 76 | 57 | 90 | 68 | 89 | 70 | 56 |
| 87 | 75 | 51 | 61 | 55 | 70 | 77 | 63 | 75 | 78 | 86 | 70 |

**a** Copy and complete the following frequency table.

| Pulse rate | 41–50 | 51–60 | 61–70 | 71–80 | 81–90 | 91–100 |
|---|---|---|---|---|---|---|
| Tally | | | | | | |
| Frequency | | | | | | |

**b** Which is the modal class?

**c** What percentage of the pupils are in the modal class?

**7 a** Find the mode of this set of numbers.

   18   15   20   16   15   20   18   16   20

**b** Do you think that the mode is typical of the data in this case? Explain your answer.

**c** Choose a value that you think is more typical of the data. Describe how you made your choice.

**8** These are the times in minutes that seven people waited at a doctor's surgery.

   1   5   6   7   10   11   15

**a** Explain why the mode is not a suitable average in this case.

**b** Choose a value that you think is typical of the data. Describe how you made your choice.

explanation 3a    explanation 3b

**9**

| 1.38 m | 1.41 m | 1.45 m | 1.49 m | 1.52 m |

What is the median height of this group of friends?

**10** Jim is finding the median shoe size for the boys in his class. He writes down
each shoe size and finds the middle one.

$7, 6, 9, 8, 7\frac{1}{2}, 10, 9, 7, 10, 8, 9\frac{1}{2}, 10$

MEDIAN SHOE SIZE FOR BOYS = $9\frac{1}{2}$

**a**  Why is Jim's calculation wrong?

**b**  Work out the correct median shoe size.

**c**  Find the modal shoe size.

**d**  Which average best describes this data?

**e**  Find the median shoe size for the girls.

GIRLS' SHOE SIZE

$6, 4, 7, 8, 4, 5, 5\frac{1}{2}, 8, 6, 4, 5, 8, 5$

**11** Find the median of each set of numbers.

> Remember to put the data in order of size first.

    **a**  32  37  28  31  33  29  33  37  32

    **b**  24  19  25  23  25  20  26  19  27  23  24

    **c**  1.6  1.4  1.2  0.9  1.3  1.2  1.4  1.5  1.3  1.2  1.0  0.9  1.1

    **d**  53  47  55  48  59  56  49  50  47  54

    **e**  2.5  2  2.7  2.7  2.9  2.5  2.6  2.8  2.5  2.78

**12** One class took part in a survey to find out how much time they spent on homework each week. The results are shown in the bar charts below.

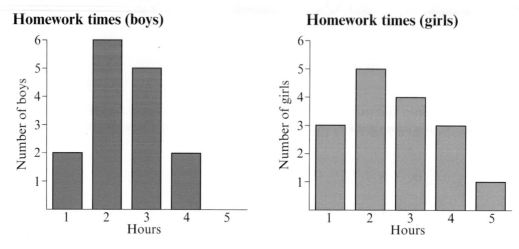

    **a**  Use the boys' chart to list their times in order.

    **b**  Find the median time that the boys spent on homework.

    **c**  Use the girls' chart to list their times in order.

    **d**  Find the median time that the girls spent on homework.

**13** Each member of a class brought a small bag of chocolate buttons and counted them. This table shows their results.

| Number of chocolate buttons | 26 | 27 | 28 | 29 | 30 | 31 |
|---|---|---|---|---|---|---|
| Number of bags | 3 | 4 | 6 | 8 | 2 | 1 |

    **a**  How many students are in the class?

    **b**  Find the median number of chocolate buttons in a bag.

    **c**  The teacher has a small bag of buttons. How many buttons do you expect to be in it?

**14** The data shows the price, in pence, of a litre of unleaded petrol at service stations along the M1. Find the median price of a litre of unleaded petrol.

95.1   94.5   98.4   96.5   96.8   94.5   94.0   98.5   96.4   96.5

**15 a** Write down the value of the median for this set of numbers.

3   6   9   10   24   48   96

**b** Do you think that the median is typical of the data in this case? Explain your answer.

**c** What happens to the median if the 48 is replaced with 76?

**d** Explain why the mode cannot be used here.

explanation 4a    explanation 4b

**16** The picture shows the weight of eight athletes.

49 kg        52 kg        58 kg

70 kg        76 kg        73 kg        70 kg        120 kg

**a** Find the mean weight of all eight athletes.

**b** Find the mean weight of the three female athletes.

**c** Find the mean weight of the five male athletes.

**d** Find the median weight of the five male athletes.

**e** Which is the best measure of average weight for the male athletes? Give a reason.

**17** Six girls and seven boys in one class had their heights measured in metres.

Girls: 1.48   1.56   1.62   1.45   1.49   1.58

Boys: 1.59   1.60   1.44   1.45   1.48   1.55   1.46

**a** Find the mean height of the girls and the mean height for the boys.

**b** Comment on the height of girls and boys in the class.

**18** The mean of 10 numbers is 2.76. What do the numbers add up to?

**19** The mean of the numbers 3.8  2.7  ☐  5.1 and 5.3  is 4.
What is the value of the missing number?

**20 a** The three sides of this triangle have a mean
length of 10 cm. Find the length of side AC.

**b** Write down five different numbers that have
a median of 7 but have a mean of 6.

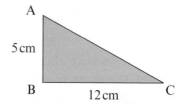

**21** Use a calculator to find the mean of each of these sets of data.
Where necessary, round your answers to one decimal place.

**a** 1   0   1   1   2   0   2   5

**b** 14   12   17   21   18   19   13   20   16   15   18

**c** 0.8 cm   0.3 cm   0.0 cm   0.5 cm   0.0 cm   0.0 cm   0.4 cm

**d** 7.8 kg   4.3 kg   6.1 kg   7.2 kg   8.7 kg   9.8 kg   8.5 kg   6.7 kg

**22** The mean of seven numbers is 12.8.

One of the numbers is removed. Find the value of this number if

**a** the mean is reduced to 11.7

**b** the mean is unchanged

**c** the mean increases to 12.9

explanation 5

**23** The youth club football team played 12 matches last season.

The table shows the number of goals that they scored.

| Goals scored per match | Number of matches | G × N |
|---|---|---|
| 0 | 1 | |
| 1 | 4 | |
| 2 | 3 | 6 |
| 3 | 2 | |
| 4 | 2 | |
| | Total = | Total = |

**a** Copy the table and fill in the missing values.

**b** Copy and complete the following statement to work out the mean number of goals per match.

Mean number of goals per match $= \dfrac{\text{Total number of ...}}{\text{Total number of ...}} = \dfrac{\square}{\square} = \square$

**24** Tickets for a theatre performance of *The Lion King* were sold at three prices.

The table shows the number of tickets sold at each price for one performance.

| Ticket price | Number of tickets sold | T × N |
|---|---|---|
| £28.50 | 396 | |
| £38.50 | 180 | |
| £48.50 | 164 | |
| | Total = | Total = |

**a** Copy the table and use a calculator to fill in the missing values.

**b** Copy and complete the following statement to work out the mean price per ticket to the nearest penny.

Mean price per ticket $= \dfrac{\text{Total cost of ...}}{\text{Total number of ...}} = \dfrac{\square}{\square} = \square$

**25** Mrs Brown keeps a record of the number of merit slips awarded to her pupils for good work. The table shows the number of merits awarded in one day.

| Merit slips awarded | Number of pupils | M × N |
|---|---|---|
| 0 | 6 | |
| 1 | 4 | |
| 2 | 10 | |
| 3 | 7 | |
| 4 | 2 | |
| | Total = | Total = |

a   Copy and complete the table. How many pupils are there in the class?

b   How many merit slips were awarded on this day?

c   Use a calculator to work out the mean number of merit slips per pupil to one decimal place.

d   On the same day last week, the mean was 1.6 to one decimal place. Has her class improved?

e   What if Mrs Brown calculated the means to the nearest whole number?

**26** 31 pupils are doing a project on wine gums. Each pupil brings a 200 g bag and counts the number of wine gums. The results are put in a table.

| Number of wine gums | Frequency | Total ... × ... |
|---|---|---|
| 49 | | |
| 50 | 10 | |
| 51 | 8 | |
| 52 | 6 | |
| 53 | 4 | |
| | Total = | Total = |

a   How many bags contained 49 wine gums?

b   Copy and complete the table.

c   Use a calculator to work out the mean number of wine gums in a bag, to one decimal place.

27  Use the information in the table to calculate the mean number of cars per family, correct to one decimal place.

| Number of cars | 0 | 1 | 2 | 3 | 4 |
|---|---|---|---|---|---|
| Number of families | 3 | 9 | 10 | 6 | 4 |

28  These are the hourly rates of pay of seven workers at a small company.

£6.80    £7.30    £6.20    £6.60    £6.20    £30.00    £6.90

a   Work out the mean hourly rate.

b   Do you think that the mean is a good average to use here? Explain your answer.

c   Find the median and the mode. Which type of average is most typical of the data?

explanation 6

29  Find the range of each set of data below.

a   24    32    31    19    21    25    20    29

b   4.7    4.8    3.6    5.1    4.7    3.8    5.4

c   9 cm    11 cm    6 cm    12 cm    14 cm    13 cm    10 cm

d   28.4 m²    27.6 m²    24.9 m²    26.7 m²    29.9 m²

30  The tallest person in Luke's class has a height of 1.6 m.

The range of the heights is 0.18 m.

What is the height of the shortest person in Luke's class?

31  The range of these five numbers is 5.4.

11.3    ☐    12.7    9.1    13.6

What are the two possible values of the missing number?

**32**  The mode of these seven numbers is 9.2. What is their range?

9.7    9.8    9.2    ☐    9.8    9.6    9.2

> First use the information about the mode to work out what the missing number is.

**33**  The range of these five numbers is 11 and their median is 124.

124    132    ☐    123    125

What is the missing number?

**34**  Write down four numbers that have a range of 2 and a mean, median and mode of 10.

**35**  **a**  Write down five numbers with a range of 0.5 and a median of 16.

   **b**  Copy and complete each statement below using the words in one of these boxes.

   **i**  If the range of a set of numbers is small then ...

   **ii**  If the range of a set of numbers is large then ...

> ...all of the numbers must be far apart.

> ...all of the numbers must be close together.

> ...not all of the numbers can be close together.

**36**  Pupils in one class recorded how long they can hold their breath in seconds.

Boys:    59    55    44    60    53    43    30    45    40    53

Girls:    44    35    61    23    56    47    36    26    52    35    30    27

   **a**  Find the mean, median and range of the boys' data.

   **b**  Find the mean, median and range of the girls' data.

   **c**  Put these statistics in a table and use them to compare the two sets of data.

# Representing data

- Interpreting various types of chart used in statistics
- Drawing a compound bar chart
- Drawing a frequency diagram for grouped data
- Drawing a pie chart

Keywords

You should know

explanation 1

**1** The pictogram shows how many people attended the school play.

**a** How many people attended the play on the following days?

   **i** Monday           **ii** Thursday

**b** Which day was the most popular?

**c** What is the range of the attendance figures?

**d** How many people went to the play altogether?

2   Internet search engines handle a huge number of enquiries every day.

The bar-line graph shows some of the most popular enquiries on one particular day.

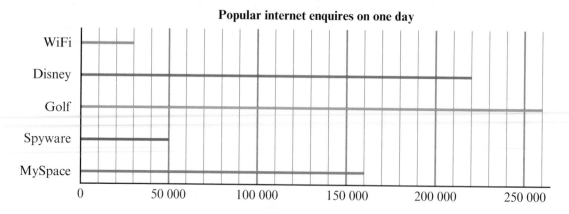

**Popular internet enquires on one day**

a   How many enquires were there for Disney?

b   Which enquiry was the mode?

c   What is the total number of enquiries for the items shown?

3   The table below shows the highest speeds reached by some rides at Alton Towers. Draw a bar-line graph to show this information.

| Ride | Speed (mph) |
| --- | --- |
| Air | 46 |
| Beastie | 9 |
| Corkscrew | 40 |
| Nemesis | 50 |
| Oblivion | 68 |
| Rita – Queen of speed | 61 |
| Runaway train | 22 |

explanation 2a    explanation 2b

**4**  100 girls in primary schools and 100 girls in secondary schools were asked to name their favourite subject. The following bar chart shows the results.

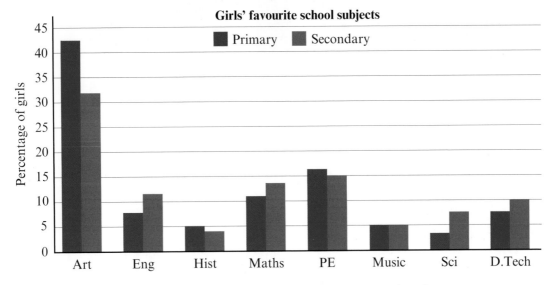

Girls' favourite school subjects

a   Which subjects lost popularity from primary to secondary?

b   Which subject maintained the same level of popularity?

c   List the subjects in order of popularity at primary level.

d   List the subjects in order of popularity at secondary level.

e   Which subject showed the greatest increase in popularity from primary to secondary?

**5**  A group of pupils was asked about things that they might do at some point in the future. The table below shows their responses.

Draw a bar chart to represent this data.

| To do | Boys % | Girls % |
| --- | --- | --- |
| Learn to drive | 100 | 90 |
| Go to university | 33 | 40 |
| Get married | 74 | 92 |
| Bungee jump | 44 | 55 |
| Run a marathon | 38 | 40 |

**6** This compound bar chart shows the results of a survey about different types of mobile phone.

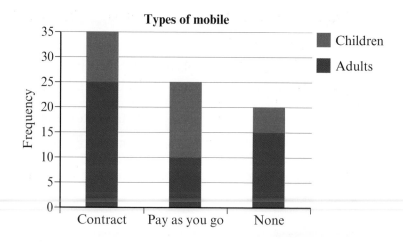

**a** How many children have a pay as you go phone?

**b** How many children took part in the survey?

**c** What is the modal type of phone for adults?

**d** What percentage of adults have a pay as you go phone?

**7** Draw a compound bar chart like the one in question **6** to show what devices people use to listen to music.

|  | MP3 player | Phone | Radio | CD player |
|---|---|---|---|---|
| **Girls** | 6 | 8 | 10 | 2 |
| **Boys** | 8 | 10 | 6 | 4 |

Use the data shown in this table.

**8** This compound bar chart shows how pupils get to school.

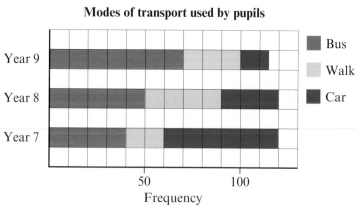

**a** How many pupils are in Year 9?

**b** What type of transport seems to decline as pupils get older?

**c** How many Year 8 pupils walk to school?

**d** What fraction of pupils in Year 8 walk to school?

**e** How many pupils come to school by car?

**9** Draw a compound bar chart to illustrate how pupils travel to school.

Use the data in this table.

|  | Bus | Walk | Car |
|---|---|---|---|
| **Boys** | 65 | 35 | 5 |
| **Girls** | 60 | 45 | 10 |

**10** This compound bar chart shows the music preferences of 200 pupils.

Music preferences of 200 pupils

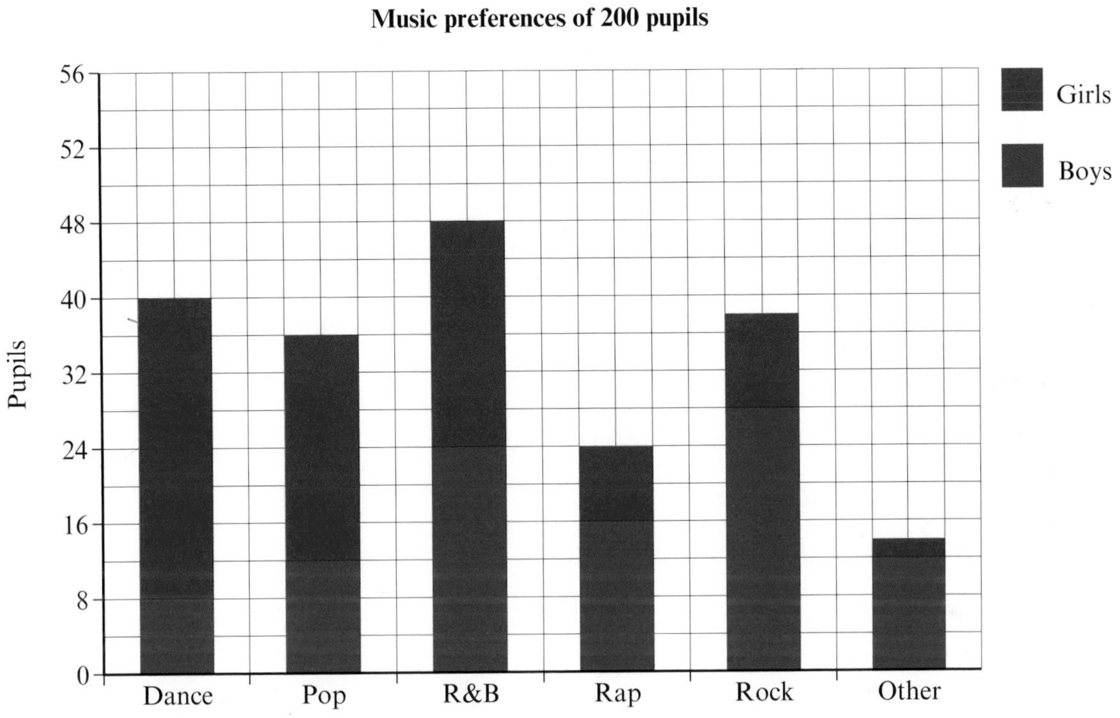

a   Overall, which type of music is the most popular?

b   Which type of music is most popular with boys?

c   Which type of music do girls like the most?

d   What percentage of girls prefer rock music?

e   What percentage of boys like R&B?

f   What percentage of girls like dance music?

explanation 3a explanation 3b

**11**  A prize was offered at a school fair for the best estimate of the number of sweets in a large jar. The estimates were:

| | | | | | | | |
|---|---|---|---|---|---|---|---|
| 147 | 138 | 124 | 150 | 97 | 134 | 110 | 137 |
| 82 | 115 | 142 | 163 | 158 | 133 | 117 | 155 |
| 136 | 149 | 112 | 160 | 98 | 125 | 158 | 142 |
| 140 | 156 | 128 | 167 | 144 | 131 | 138 | 150 |
| 129 | 131 | 146 | 140 | 149 | 98 | 111 | 146 |
| 139 | 140 | 150 | 109 | 167 | 130 | 135 | 152 |

**a**  Copy and complete the table using equal-sized class intervals.

| Estimate | 80–99 | 100–119 | | | |
|---|---|---|---|---|---|
| Tally | | | | | |
| Frequency | | | | | |

**b**  Draw a frequency diagram to represent the data.

**c**  What is the modal class?

**d**  What is the range of the estimates?

**e**  How many estimates were less than 140?

**12**  The table shows the number of Christmas raffle tickets sold by members of a class.

| Number of tickets sold | 1–5 | 6–10 | 11–15 | 16–20 | 21–25 | 26–30 |
|---|---|---|---|---|---|---|
| Frequency | 5 | 11 | 6 | 3 | 1 | 2 |

**a**  Draw a frequency diagram to represent the data.

**b**  What is the modal class?

**c**  Explain why the range cannot be found exactly.

**d**  There are 30 pupils in the class. How many didn't sell any tickets?

**e**  How many pupils sold more than 15 tickets? What percentage of the class is this?

**13** Earthworms are known to improve the quality of soil. The number of earthworms present in an area gives one measure of the quality of the soil.

The table shows how the number of worms varied in an area of pasture.

| Worms/m² | 100–199 | 200–299 | 300–399 | 400–499 | 500–599 |
|---|---|---|---|---|---|
| Frequency | 9 | 13 | 19 | 12 | 7 |

**a** Draw a frequency diagram to represent the data.

**b** What is the modal class?

**c** Which class contains the median?

**d** What percentage of the sample area had less than 200 worms per square metre?

explanation 4a     explanation 4b

**14** This pie chart shows the reading preferences of pupils in one year.

**a** What percentage of pupils chose romance?

**b** What was the modal choice?

**c** If 26 pupils chose fantasy, how many chose crime?

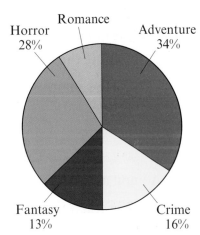

**Favourite books**

**15** This pie chart shows the mix of boys and girls who joined an after-school dance class.

**a** What percentage of the class were boys?

**b** If there were 27 girls in the class, how many pupils attended altogether?

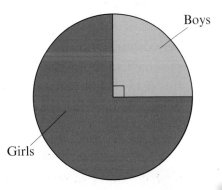

**Dance class members**

**16** Equal numbers of boys and girls were asked how many cans of drink they had drunk in the last two days. These pie charts show the results.

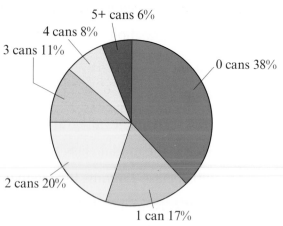

Cans drunk by boys

5+ cans 6%
4 cans 8%
3 cans 11%
0 cans 38%
2 cans 20%
1 can 17%

**a** Did more boys or girls drink 1 can in the last two days?

**b** Overall, did boys or girls drink the most cans?

**c** What is the modal number of cans drunk?

**d** 32 girls drank 2 cans in the last two days.

    **i** How many boys drank 2 cans?

    **ii** How many girls drank less than 2 cans?

    **iii** How many boys drank more than 3 cans?

    **iv** How many pupils took part?

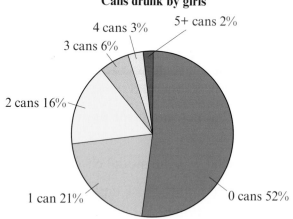

Cans drunk by girls

4 cans 3%  5+ cans 2%
3 cans 6%
2 cans 16%
0 cans 52%
1 can 21%

**17** A pupil achieved two A*s, three As, four Bs and one C in her examinations.

    **a** What fraction of the pupil's grades were Cs?

    **b** Draw a pie chart to illustrate her results.

**18** This table shows the results of a survey of eye colour. Draw a pie chart to represent this data. What percentage of people have hazel eyes?

| Eye Colour | Blue | Brown | Hazel | Green |
|---|---|---|---|---|
| Frequency | 10 | 13 | 3 | 4 |

**19** The pie chart shows the types of transport used
    by a group of England supporters to go to an
    away match.

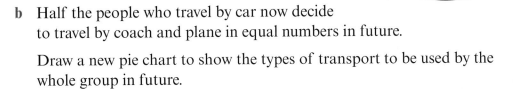

   **a**  **i**   What percentage travelled by car?

   **ii**   What percentage travelled by train?

   **iii**   If 86 travelled by coach, how many were
          in the group altogether?

   **b**  Half the people who travel by car now decide
        to travel by coach and plane in equal numbers in future.

   Draw a new pie chart to show the types of transport to be used by the
   whole group in future.

**20** In a class, $\frac{1}{3}$ of the pupils have a pet dog, $\frac{1}{4}$ have a cat, $\frac{1}{6}$ have fish and the rest
    do not have a pet. Draw a pie chart to illustrate this information.

explanation 5

**21** In 1982 the California Condor was on the brink of extinction. Between 1982
    and 1987 the remaining 27 birds were captured. The line graph tells the story
    between 1987 and 2007.

   **a**  In 1992 some birds were
        re-introduced to the wild.
        How many?

   **b**  What was the total
        population of California
        Condors in 1997?

   **c**  Explain the dip in the
        captive population shown
        between 2002 and 2007.

   **d**  What was the total
        population in 2007?

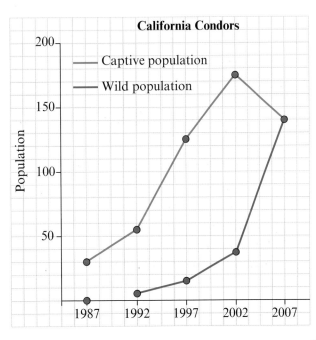

# Chance and probability

- Describing situations involving chance
- Identifying the possible outcomes for a situation
- Recognising when the outcomes are equally likely
- Calculating the probability of an event for equally likely outcomes

Keywords

You should know

explanation 1

**1** The diagram below shows a scale ranging from impossible to certain.

The letters **a**, **b**, **c** and **d** are positioned on this scale to match these labels.

| likely | unlikely | very likely | very unlikely |
|---|---|---|---|

Match up the letters and labels.

```
        a              b                    c        d
   ┌──────────────────────────────────────────────────────┐
   Impossible           Even chance                  Certain
```

**2** Which of the following labels best describes each event below?

impossible  very unlikely  unlikely  even chance  likely  very likely  certain

**a** You correctly guess the answer to a multiple choice question with 3 options.

**b** The winner of a television phone-in competition is a woman.

**c** You score more than 2 when you roll an ordinary dice.

**d** A stone thrown up into clear air will fall back down.

**e** One day, you will win the jackpot in the lottery.

**f** A monkey will spell out I LUV MATHS when playing with a keyboard.

**g** A world record will be broken at the next Olympics.

**h** You score 7 when you roll an ordinary dice.

**3** Arrange these outcomes in order from the least likely to the most likely.

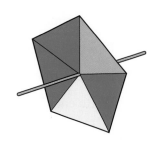

   **A** This spinner lands on blue.

   **B** A coin lands heads up.

   **C** This spinner lands on green.

   **D** You score 3 when you roll an ordinary dice.

**4** Say whether the chance of each of these events happening is *better than even* or *less than even*.

   **a** You correctly guess a person's favourite colour.

   **b** A learner driver passes the driving test first time.

   **c** At least one goal is scored in a selected football match.

   **d** The next person to enter the room is right-handed.

**Around 43% of people pass their driving test first time.**

( explanation 2 )

**5** At the start of his mind-reading act, Alfonso turns his back on the audience and throws a teddy bear over his shoulder. The person who catches the teddy bear is then invited onto the stage to take part in the act.

   **a** Why doesn't Alfonso just ask for a volunteer?

   **b** Why doesn't he face the audience to throw the teddy bear?

   **c** Do you think that selecting a person this way will give Alfonso any unfair advantage?

**6** Here are some of the ways of selecting one person from a group of people.

  **A** Pick the tallest.

  **B** Pick the one whose surname is first alphabetically.

  **C** Write each name on a piece of paper and choose one without looking.

  **D** Pick the one that you like the most.

  **a** Which one of these is the only way to select a person at random?

  **b** What precaution would you take to make sure that the selection was fair?

**7** An ordinary dice is rolled. List the outcomes for each of these events.

  **a** An odd number is scored.

  **b** A prime number is scored.

  **c** The score is less than 5.

  **d** The score is not less than 5.

  **e** At least 2 is scored.

**8** One of these six coloured digit cards is selected at random.

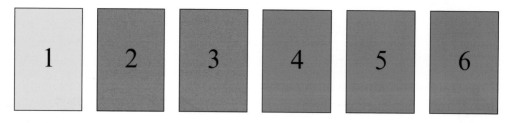

  Write down the number of possible outcomes for these events.

  **a** The number on the card is at least 4.

  **b** The card is blue.

  **c** The card is not yellow.

  **d** The card is blue and the number is even.

**9**   Tarek is making a list of all the possible outcomes when three coins are flipped.

There are eight possible outcomes. Complete his list.

HHH

HHT

HTH

.............

.............

.............

.............

.............

explanation 3

**10**  **a**  How many possible outcomes are there for a single spin of this spinner?

   **b**  How many of these outcomes are green?

   **c**  Find the probability that the spinner lands on

   **i**   green

   **ii**  blue

   **iii** any number apart from 4

   **iv**  a blue odd number

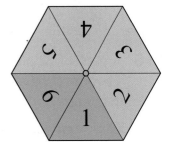

**11**  Find the probability that this spinner lands on

   **a**  red

   **b**  purple

   **c**  either red or purple

   **d**  any colour apart from red

**12**  **a**  What is the probability of an event that is certain to happen?

   **b**  What is the probability of an event that cannot happen?

**13**  Copy this probability scale and fill in the missing labels.

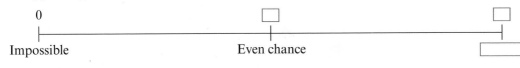

**14** Aisha rolls a fair ordinary dice. Find the probability that she scores

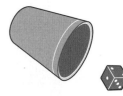

    **a**   a prime number

    **b**   a number greater than 4

    **c**   a number less than 7

    **d**   a number greater than 6

**15 a**   Describe the contents of a pack of
       52 playing cards.

    **b**   If one card is chosen at random,
       find the probability that it is

       **i**   a king       **ii**   a spade

      **iii**   a red card       **iv**   a red ace

**16** A pack of 52 playing cards is shuffled and the first five cards are set apart. They are the 2 of clubs, 3 of spades, 3 of hearts, 9 of spades and Queen of diamonds.

These cards are mixed up and placed face down. The next card from the pack is turned over; it is the 7 of clubs.

One of the five cards is now chosen at random. Find the probability that it is

    **a**   higher than the 7 of clubs       **b**   lower than the 7 of clubs

    **c**   the same suit as the 7 of clubs       **d**   the same colour as the 7 of clubs

**17** Repeat question **16** if the 7 of clubs is replaced by the Queen of hearts.

**18** This spinner has three possible outcomes.

Simon says that one outcome out of three is yellow, so the probability that the spinner lands on yellow is $\frac{1}{3}$.

Do you think that Simon is right? Explain your answer.

**19** A bag contains three red counters and two blue counters. The counters are identical apart from their colour. One counter is selected at random.

a   Write the probability that the counter is red as

   i   a fraction       ii   a decimal       iii   a percentage

b   Write the probability that the counter is either red or blue as a percentage.

c   What is the probability that the counter is green?

**20** Copy and complete this table, then comment on your answers.

| Event | P(event happens) | P(event doesn't happen) |
|---|---|---|
| You score a two when you roll a fair dice. | | |
| You choose a heart from a pack of cards. | | |
| You get a tail when you flip a coin. | | |
| It will rain today. | 0.65 | |
| You score double six when you roll two dice. | | |
| It will snow in December. | 48% | |

P(event happens) means 'the probability that the event happens'.

**21** The probability that a bus is early is 10% and the probability that it is late is 30%.

What is the probability that it is on time?

**22** This bar chart shows the shoe sizes of pupils in one class.

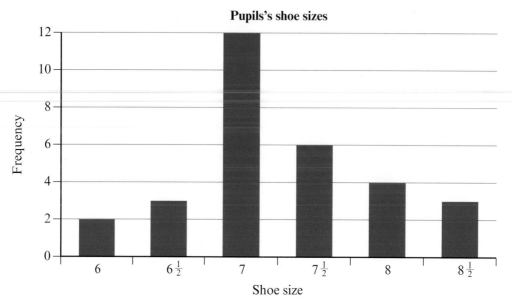

One pupil is chosen at random.

Find the probability that the chosen pupil takes

**a** size 6

**b** a half size (give your answer as a percentage)

**c** at least a size 7

> A half size means one that is not a whole number. For example, $6\frac{1}{2}$ or $7\frac{1}{2}$.

**23** Sally is making a list of all the possible outcomes when two coins are flipped.

H H     H T     …………

Complete her list.

Find the probability of getting two tails.

# Formulae

- Using a formula
- Simplifying expressions in algebra
- Building and simplifying a formula

Keywords

You should know

explanation 1a  explanation 1b

**1** Work these out.

a  $-1 - 4 + 7 - 10$    b  $5 - (-6) + 2 - (+12)$    c  $4 - 12 \div 2$

d  $2 + 3 \times 4$    e  $6 - 2 \times 9$    f  $5(2 + 6)$

g  $3 \times 5 + 6 \times 4$    h  $7 + 6 \div 2$    i  $(7 - 10) \div 2$

**2** $x = 5$. Find the value of each expression.

a  $x + 3$    b  $3x$    c  $4x - 27$

d  $10 - x$    e  $3(x - 7)$    f  $(x - 1)^2$

**3** $x = 12$. Find the value of each expression.

a  $\dfrac{x}{3}$    b  $\dfrac{x + 8}{4}$    c  $\dfrac{3x}{4}$

d  $\dfrac{60}{x}$    e  $\dfrac{18}{x - 3}$    f  $\dfrac{24}{20 - x}$

**4** Find the values $w$, $x$, $y$ and $z$ that make each expression equal to 30.

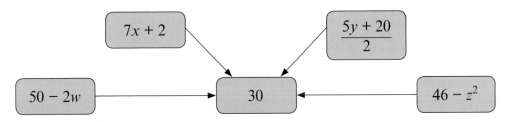

**5** $a = 3$ and $b = 5$. Find the value of each expression.

a  $a^2 + b^2$    b  $2a^2$    c  $3b^2$

d  $1 - a + b$    e  $a^2 - b^2$    f  $2b^2 - a$

**6** Copy and complete the sentences.

   **a** When $y$ is 4, $5y$ is $\square$.　　**b** When $y$ is 3, $10y^2$ is $\square$.

   **c** When $y$ is 3, $\square y^2 - \square$ is 89.

**7** $x = 2$ and $y = 5$. Use $x$ and $y$ to write three different expressions that have a value of 20.

explanation 2a　explanation 2b

**8** Simplify these expressions.

  **a** $x + 2 + 3$　　**b** $x + 9 - 2$　　**c** $x + 3 \times 4$

  **d** $x + x$　　**e** $x + x + x$　　**f** $x + x - x$

  **g** $2x + x$　　**h** $2x - x$　　**i** $2x + 3x$

  **j** $3x - 5x$　　**k** $5x + 3x - x$　　**l** $9x - 2x - 4x$

**9** Copy and complete.

  **a** $39 + 27 + 1 = 39 + 1 + \square = \square$

  **b** $28 + 75 + 25 + 11 = 28 + \square + 11 = \square$

  **c** $327 - 98 - 2 + 30 = 327 - \square + 30 = \square$

  **d** $579 + 86 - 79 = 579 - \square + \square = \square$

  **e** $49 + 78 + 51 + 65 + 22 = 49 + \square + 78 + \square + 65 = \square$

**10** Explain what question **9** shows about addition and subtraction.

**11** Work out these calculations.

  **a** $75 + 49 + 25 + 51 + 88$　　**b** $78 + 67 - 18 + 40$

  **c** $32 - 54 - 16 + 68$

**12** Simplify these expressions.

  **a** $x + 3 + x$　　**b** $x + 4 + x + 6$　　**c** $2x + 5 + x - 3$

  **d** $x + x - x + x - x$　　**e** $5x + 7 - x - 3$　　**f** $4 + 7x - 4 - 2x$

**13** Simplify these expressions.

a $x + y + y$

b $2x - y + y$

c $3x + y - x + y$

d $x + 3 + y + 5$

e $x - y + y + x + 3$

f $2x + y - 3 - x + 4y$

g $xy + xy$

h $2xy + 3xy$

i $xyz + xyz$

**14** a Explain the phrase like terms.

b Simplify this expression.

$x^2 + 5y^2 + 3x + 7 + 4y + 2x^2 - y^2 - x + y$

c What happens to the number 7? Why?

**15** David uses number lines to help him collect like terms and simplify this expression.

$-5k + 3k - 6m - k + 7m + 10 = -3k + m + 10$

like      like

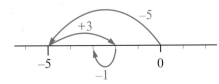 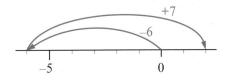

Use this method to simplify these expressions.

a $k + k + m - k - k - 5m$

b $3k + 2 + m - 10k - 4m$

c $k - 6k + 2 - 5m + 4 + 12m$

d $10 - p + 7q - 8p + 1 + q$

e $-2q + 5 + p + 7q + 3p - 11$

f $9p - 3q - 7 - 8p - 10$

g $-k - 3 - 3k + n - 5$

h $-k + 8k - 1 + 7n - 2k + 3$

i $10k - 4 - n + k + 6n - 1$

j $x^2 + x - 1 + x^2 + 7 + 2x$

k $y + y^2 - 2y + 3y^2$

l $a^2 + 10a - 4 + 4a^2 + a + 5$

explanation 3a    explanation 3b

**16** Find and simplify a formula for the perimeter, $P$, of each shape.

a
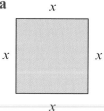

b
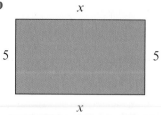

c
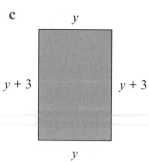

**17** Find and simplify a formula for the perimeter, $P$, of each shape.

a
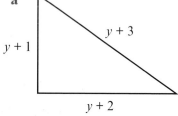

b
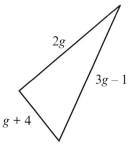

c
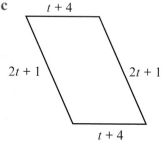

d
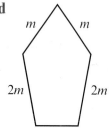

e
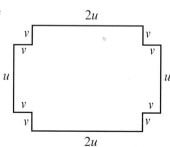

f
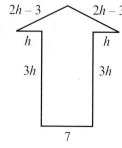

**18** On the pinboard there are two lengths $k$ and $m$.
The red shape has a perimeter of $4m + 3k$.

Draw shapes that have these perimeters.

a   $4k$          b   $6m + k$

c   $4m + 2k$     d   $2m + 3k$

e   $8m + k$      f   $2m + 4k$

$P = 4m + 3k$

**19** Each card shows an algebraic expression.

A $2x$  B $x + 3$  C $x - 5$  D $7 - x$  E $4 - 2x$  F $3x + 1$

  **a** Choose two of the cards to give a total of $4x + 4$.

  **b** Choose two of the cards to give a total of $7 - x$.

  **c** Choose two of the cards to give a total of $4$.

  **d** Choose two of the cards to give a total of $10$.

  **e** Choose three of the cards to give a total of $12$.

  **f** Choose three of the cards to give a total of $3x + 11$.

  **g** What is the total of all of the expressions on the cards?

explanation 4

**20** Use the formula $s = \frac{d}{t}$

  **a** Find $s$ when $d = 12$ and $t = 3$.   **b** Find $s$ when $d = 56$ and $t = 8$.

  **c** Find $s$ when $d = 150$ and $t = 25$.   **d** Find $d$ when $s = 20$ and $t = 11$.

**21** Use the formula $F = ma$.

  **a** Find $F$ when $m = 3$ and $a = 10$.   **b** Find $F$ when $m = 4.8$ and $a = 10$.

  **c** Find $F$ when $m = 5$ and $a = 1.3$.   **d** Find $m$ when $F = 24$ and $a = 4$.

**22** Use the formula $m = \frac{x + y}{2}$.

  **a** Find $m$ when $x = 10$ and $y = 12$.   **b** Find $m$ when $x = 4$ and $y = 5$.

  **c** Find $m$ when $x = -2$ and $y = 10$.   **d** What does this formula do?

**23** The formula $d = 5t^2$ works out approximately the distance, in metres, a stone falls after $t$ seconds.

  **a** Find $d$ when $t = 3$.   **b** Find $d$ when $t = 4$.   **c** Find $d$ when $t = 6$.

  **d** The Eiffel Tower is 300 m high. A stone is dropped from the top. Use the formula to work out approximately how many seconds it would take the stone to fall to the ground.

**24** Use a calculator for this question.

The formula for stopping distances is $d = \dfrac{v^2}{20f}$.

  **a**  When $v = 10$ and $f = 0.8$, check that $d = 6.25$ and explain how to use the formula.

  **b**  Find $d$ when $v = 13.2$ and $f = 0.75$.

  **c**  Find $d$ when $v = 15$ and $f = 0.6$.

**25** Use a calculator for this question.

Copy and complete the table using the formula $V = IR$.

| I | R | V |
|---|---|---|
| 3 | 12 | 36 |
| 0.24 | 80 | |
| | 96 | 12 |
| 0.48 | | 240 |
| | 550 | 220 |

**26** In each diagram below
- $D$ represents the number of red dots
- $A$ represents the number of arcs or lines
- $R$ represents the number of regions or spaces

| D | A | R |
|---|---|---|
| 3 | 4 | 3 |
| | | |
| | | |
| | | |
| | | |

The table shows the values of $D$, $A$ and $R$ for the first diagram. Notice that the outside of the diagram counts as a region, so $R = 3$.

  **a**  Copy and complete the table for the other two diagrams.

  **b**  Draw some diagrams of your own and fill in the table.

  **c**  Find a formula connecting $D$, $A$ and $R$. Check that your formula works for all the values in the table.

# Functions and equations

- Representing an equation using a flow diagram
- Solving an equation using inverse operations
- Solving an equation using algebra

Keywords

You should know

explanation 1

**1** Write an expression for the output of each function machine.

a  $x \rightarrow \boxed{+\ 2} \rightarrow$

b  $x \rightarrow \boxed{\div\ 3} \rightarrow$

c  $w \rightarrow \boxed{\times\ 5} \rightarrow$

d  $p \rightarrow \boxed{-\ 9} \rightarrow$

**2** Write an expression for the output of each function machine.

a  $x \rightarrow \boxed{\times\ 6} \rightarrow \boxed{+\ 5} \rightarrow$

b  $x \rightarrow \boxed{\times\ 4} \rightarrow \boxed{-\ 3} \rightarrow$

c  $x \rightarrow \boxed{\div\ 3} \rightarrow \boxed{-\ 7} \rightarrow$

d  $x \rightarrow \boxed{\div\ 8} \rightarrow \boxed{+\ 1} \rightarrow$

e  $x \rightarrow \boxed{+\ 4} \rightarrow \boxed{\times\ 5} \rightarrow$

f  $x \rightarrow \boxed{-\ 5} \rightarrow \boxed{\div\ 10} \rightarrow$

g  $x \rightarrow \boxed{\times\ 7} \rightarrow \boxed{-\ 3} \rightarrow$

h  $x \rightarrow \boxed{\div\ 2} \rightarrow \boxed{+\ 1} \rightarrow$

i  $x \rightarrow \boxed{-\ 1} \rightarrow \boxed{\times\ 6} \rightarrow$

j  $x \rightarrow \boxed{+\ 5} \rightarrow \boxed{\div\ 2} \rightarrow$

**3** Draw a function machine to represent each expression.

a  $2g + 7$

b  $3(h - 9)$

c  $4(t + 3)$

d  $5r - 10$

e  $\dfrac{x}{4} - 5$

f  $\dfrac{m}{9} + 6$

g  $\dfrac{f + 4}{2}$

h  $\dfrac{k - 12}{7}$

i  $4a + 3$

j  $\dfrac{w}{2} + 12$

k  $8(b - 1)$

l  $\dfrac{s + 1}{10}$

explanation 2

**4** Here are two reverse function machines. Write the value of $x$ for each.

a  $x \leftarrow \boxed{+\ 4} \leftarrow \boxed{\times\ 5} \leftarrow 7$

b  $x \leftarrow \boxed{\div\ 9} \leftarrow \boxed{+\ 7} \leftarrow 11$

**5** Write the inverse of each operation.

    **a**  Add 6       **b**  Multiply by 5      **c**  Subtract 1       **d**  Divide by 2

    **e**  $+5$          **f**  $\times 6$            **g**  $\div 3$            **h**  $-9$

    **i**  $\times 10$       **j**  $+3.4$         **k**  $-9.8$        **l**  $\div 7.2$

**6** This function machine represents the equation $\frac{x}{4} - 5 = 6$.

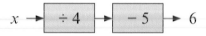

    **a**  Copy and complete the reverse function machine. Use inverse operations.

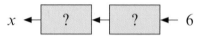

    **b**  Use the reverse function machine to solve the equation $\frac{x}{4} - 5 = 6$.

**7**  **i**  Draw a function machine for each of the following equations.

    **ii**  Draw the reverse function machine for each.

    **iii**  Use the reverse function machine to solve the equation.

    **a**  $4x + 12 = 20$       **b**  $3n - 14 = 22$      **c**  $5y - 7 = 43$

    **d**  $4p + 1 = 25$        **e**  $2t + 9 = 20$       **f**  $2(m - 8) = 3$

    **g**  $5(y - 7) = 45$     **h**  $\frac{r}{10} + 1 = 16$     **i**  $\frac{a}{3} - 9 = 5$

> explanation 3a    explanation 3b

**8** Sam is solving the equation $2(m - 3) = 9$.
He divides both sides by 2. This removes
the 2 that is multiplying the bracket.
He is not sure what to do next.

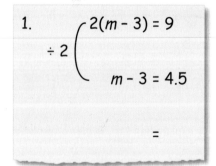

    **a**  Sarah suggests adding 3 to both sides to
remove the subtract 3. Is she right?

    **b**  What is the answer?

    **c**  Solve $5(p + 12) = 100$. Explain each step.

**9** A teacher explains how to solve
$2m + 4 = 17$.
Solve the following equations.
Show your method.

a   $6t + 9 = 51$      b   $2n - 15 = 25$

c   $9m + 3 = 48$      d   $6y - 8 = 4$

e   $2(p + 3) = 11$    f   $4x - 16 = 24$

g   $2w + 2 = 7$       h   $7m - 3 = 4$

i   $3(x + 8) = 21$

Objective: Be able to solve
    equations using
    inverse operations

Solve $2m + 4 = 17$

$$2m + 4 = 17$$

$-4$

$$2m = 13$$

$\div 2$

$$m = 6.5$$

**10** Rashid is solving the equation $6y - 7 = 11$. Look at his working out.
The teacher has marked some of his first line wrong.

$$6y - 7 = 11$$

$\checkmark$
$+ 7$

$$6y \quad = 4 \; ✗$$

a   Explain what Rashid has done wrong.

b   Show Rashid how to solve the equation correctly.

**11** Katherine is solving the equation $2x + 7 = 16$. Look at Katherine's attempt.

$$2x + 7 = 16$$

$\div 2$

$$x + 7 = 8 \; ✗$$

a   Explain what Katherine has done wrong.

b   Show Katherine how to solve the equation correctly.

## Angles

- Looking at different types of angle (acute, obtuse, reflex and right angles)
- Measuring angles
- Calculating angles

Keywords

You should know

explanation 1

**1** Describe each of these angles. The first one has been done for you.

a

Acute

b
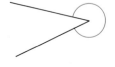

c

d

e

f

g

h

i

explanation 2a    explanation 2b    explanation 2c

**2** Sophie is measuring an *acute* angle between two lines with a 180° protractor.

The diagram shows part of the protractor scale and one of the lines.

Read the scale to find the size of the angle.

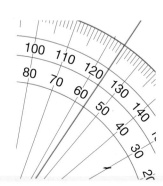

**3** Find the acute angles shown on these protractor scales.

a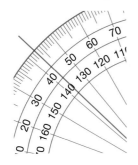

b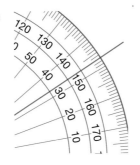

c

**4** Find the obtuse angles shown on these protractor scales.

a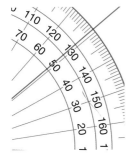

b

c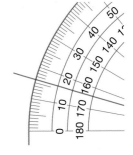

**5** Ben is measuring a *reflex* angle between two lines with a 360° protractor.

The diagram shows part of the protractor scale and one of the lines.

Read the scale to find the size of the angle.

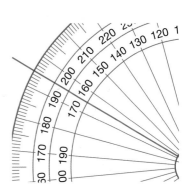

**6** Use the information given on the following diagrams to find the unknown angles.

a

Obtuse

b

Reflex

c

Obtuse

d

Reflex

**7** Measure the following angles with a protractor.

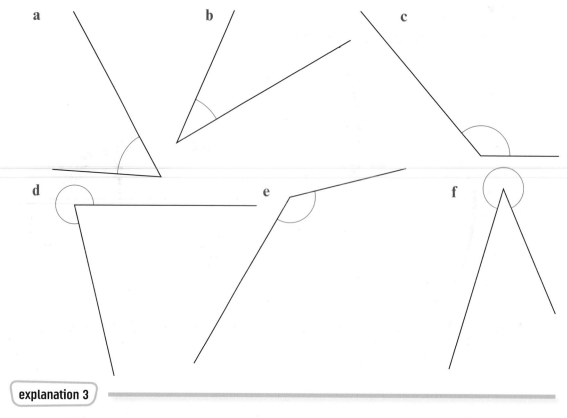

a  b  c

d  e  f

explanation 3

**8** Draw a rectangle 12 cm by 8 cm on
squared paper. Then complete the
diagram shown as accurately as
possible.

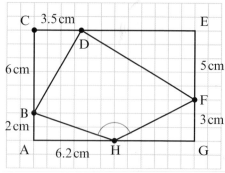

The angle BHF is marked in red. This angle can also be written as ∠BHF.

**a** Use a protractor to measure the following angles to the nearest degree.

   **i**  ∠BHF     **ii**  ∠HFD     **iii**  ∠BDF     **iv**  ∠HBD

   **v**  ∠HFE     **vi**  ∠BHA     **vii**  ∠BDE     **viii**  ∠ABD

**b** The angle marked in red is one of the four angles inside the quadrilateral
   BDFH.

   Find the sum of the four angles inside the quadrilateral BDFH.
   Comment on your answer.

explanation 4a    explanation 4b

**9** Here are some angles marked with letters.

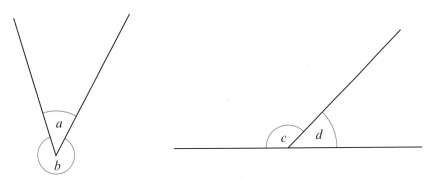

What is the value of $a + b$?

What is the value of $c + d$?

**10** Work out the size of each angle marked with a letter in the diagrams below.

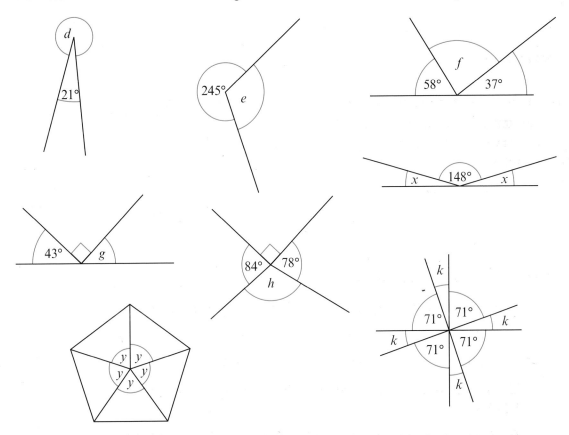

**11** Work out the size of each angle marked with a letter in the following diagrams.

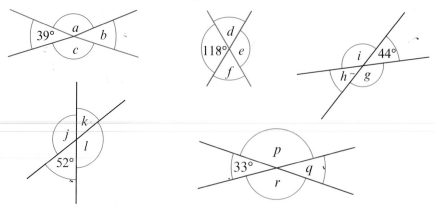

**12** Work out the angles marked with letters in the diagrams below.

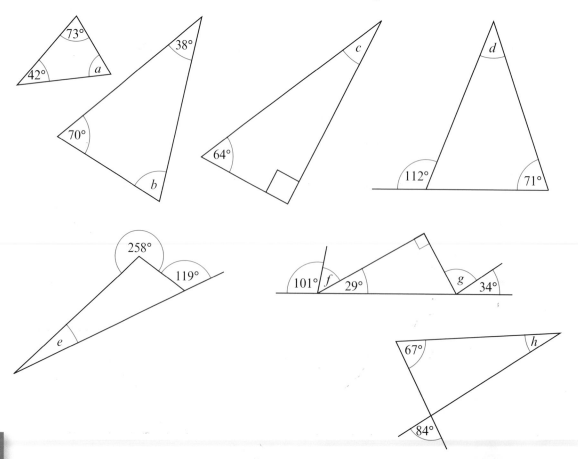

**13** Find the sizes of the angles marked with letters in the diagrams below.

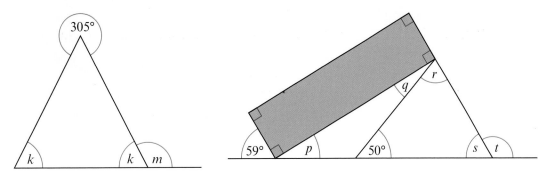

explanation 7

**14** Work out the angles marked with letters in these diagrams.

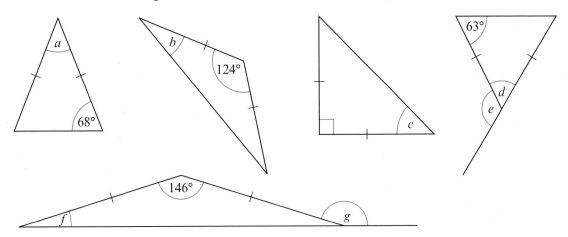

**15** Work out the angles marked with letters in the following diagrams.

**16**  How high is the tree shown in this diagram?

Explain how you know.

45°

17 m

**17  a**  Through what angle does the minute hand of a clock turn in 30 minutes?

  **b**  Through what angle does the hour hand of a clock turn in 30 minutes?

  **c**  What is the obtuse angle between the hands of a clock at 12:30?

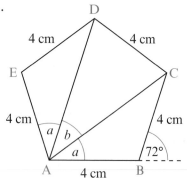

**18  a**  Find the perimeter of the pentagon ABCDE.

  **b**  Work out the value of angle $a$.

  **c**  What is the size of the angle BAE?

  **d**  Work out the value of angle $b$.

  **e**  What can you say about the lines AD and BC?

  Explain your answer.

D

4 cm        4 cm

E                    C

4 cm        4 cm

$a$ $b$

$a$        72°

A    4 cm    B

**19**  ADEF is a rectangle 8.7 cm by 5 cm and CE is a straight line 10 cm long.

  **a**  Find the value of the angle $x$.

  **b**  Find the value of the angle $y$.

  **c**  Find the value of angle $z$.

  **d**  Find the perimeter of the triangle ABD.

  Explain how you got each answer.

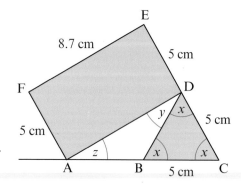

E

8.7 cm

5 cm

F                    D

$y$  $x$      5 cm

5 cm

$z$      $x$        $x$

A        B   5 cm   C

# Shape

- Investigating properties of parallel lines
- Recognising line symmetry
- Recognising different types of quadrilateral
- Plotting coordinates in four quadrants

Keywords

You should know

explanation 1a    explanation 1b

**1** Use a tennis court to give examples of lines that are

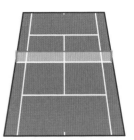

    **a** Parallel

    **b** Perpendicular

    **c** Horizontal

    **d** Vertical

**2** Copy the 16 dot diagram with the red line and the point P.

    **a** Find a dot on the diagram and label it Q so that PQ is parallel to the red line. Draw the line PQ.

    **b** Find another dot on the diagram and label it T so that PT is perpendicular to the red line. Draw the line PT.

**3**  **a** Draw a line and mark a point P which is not on the line. Use a set square and ruler to draw a new line through P which is parallel to the first line.

    **b** Copy the diagram and describe the shortest distance from the point R to the line AB.

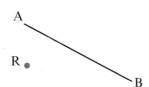

explanation 2

**4** This quadrilateral drawn on squared paper has exactly two equal sides and two right angles. The equal sides are marked by a small dash.

   **a** What is the name of this quadrilateral?

   **b** On squared paper draw and name

      **i** a quadrilateral that has exactly two equal sides and one pair of parallel sides

      **ii** three different quadrilaterals that have perpendicular diagonals

   **c** Use these four triangular tiles to make three different quadrilaterals.

explanation 3

**5** Copy and complete each diagram so that the dotted line is a line of symmetry.

   **a**

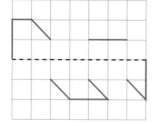 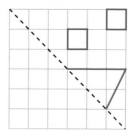

   **b** On squared paper draw a quadrilateral that has only one right angle and only one line of symmetry.

   **c** State whether the dotted lines are lines of symmetry. Justify your answers.

   **i**        **ii**        **iii**

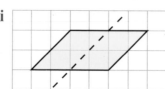 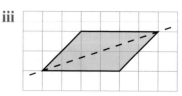

**6** **a** Draw two trapeziums, one with and one without a line of symmetry.

   **b** Draw and name two other quadrilaterals with exactly one line of symmetry.

   **c** Draw and name a quadrilateral that has no lines of symmetry.

   **d** Draw and name two different quadrilaterals that have exactly two lines of symmetry.

explanation 4

**7 a** Write down the coordinates of each of the labelled points.

**b** The point (−3, 3) is the midpoint of GF. Write down the coordinates of the midpoints of these lines.

    **i**  KH      **ii**  HB

    **iii**  EC     **iv**  GC

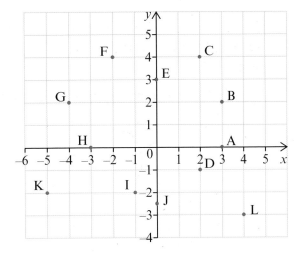

**8** The coordinates of the top corner of the second

    red parallelogram are (4, 2)
    green rectangle are (−2, 3)
    purple rectangle are (−3, −2)
    blue parallelogram are (2, −4)

**a** What are the coordinates of the top corner of the fourth

    **i**  red parallelogram

    **ii**  green rectangle

    **iii**  purple rectangle

    **iv**  blue parallelogram

**b** What are the coordinates of the top corner of the tenth

    **i**  red parallelogram      **ii**  green rectangle

    **iii**  purple rectangle    **iv**  blue parallelogram

**9** On squared paper draw *x*- and *y*-axes labelled from −10 to 10. Plot the points and join them up in order to form a shape. Name each shape and use dotted lines to draw any lines of symmetry. Shape 1 has been done for you.

Shape 1   (5, 2)      (7, 4)      (9, 2)      (7, 0)

Shape 2   (−6, 8)     (−6, 10)    (−3, 10)    (−3, 8)

Shape 3   (0, 6)      (2, 10)     (4, 6)

Shape 4   (−8, 1)     (−6, 3)     (−2, 3)     (−4, 1)

Shape 5   (−5, −1)    (−6, −4)    (−5, −7)    (−4, −4)

Shape 6   (0, −4)     (4, −4)     (3, −2)     (1, −2)

Shape 7   (1, −6)     (2, −5)     (5, −6)     (2, −7)

Shape 8   (6, −2)     (6, −5)     (8, −5)     (8, −3)

**10** Draw *x*- and *y*-axes labelled from −6 to 6.

   **a**  Plot the points (1, 1) (−1, −1) and (−1, 1).

   **b**  What are the coordinates of a fourth point that would make a square?

   **c**  What are the coordinates of a fourth point that would make a parallelogram?

   **d**  What are the coordinates of a fourth point that would make a kite?

   **e**  What are the coordinates of a fourth point that would make an arrowhead?

# Surveys and experiments

- Planning and conducting a survey
- Conducting a mathematical experiment
- Using an appropriate type of data for a given purpose

Keywords

You should know

explanation 1

**Mobile explosion**

**Has everybody got a mobile phone?**

A school starts a project to find out more information about the use of mobile phones in their community and they think of some questions.

What type of contract do you have?

Do you have a mobile?

What do you use your mobile for?

How much time do you spend on your phone?

Who should we ask?

?

**1** Discuss these questions in a group. Write down some more questions that you think should be considered.

**2** Make a list of groups of people that should be consulted in this survey.

Write down some questions that you might ask each group.

explanation 2

**3** Take a look at these questions. In pairs discuss why each one would not be suitable for a survey in its present form. Write down why you think they are unsuitable.

   **a** Most people want more car parking space available in the town. Do you agree?

   **b** How much do you earn?

   **c** How old are you?

   **d** Are you in favour of making animals suffer for medical research?

   **e** What are your views on the state of the economy?

   **f** What do you think about young people?

   **g** What qualifications do you have?

   **h** Why do you think women make better drivers than men?

   **i** How could recycling be made more effective?

**4** You can sometimes avoid making questions too personal by offering choices.

> Offering choices may also make the question easier to answer, while providing you with enough information.

Instead of simply asking for a person's age, for example, you could ask them to select an age-range.

Less than 18     18 to 25     over 25

Write some suitable choices for each of these questions.

   **a** How much time do you spend each day watching television?

   **b** Approximately, how many times have you visited a cinema in the last year?

   **c** What is your view on the statement that computers have helped to raise standards in education?

   **d** How many miles do you travel by car in a typical year?

   **e** Do you think that calculators should be used in primary schools?

**5** The following question is politely phrased and offers choices, but there is still something wrong.

**Please select the number of times per week that you eat meat.**
**Once        Twice        Three times or more**

What is the problem?

**6** Explain why it wouldn't be easy to write suitable choices for the following question.

What is your favourite holiday resort?

**7** Compare pairs of questions in these two questionnaires.

| |
|---|
| **1** How old are you?<br><br>........................................................<br><br>**2** Do you have a mobile phone?<br><br>   Y/N<br><br>**3** What was the main reason for buying a mobile?<br>   ☐ to keep in touch with friends<br>   ☐ security reasons<br><br>**4** Is your phone a contract phone?<br><br>........................................................ |

| |
|---|
| **1** Are you?<br>   ☐ under 16      ☐ 16–35<br>   ☐ 36–60        ☐ over 60<br><br>**2** Do you own a mobile phone?<br>   ☐ yes          ☐ no<br><br>**3** What was the main reason for buying a mobile?<br>   ☐ keep in touch with friends<br>   ☐ security      ☐ entertainment<br>   ☐ internet      ☐ other<br><br>**4** What type of phone do you have?<br>   ☐ Pay & Go      ☐ contract |

( explanation 3a )  ( explanation 3b )

**8** Look back at question 5 and also questions 1 and 2 about the project on mobile phones.

 **a** Try to improve your questions and add some new ones.

 **b** Design a questionnaire to investigate the use of mobile phones.

 **c** Test your data collection sheet with a small group of people.

   Make any changes needed to improve it.

**9** Carry out a survey using either your questionnaire on mobile phones *or* a new data collection sheet based on a different enquiry.

Make sure that the data collected represents the situation fairly.

Be aware that the day, time and location all affect who is available to answer your questions.

Use a variety of charts to present your data.

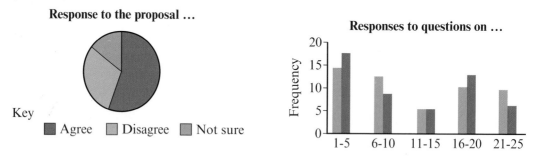

Make some statements about what your survey shows.

Treat all of the information fairly – even if you disagree with it!

Try to draw some conclusions relating to the purpose of the survey.

> explanation 4

**10** Decide whether you would use primary data, secondary data or experimental data to investigate the following questions.

**a** Do more people visit the cinema regularly now than 10 years ago?

**b** Do people feel that traffic speed cameras make the roads safer?

**c** Is the population of the UK increasing or decreasing?

**d** Is a piece of toast more likely to land jam side down?

**11  a**  Cut out a square of card with sides 4 cm.
Draw the diagonals on the square and label its
sides from 1 to 4.
Push a cocktail stick through the centre to make
a spinner.

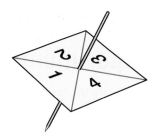

**b**  In an experiment, the spinner is spun and the results are recorded.
If you carry out lots of trials, what would you expect in terms of the
frequency of each possible score?

**c**  Copy the table.
Carry out 40 trials and record your results in the table.
Comment on your results. Are they what you expected?

| Score | Tally | Frequency |
|-------|-------|-----------|
| 1 | | |
| 2 | | |
| 3 | | |
| 4 | | |

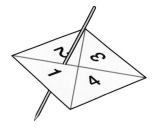

**d**  Move the cocktail stick about 0.8 cm from the centre along the diagonal
between 1 and 2.

Describe how you think this might affect the results.

Do you think the direction of spin will make a difference?

**e**  Carry out 40 trials, spinning clockwise each time.

Record your results in a table.

Comment on your results.

**f**  Carry out another 40 trials, spinning anticlockwise each time.

Record your results in a table.

Does the direction of spin appear to make a difference?

Compare your results with others in the class.

# Experiments and probability

- Using the results of a large number of trials
- Using random numbers to simulate throwing a coin or dice
- Estimating a probability

Keywords

You should know

explanation 1a  explanation 1b

1 The probability of throwing a six when a fair dice is rolled is $\frac{1}{6} = 0.167$ to 3 d.p. This is called the theoretical probability of rolling a six.
Yasmin rolls a fair dice ten times. The outcome of each throw is shown below. She uses this information to find the experimental probability of getting a six.

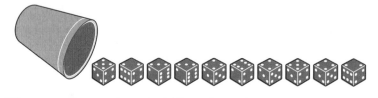

The experimental probability of getting a six based on these ten trials is

$$\frac{\text{the number of times the event occured}}{\text{the number of trials}} = \frac{1}{10} = 0.1$$

a Leon thinks he can get a better result by rolling the dice 20 times. He gets three sixes. Calculate the experimental probability of getting a six based on his results.

b Ben put his results in a table.

i How many times did he roll the dice?

| OUTCOME | SIX | NOT A SIX |
|---|---|---|
| FREQUENCY | ЖЖ ||| | ЖЖ ЖЖ ЖЖ ЖЖ ЖЖ ЖЖ ЖЖ || |

ii Calculate the experimental probability of rolling a six based on Ben's results.

c Whose result is the most reliable and why?

d The three pupils put their results together. Calculate a new estimate of the probability of rolling a six.

e What happens to the experimental probability as the number of trials increases?

**2** A group of children perform an experiment at school. They butter pieces of toast and push them off the edge of a table one at a time. They record the results in a table.

| Outcome | Landed butter-side down | Landed butter-side up |
|---|---|---|
| Frequency | 33 | 27 |

Calculate the experimental probability that toast lands

**a** Butter-side down

**b** Butter-side up

**3** Draw a square 6 cm by 6 cm and shade in the grey region accurately. Get a paper clip and a pencil, place the point of the pencil inside the paper clip at the centre of the square so that the paper clip is free to spin around.

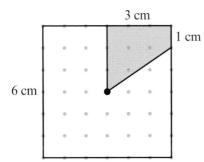
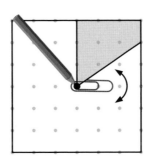

Flick the paper clip so that it spins round. When it stops, note if the middle of the paper clip lies in the shaded region. Repeat this about 60 times and summarise your results in a table.

| Outcome | Stops inside shaded region | Stops outside shaded region |
|---|---|---|
| Tally | | |
| Frequency | | |

**a** Calculate the experimental probability that the paper clip lands in the shaded region.

**b** Measure the angle of the shaded region at the centre.

**c** Calculate the theoretical probability of the paperclip landing in the shaded region.

**d** Compare your answers to parts **a** and **c**.

**4** A box contains 80 plastic spoons. The box is shaken and turned upside-down so that the spoons fall out.

28 of them land spoon-up, the rest land spoon-down. What is the experimental probability that a plastic spoon lands spoon-down?

**5** A man flips a coin 200 times and a head occurs 60 times. What is the experimental probability of getting a head with this coin? Is the coin fair?

**6** Put a small amount of Blu-Tack on one side of a 10p coin. Spin the coin about 50 times and note which side lands facing up. Summarise your results in a table and use the information to find the experimental probability that the coin lands with the Blu-Tack facing up.

explanation 2

**7** Scientific calculators have a key, usually labelled Ran# or Random, that will display a random decimal between 0 and 0.999

  **a** A tetrahedral dice has four faces labelled 1 to 4. Explain how you could use the Ran# key to simulate rolling one of these dice.

  **b** Describe a way of using the random number key to behave like a coin.

  **c** Describe how you could produce a list of random numbers from 1 to 99.

**\*8** Raffle tickets numbered from 400 to 725 inclusive have been sold. Describe how you could use a calculator to choose the winning number.

# Mental methods

- Organising a calculation so that you can work it out mentally

Keywords

You should know

explanation 1

**1** Copy the diagrams to show the calculations and fill in the missing numbers.

a 129 + 64

b 56 + 49

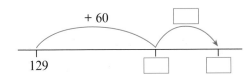

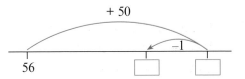

**2** Work out these additions.

a 37 + 54    b 426 + 69    c 428 + 239

d 278 + 188    e 337 + 453    f 112 + 344

**3** Copy the diagrams to show the calculations and fill in the missing numbers.

a 220 − 63

b 473 − 19.38

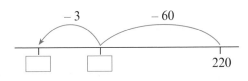

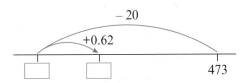

**4** Work out these subtractions.

a 100 − 68    b 625 − 219    c 817 − 472

d 563 − 418    e 10 − 3.65    f 78.5 − 9.27

**5** Copy and complete.

a   $4.36 + \square = 10$  b   $87.4 + \square = 100$  c   $41.8 + \square = 100$

d   $£7.80 + \square = £10$  e   $£4.68 + \square = £10$  f   $£34.80 + \square = £100$

**6 a** Work out in your head the cost of four portions of chips, one pudding, one fish, one tub of gravy and two tubs of curry.

| Fish | £2.20 |
|------|-------|
| Chips | £0.95 |
| Pudding | £1.00 |
| Gravy/Curry | £0.55 |

  **b** What is the change from a £10 note?

  **c** How many portions of fish and chips can you buy for £20 and how much change will you get?

**7** Copy and complete these arithmagons so that each number in a rectangle is the sum of the numbers in the circles on either side.

a

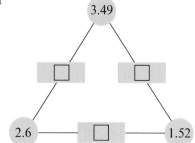

b

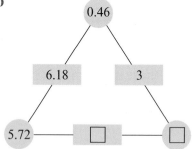

explanation 2

**8** These calculations show some different ways to partition a multiplication.

Copy and complete.

a   $43 \times 6 = (40 \times 6) + (\square \times 6)$

$\phantom{43 \times 6} = \square + \square$

$\phantom{43 \times 6} = \square$

b   $39 \times 7 = (40 \times 7) - (\square \times 7)$

$\phantom{39 \times 7} = \square - \square$

$\phantom{39 \times 7} = \square$

c   $3.7 \times 11 = (3.7 \times 10) + (3.7 \times \square)$

$\phantom{3.7 \times 11} = \square + \square$

$\phantom{3.7 \times 11} = \square$

d   $5.8 \times 9 = (5.8 \times 10) - (5.8 \times \square)$

$\phantom{5.8 \times 9} = \square - \square$

$\phantom{5.8 \times 9} = \square$

**9** Use similar methods to those in question **8** to work these multiplications out mentally.

   **a**  23 × 8          **b**  99 × 7          **c**  6 × 54

   **d**  12 × 38         **e**  198 × 3         **f**  6.8 × 11

   **g**  5.7 × 9         **h**  10.1 × 36       **i**  48 × 9.9

**10** On average 58 babies are born in the maternity unit each week.

Sally uses a mental method to work out how many babies are born in the department each year.

58 × 100 ÷ ☐ + ☐ + ☐

Explain and complete her method. Write down other ways this can be done and check your ideas with a partner.

explanation 3

**11** Copy and complete.

   **a**  25 × 36 = (25 × 4) × ☐
   
   = ☐ × ☐
   
   = ☐

   **b**  2.5 × 24 = (2.5 × 4) × ☐
   
   = ☐ × ☐
   
   = ☐

   **c**  125 × 12 = (125 × 4) × ☐
   
   = ☐ × ☐
   
   = ☐

   **d**  12.5 × 16 = (12.5 × 2) × ☐
   
   = ☐ × ☐
   
   = ☐

   **e**  6.4 × 30 = (6.4 × 10) × ☐
   
   = ☐ × ☐
   
   = ☐

   **f**  0.92 × 400 = (0.92 × 100) × 4
   
   = ☐ × ☐
   
   = ☐

**12** Work these out.

   **a**  25 × 16       **b**  25 × 17       **c**  25 × 14

   **d**  125 × 8       **e**  125 × 9       **f**  125 × 32

   **g**  2.5 × 12      **h**  7.5 × 12      **i**  1.25 × 24

   **j**  3.2 × 40      **k**  0.72 × 300    **l**  0.75 × 400

> Look for connections between the questions that may help you work out the answers.

**13** Copy and complete.

   **a**  $4.86 \times 50 = \square \times 100$

             $= \square$

   **c**  $£7.50 \times 60 = £15 \times \square$

             $= \square$

   **b**  $12.5 \times 14 = 25 \times \square$

             $= \square$

   **d**  $£6.25 \times 44 = £25 \times \square$

             $= \square$

**14** In the UK speed limit signs are in miles per hour but in Europe they are in kilometres per hour. Work out what these speed limits are in kilometres per hour.

> 1 mile is approximately 1.6 km.

   **a**  40 mph

   **b**  70 mph

**15** Tarun works 5 days per week. He saves £7.50 each day by walking to work instead of driving. How much will Tarun save in 1 week?

**16** Work out these calculations.

   **a**  $4.5 \times 8$
   **b**  $11.5 \times 12$
   **c**  $£2.25 \times 16$

   **d**  $£32 \times 1.25$
   **e**  $£96 \times 1.125$
   **f**  $96 \times £7.50$

**17** Samir is working out $25^2$ in his head with a few jottings. Look at his jottings and use a similar method to find these square numbers.

> $25^2 = 25 \times 25$
> $= 25 \times 10 \times 2 + 25 \times 4 + 25$
> $= 500 + 100 + 25$
> $= 625$

   **a**  $16^2$
   **b**  $17^2$
   **c**  $15^2$

   **d**  $19^2$
   **e**  $36^2$
   **f**  $27^2$

**18** A carton of orange costs 76p.

   **a**  Work out $76 \times 10$ and $76 \times 20$.

   **b**  How many cartons of orange juice can you buy for £20? Explain your method.

   **c**  How much change will you get from a £20 note?

**19** A chocolate bar costs 36p. How many can you buy for £8?

explanation 4

20 Use the fact that $139 \times 48 = 6672$ to find the answers to these.

a  $139 \times 24$          b  $139 \times 480$          c  $139 \times 16$

d  $1.39 \times 48$          e  $13.9 \times 0.48$          f  $13.9 \times 24$

21 Copy these calculations and fill in the gaps to make them equal to $2.75 \times 400$.

a  $275 \times \square$          b  $5.5 \times \square$          c  $11 \times \square$

22 Use the fact that $24 \times 136 = 3264$.

a  What are the answers to these?

i  $3264 \div 24$          ii  $3264 \div 136$          iii  $3264 \div 48$

iv  $3264 \div 12$          v  $3264 \div 68$          vi  $6528 \div 272$

b  Find the value of a gold watch in euros that cost
$3264 (Canadian dollars) when €1 = $1.36.

23 Look at the jottings in the box.
Work out these calculations.

a  $0.4 \times 6$          b  $0.4 \times 0.6$

c  $7 \times 0.9$          d  $0.3 \times 0.9$

e  $0.2 \times 0.4$          f  $0.8^2$

g  $0.4^2$          h  $1.2^2$

i  $8 \times 0.7$          j  $0.5 \times 0.09$

$3 \times 5 = 15$
$0.3 \times 5 = 3 \times 5 \div 10 = 1.5$
$0.3 \times 0.5 = 3 \times 5 \div 100 = 0.15$

explanation 5

24 a  Which of these numbers are divisible by 3?

1467     2513     8215     7324     6543     5437

b  Are any of the numbers divisible by 6? Explain your answer.

25 Write a 6-digit number that is divisible by 30.

**26** Only one of the numbers below is divisible by 15.

42 368    76 542    97 650    86 735

65 874    98 124    31 576

a   Describe an efficient way to find the number.

b   Which number is it?

**27** Write a 5-digit number divisible by each of these numbers.

a   9          b   18          c   45          d   18 and 45

**28** a   Work out the value of $5^3$, $5^4$ and $5^5$. Remember $5^1 = 5$, $5^2 = 5 \times 5$ and so on.

b   Find the value of $5^n - 2^n$ for values of $n$ from 1 to 5.

c   What do you notice about your answers?

---

**explanation 6**

---

**29** Copy and complete these calculations.

a   $1200 \div 24 = \dfrac{1200}{24}$

$= \dfrac{100}{\square}$

$= \square$

b   $134 \div 50 = \dfrac{\square}{50}$

$= \dfrac{\square}{100}$

$= \square$

**30** Work out these divisions.

a   $432 \div 18$      b   $8250 \div 150$      c   $6300 \div 450$      d   $920 \div 40$

e   $423 \div 50$      f   $321 \div 25$      g   $216 \div 75$      h   $186 \div 150$

**31** Callum says a quick way of dividing by 50 is to divide by 100 and double the answer.

a   Explain how to divide by 25.

b   Work out $205 \div 25$.

c   A bookcase is 205 cm high. 1 inch is approximately 2.5 cm. What is the height of the bookcase in inches?

# Written methods for multiplying and dividing

- Multiplying and dividing using written methods

Keywords

You should know

explanation 1a    explanation 1b

**1** Copy and complete the crossnumber.

**Across**

**1** $109 \times 7$

**3** $318 \times 6$

**4** $538 \times 8$

**Down**

**1** $\square \div 4 = 1787$

**2** $\square \div 9 = 334$

**2** A teacher challenges his class to improve their accuracy. The best mark was 8 out of 10. See if you can do any better.

**a** $45 \times 6$    **b** $57 \times 5$    **c** $316 \times 8$    **d** $509 \times 4$    **e** $724 \times 2$

**f** $407 \times 3$    **g** $824 \times 9$    **h** $992 \times 7$    **i** $109 \times 6$    **j** $1028 \times 7$

**3** Given that $423 \times 9 = 3807$, write down the answer to these calculations.

**a** $42.3 \times 9$    **b** $4.23 \times 9$    **c** $8.46 \times 9$

**4 a** Work out these calculations.

**i** $576 \times 4$    **ii** $812 \times 6$    **iii** $284 \times 5$

**b** Use your answers to part **a** to write down the value of these calculations.

**i** $5.76 \times 4$    **ii** $57.6 \times 4$    **iii** $81.2 \times 6$

**iv** $28.4 \times 5$    **v** $8.12 \times 6$    **vi** $2.84 \times 5$

**5** Show your method for answering these questions.

**a**

Work out
$0.71 \times 5$

**b**

Convert 4 oz to grams
1 ounce = 28.35 g

**c**

£1 = €1.47
£8 = $\square$ euro

**d**

1 foot = 30.5 cm
6 feet = $\square$ cm

131

explanation 2

**6 a**   Which calculation matches which card? Use estimation to help you.

   **i**  643 × 8        **ii**  247 × 7        **iii**  381 × 9        **iv**  734 × 6

**b**   Write the answers to these calculations.

| 3429 | 5144 | 4404 | 1729 |

   **i** 24.7 × 7        **ii**  6.43 × 8        **iii**  73.4 × 6        **iv**  3.81 × 9

**c**   A sports shop buys rugby balls for £7.34 each and the bill comes to £440.40.
They sell them in the shop for £10 each. How much profit will they make?

**7**   Siobhan is working out 4.29 × 7.

She first approximates her answer
and then sets her work out in
columns.

4.29 × 7 is approximately 4 × 7 = 28.

| × | 4 | 0.2 | 0.09 | answer |
|---|---|-----|------|--------|
| 7 | 28 | 1.4 | 0.63 | 30.03 |

**a**   Explain her method.

**b**   Use her method to work out

   **i**  3.37 × 8        **ii**  6.02 × 5        **iii**  4 × 5.81        **iv**  9.607 × 3

**8**   Jennie buys six pairs of socks costing £2.48
per pair and three T-shirts costing £9.94 each.
The shopkeeper asks for £54.70 to pay for
the items.

**a**   Use estimation to show that £54.70 is
too much for the items.

**b**   Work out how much Jennie should pay.

**9**   Amul has a £50 note. He wants to buy a set of six glasses costing £7.95 each.

**a**   Use estimation to show that Amul has enough money.

**b**   Work out how much change Amul will receive.

**10** David's grandmother weighs $7\frac{1}{2}$ stone. She wants to know her weight in kilograms.

David looks on the internet and finds that 1 stone = 6.35 kg.

   **a**  What is half a stone in kilograms?

   **b**  Convert 7 stone to kilograms.

   **c**  What is David's grandmother's weight in kilograms?

> explanation 3a    explanation 3b

**11** Work out these calculations.

   **a**  $24 \times 16$       **b**  $28 \times 65$       **c**  $63 \times 24$

   **d**  $39 \times 56$       **e**  $273 \times 18$      **f**  $407 \times 36$

   **g**  $43 \times 128$      **h**  $172 \times 216$    **i**  $127 \times 305$

**12** Sundeep earns £376 per week. How much will he earn in a year?

**13** Work out $989 \times 18$. Explain how your answer can be used to find the cost of buying 18 litres of petrol priced at 98.9 pence per litre.

**14** Samantha is working out $17.4 \times 3.6$.
Look at her working.

Use this method or the standard method to work out

   **a**  $37.1 \times 2.3$    **b**  $45.9 \times 1.4$

   **c**  $54.6 \times 3.7$    **d**  $3.11 \times 1.8$

   **e**  $1.23 \times 5.2$    **f**  $7.04 \times 8.9$

$17.4 \times 3.6$ is approximately $20 \times 4 = 80$.

| $\times$ | 10 | 7 | 0.4 | total |
|---|---|---|---|---|
| 3 | 30 | 21 | 1.2 | 52.2 |
| 0.6 | 6 | 4.2 | 0.24 | + 10.44 |
| | | | | 62.64 |

**15** Malik has €66.03 holiday money left and wants to change it back to pounds sterling.
The exchange rate is £1 = €1.42, so he works out $66.03 \div 1.42$ and gets £46.50.
Perform a calculation to check whether this answer is correct.

**16** Robert is 5'8" tall.
What is his height in centimetres?

> 5'8" means 5 feet 8 inches.
> 1 foot = 12 inches and 1 inch = 2.54 cm.

explanation 4a   explanation 4b   explanation 4c   explanation 4d

**17** Copy and complete the crossnumber.

**Across**

**1** $\square \times 8 = 2328$

**4** $\square \times 3 = 21\,324$

**Down**

**1** $\square = 1100 \div 4$

**2** $\square = 8217 \div 9$

**3** $7 \times \square = 756$

**18** The teacher challenges the class again on accuracy. The best mark, under test conditions, was 7 out of 9. Can you do better?

a   $524.4 \div 6$          b   $89.45 \div 5$          c   $2483.6 \div 7$

d   $1268 \div 4$          e   $15\,312 \div 3$          f   $752 \div 8$

g   $4095 \div 9$          h   $5448 \div 6$          i   $861 \div 7$

**19** Rizwan changes £9 into euros and receives €13.05. What was the exchange rate?

**20** Eight ice creams cost £7.76.

a   Were they more or less than £1 each?

b   Work out the price of each ice cream.

**21** Calculate the mean of 4.63, 7.25, 6.78 and 5.3.

**22** Five friends share the cost of a meal at a restaurant. The total charged is £147. How much do they each have to pay?

explanation 5a   explanation 5b   explanation 5c

**23** Write an estimate for each of these and then find the exact answer.

a   $8294 \div 13$          b   $6192 \div 12$          c   $588 \div 14$

d   $3090 \div 15$          e   $1984 \div 16$          f   $4956 \div 21$

**24** Write an estimate for each of these and then find the exact answer.

   a  $575 \div 23$          b  $871.1 \div 31$          c  $751.4 \div 17$

   d  $30.03 \div 1.3$          e  $12.432 \div 2.4$          f  $5.733 \div 0.9$

**25** Nathan cannot understand how to work out $1911 \div 14$. Rebecca tries to help by first writing down the 14 times table.

   $14 \times 1 = 14$          $14 \times 2 = 28$          $14 \times 3 = 42$          $14 \times 4 = 56$          $14 \times 5 = 70$

   $4 \times 6 = 84$          $14 \times 7 = 98$          $14 \times 8 = 112$          $14 \times 9 = 126$

   a  Explain how to work out $1911 \div 14$. Use a range of methods.

   b  Explain what happens when you work out $457 \div 14$.

**26** Copy and complete these arithmagons. The numbers in the rectangles are the products of the numbers in the circles on either side.

   a

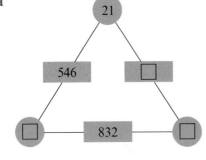

   b

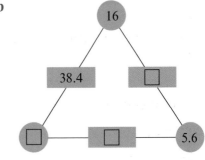

   c

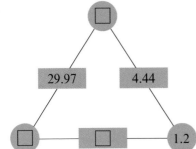

   d

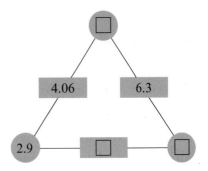

**27** The total weight of the 15 players in a rugby team is 1369 kg.

   Find the mean weight correct to 1 decimal place.

# Using a calculator (2)

- Interpreting a calculator display for the question's context
- Using a calculator with fractions, mixed numbers and decimals
- Using inverse operations to check a calculation
- Using a calculator to find remainders after division

Keywords

You should know

explanation 1a / explanation 1b

**1** Look at the interpretation of the calculator display of 2.5.

| Calculator display | Context | Interpretation | Interpretation |
|---|---|---|---|
| TAKICO   TX-55   *2.5* | money | £2.50 | 2.5p or 3p |
| | length | 2.5 m  2 m and 50 cm | 2.5 km  2 km and 500 m |
| | time | 2.5 hr  2 hr 30 min | 2.5 min  2 min 30 sec |

**a** Copy the headings of the table. Complete your table for these calculator displays.

   **i** 3.1         **ii** 0.4         **iii** 108.2

**b** Write these times in hours and minutes.

   **i** 3.25 hours      **ii** 1.75 hours      **iii** 4.8 hours

**2** The CD cover shows how long each track lasts.

**a** The time of the first track is 4:13. Explain what this means and write the time as a mixed number.

**b** Use your calculator to find how long the CD lasts. Give your answer in minutes and seconds.

**c** What is the average time of a track?

| GREATEST HITS | |
|---|---|
| **1** LOVE IS | 4:13 |
| **2** SOMEWHERE | 2:57 |
| **3** WHAT YOU GET IS TROUBLE | 4:26 |
| **4** THE HIGHEST | 3:16 |
| **5** DEEP | 5:10 |
| **6** ON FIRE | 3:04 |

**3** An athlete ran her first half-marathon (13.5 miles) in 1 hour and 38 minutes.

   **a** Write her time in hours as a mixed number.

   **b** Use the formula below to find her average speed in miles per hour.

   **c** Another competitor took 2 hours and 13 minutes.

     Find his average speed.

$$\text{average speed in miles per hour} = \frac{\text{distance in miles}}{\text{time taken in hours}}$$

**4** The formula used to work out body mass index (BMI) is

$$\text{BMI} = \frac{W}{h^2}$$

where $W$ is the weight of the person in kilograms and $h$ is their height in metres.

   **a** Work out the BMI for Peter. He is 132 cm tall and weighs 42 kg.

   **b** Peter's identical twin brother is also 132 cm tall and his BMI is 25. How much does Peter's brother weigh?

**5** Mary converts $\frac{1}{9}$ to a decimal by doing $1 \div 9$ on her calculator. The display is

   **a** Draw a calculator display for $\frac{2}{9}$ as a decimal.

   **b** What fractions are these calculator displays equivalent to?

   **i**

   **ii**

   **iii**

**6** Use inverse operations to find the missing numbers in these calculations.

a $\square \div 9 = 8.76$   b $\square + 173.89 = 312.6$   c $\square \times 1.175 = 28.905$

d $\sqrt{\square} = 16.4$   e $\square - 97.34 = 421.8$   f $(\square)^2 = 69.8896$

**7** Use inverse operations to find the missing numbers in these calculations.
Check each answer by putting it back into the original calculation.

a $\square \times 11.83 + 7.245 = 121.2862$   b $\square \div 4.25 - 19.82 = 17.18$

c $\sqrt{(\square + 9.28)} = 4.36$   d $3\frac{5}{8} \times (\square)^2 = 58$

**8** Work these out. Check your answers using inverse operations.

a $113.687 \div 14.9$   b $9.81 \times 15.6$   c $8.743^2$

d $\sqrt{41.6025}$   e $2.3 \times 7.8^2$   f $5.9 \times \sqrt{73.96}$

**9** Kevin works out $439 \times 23$ on his calculator. His answer is 11414. Immediately Zainab says this is wrong because the answer must end in 7 as $9 \times 3 = 27$. Which of the following calculations is definitely wrong?

$128 \times 322 = 41216$   $108 \times 3 = 327$   $56 \times 21 = 1176$

**10** Megan works out the mean cost of a 2 litre carton of milk.
The prices at three shops are £1.08, 96p and £1.11.
Her answer is £32.73. What mistake has she made?

**11** Find the remainder for each of these divisions.

a $546 \div 17$   b $2310 \div 9$   c $824 \div 31$

d $2562 \div 68$   e $9751 \div 53$   f $6214 \div 39$

**12** A machine is loaded with 5000 nails. It puts the nails into packs containing 27 nails each.

a How many packs of nails can be made?

b How many nails are left over?

**13** A man works out how many 23p stamps he can buy for £5. His answer is 20.

   **a** Explain why his answer is wrong.

   **b** How many 23p stamps can he buy for £5?

   **c** How much change will he receive?

**14** Three people go out for dinner. The cost of each meal is £6.85 and the total cost of drinks is £2.65. How much is the complete cost?

**15** A school day-trip is organised for 548 pupils. All of the pupils travel on coaches that can carry 47 pupils each.

   **a** How many coaches are needed?

   **b** Calculate the number of spare seats.

**16** A factory produces balloons. 16 balloons are needed to fill one bag. A machine produces 1150 balloons in one hour. How many bags can be filled in an hour?

**17** In 1949 the first non-stop flight around the world took 5641 minutes.

   **a** Convert this time to days, hours and minutes. Show each step of your method.

   **b** The entire flight was 23 452 miles. Use the formula to work out the average speed of the aeroplane.

   $$\text{average speed in miles per hour} = \frac{\text{distance in miles}}{\text{time taken in hours}}$$

**18** In 1957 a jet plane took 2719 minutes to fly around the world non-stop, covering a distance of 24 325 miles.

   **a** Find the time in hours for the non-stop flight?

   **b** Calculate the average speed of the jet plane in miles per hour.

**19** 45 divides into 990 exactly, so the remainder is 0.

   **a** What is the remainder when 1000 is divided by 45?

   **b** Write down the remainder when 1035 is divided by 45?

   **c** What is the remainder when 989 is divided by 45?

# Expressions and equations

- Simplifying algebraic expressions
- Solving equations using inverse operations
- Expanding brackets

Keywords

You should know

explanation 1a   explanation 1b

**1** Write an expression for each set of instructions. Start with $x$.

   **a** Subtract 11, then divide the answer by 5.

   **b** Add 7, then multiply the answer by 2.

   **c** Multiply by 3, then add 5 and divide the answer by 4.

   **d** Subtract from 10 and multiply the answer by 3.

   **e** Divide by 3, then add 5.

**2** Write expressions for each set of instructions.
Use the letter $n$ for the number in each case.

   **a** 100 minus a number.

   **b** Multiply a number by 2 and then subtract 1.

   **c** Divide a number by 7 and then add 10.

   **d** Add 3 to a number and then multiply by 2.

   **e** Multiply a number by itself and then divide by 2.

**3** A hotdog costs £$x$, a bag of popcorn costs £$y$ and a bag of fruit costs $w$ pence.
A group of seven friends buy six hotdogs and five bags of popcorn.
Write an expression for each of the following.

   **a** The total cost in pounds.

   **b** The change from a £20 note.

   **c** The amount each friend pays if they share the cost equally.

   **d** The cost of one bag of fruit in pounds.

   **e** The cost of one hotdog and three bags of fruit in pounds.

**4** Write a set of instructions in words for each expression.

    **a**   $2(x - 5)$         **b**   $21 - 5x$         **c**   $\dfrac{x}{3} + 4$

    **d**   $\dfrac{x + 8}{4}$         **e**   $35 - 4(x + 1)$         **f**   $\dfrac{18}{x - 3}$

**5** In the following diagram, each $\square$ stands for a number. Copy the diagram and fill in the missing numbers to make all the expressions equal to 60 when $k = 5$.

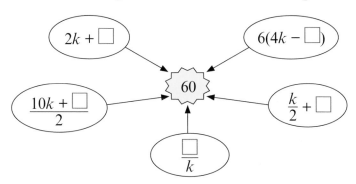

**6** Find the missing number to make each of these statements true when $p = 4$.

    **a**   $p + \square = 2p + 6$         **b**   $2p + \square = p + 5$         **c**   $p + \square = 5p - 4$

---

**explanation 2**

---

**7** Simplify each of these expressions.

    **a**   $2x - 3 + 3$         **b**   $\dfrac{x}{4} + 7 - 7$         **c**   $\dfrac{5x}{5}$

    **d**   $\dfrac{3x}{3}$         **e**   $\dfrac{x}{4} \times 4$         **f**   $\dfrac{x + 3}{7} \times 7$

**8** Each $\square$ represents a number. Each expression simplifies to $x$.
Copy and complete the expressions.

    **a**   $x + 8 - \square$         **b**   $x - 9 + \square$         **c**   $x - \square + 6$

    **d**   $\dfrac{4x}{\square}$         **e**   $\dfrac{4x}{\square} + 5 - \square$         **f**   $\dfrac{x - 9}{7} \times \square + \square$

**9** Each ☐ represents a number and each ◇ represents an operation.
Each expression simplifies to $y$. Copy and complete each expression.
The first one has been done for you.

a  $y - 4 \boxed{+} \boxed{4}$

b  $y + 12 \diamond \square$

c  $y - 3 \diamond \square$

d  $\dfrac{2t}{\square}$

e  $\dfrac{y}{5} \diamond \square$

f  $\dfrac{6y}{\square}$

---

**explanation 3**

---

**10** Copy and complete each diagram to solve the equations.

a  $\dfrac{x}{5} = 23$

| × 5 | × 5 |
|---|---|

$x = \square$

b  $4y + 11 = 39$

| ☐ | ☐ |
|---|---|

$4y = \square$

| ☐ | ☐ |
|---|---|

$y = \square$

c  $\dfrac{n}{3} - 7 = 118$

| ☐ | ☐ |
|---|---|

$\dfrac{n}{3} = \square$

| ☐ | ☐ |
|---|---|

$n = \square$

**11** Solve the equations. Draw diagrams as you did in question **10**.

a  $\dfrac{x}{10} = 17$

b  $4x = 64$

c  $p + 99 = 147$

d  $2x - 13 = 17$

e  $\dfrac{m}{2} + 7 = 20$

f  $12n + 9 = 45$

**12** Harry wants to work faster.
Look at his work.

a  Explain each step.

b  Solve the equations using
this method.

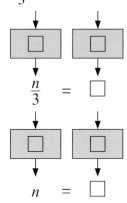

Solve the equation  $2x - 4 = 18$

Step 1

$2x - 4 = 18$

$2x = 22$

Step 2

$x = 11$

    i  $2x + 5 = 18$      ii  $5x - 3 = 42$

    iii  $\dfrac{x}{2} + 11 = 25$      iv  $4x - 17 = 35$

**13** Copy and complete each step to solve the equations.
Each ☐ represents a number.

a $3x - 17 = 16$

$3x = \square$

$x = \square$

b $2(y + 12) = 68$

$y + 12 = \square$

$y = \square$

c $\dfrac{x}{5} + 112 = 126$

$\dfrac{x}{5} = \square$

$x = \square$

d $\dfrac{5x}{3} = 15$

$5x = \square$

$x = \square$

e $11 = \dfrac{x - 19}{6}$

$\square = x - 19$

$x = \square$

f $75 = 5(p - 32)$

$\square = p - 32$

$p = \square$

**14** Solve the equations.

a $\dfrac{x - 24}{8} = 7$

b $9x + 73 = 109$

c $11(x + 14) = 220$

d $17 = \dfrac{x}{4} - 53$

e $25 = \dfrac{x + 81}{4}$

f $40 = \dfrac{3p}{5}$

---

| explanation 4 |

**15** Solve the equations. Give your answers as fractions in their simplest form.

a $10x = 5$

b $3x + 1 = 9$

c $5x - 2 = 1$

d $12x + 10 = 19$

e $25x - 9 = 11$

f $24 = 18x + 12$

---

| explanation 5 |

**16** The perimeter of the rectangle is 76 cm.

a Write this information as an equation and simplify it.

b Solve the equation.

c Find the length of the longest side of the rectangle.

17 cm

$3x$ cm

**17 a** Write and simplify an equation for the sum of the angles of this triangle.

**b** Solve the equation.

**c** Find the angles of the triangle.

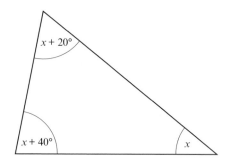

**18** In this diagram, AB is a straight line.

**a** Write and simplify an equation for the sum of the labelled angles.

**b** Solve the equation.

**c** What is the size of each of the labelled angles?

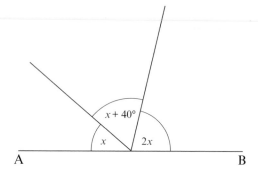

**19** There are 29 chocolates in total on two trays. The second tray has seven fewer chocolates than the first tray. Let $n$ stand for the number of chocolates on the first tray.

**a** Write an expression for the number of chocolates on the second tray.

**b** Write an equation for the total number of chocolates and simplify it.

**c** Solve the equation.

**d** How many chocolates are there on each tray?

explanation 6

**20** Solve the equations.

**a** $3x + 5 = x + 12$        **b** $10k - 8 = 3k + 34$        **c** $7n + 14 = 2n + 69$

**d** $4m - 10 = 3m + 7$        **e** $10 + 3p = p + 12$        **f** $7y - 39 = 3y - 11$

**g** $u + 15 = 2 + 3u$        **h** $7x - 61 = 2x - 1$        **i** $4y - 3 = 2y - 11$

**j** $2x - 15 = 3 - x$        **k** $t + 2 = 26 - 2t$        **l** $11y + 16 = 42 - 2y$

**explanation 7**

**21** Simplify each expression.

    **a** $xy + 2yx$       **b** $5zx + xz$       **c** $2xy + 3yx - xy$

    **d** $5pq - 3qp$       **e** $rp + 6pr - 2$       **f** $pq + qp + pr$

**22 a** Work out these products.

      **i** $(5 \times 4) \times 3$     **ii** $5 \times (4 \times 3)$     **iii** $5 \times 4 \times 3$

    **b** What do you conclude about the values of $(xy)z =$ and $x(yz)$?

**23 a** Choose your own numbers for $x$, $y$ and $z$ and work out the value of each expression.

      **i** $zxy$       **ii** $x(yz)$       **iii** $yxz$       **iv** $y(zx)$

    **b** Explain why these expressions are all equal to $xyz$ for any values of $x$, $y$ and $z$.

**24** Simplify these expressions.

    **a** $3pqr + 2rpq$       **b** $p(qr) + 6rpq$       **c** $10r(qp) - pqr$

**25** Simplify these expressions. The first one has been done for you.

    **a** $2 \times 4p = (2 \times 4)p = 8p$     **b** $3 \times 5q$     **c** $4 \times 7t$

    **d** $8r \times 3$                     **e** $9n \times 4$     **f** $10k \times 3$

**26** Simplify these expressions. The first one has been done for you.

    **a** $4 \times 3g + 5 \times 2g = 12g + 10g$     **b** $3 \times 4w + 2 \times 7w$
                            $= 22g$

    **c** $5 \times 4v - 3 \times 3v$           **d** $7 \times 3x - 5x \times 4$

    **e** $6 \times 4y + y - 3 \times 2y$       **f** $a + 3a \times 5 - 2 \times 4a$

**27** Find and simplify an expression for the coloured area of each shape.

**a**
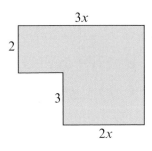

**b**
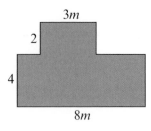

**c**
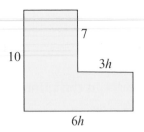

**d**
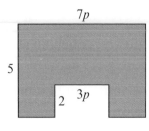

**e**
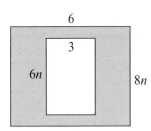

**f**
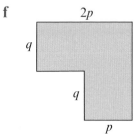

**28** Copy and complete the statement to show the total area in two different ways.
Each ☐ stands for a number.

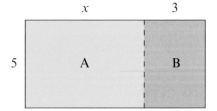

   Total area = area A + area B

   $5(x + ☐) = 5x + ☐$

**29** Copy and complete the statement to show the coloured area of the rectangle in two different ways. ♥ stands for a number and ♦ stands for an expression.

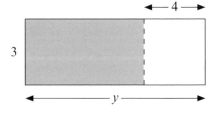

   Coloured area = total area − white area

   $3(y - ♥) = ♦ - 12$

explanation 8a  explanation 8b

**30** Copy and complete the steps to work out $24 \times 19$.

$24 \times 19 = 24 \times (20 - \square)$

$= 24 \times \square - 24 \times \square$

$= \square - \square$

$= \square$

**31** Adapt the method you used in question **30** to help you do the following calculations.

a $32 \times 29$ b $14 \times 49$ c $18 \times 9.9$

**32** Expand the brackets in the expressions.

a $4(x + 5)$ b $6(n - 4)$ c $3(5 + t)$

d $10(12 - h)$ e $8(7 + p)$ f $9(11 - b)$

g $x(3 + y)$ h $r(5 - t)$ i $k(n + 2)$

**33** Jim got the first answer right and all the others wrong. Look at his work.

a Why are his answers wrong?

b Write the correct answers.

Expand the brackets.

i $2(p \times 3) = 2p \times 6$ ✓

ii $4(2y + 1) = 8y + 1$ ✗

iii $7(3m - 2) = 21m - 2$ ✗

iv $8(5n + 4) = 40n + 4$ ✗

v $3(1 - 2k) = 3 - 2k$ ✗

**34** Expand the brackets in the expressions.

a $3(2x + 1)$ b $4(3n - 2)$ c $5(4 - 2k)$

d $6(10 + 3j)$ e $2(9 - 5e)$ f $7(3d + 4)$

g $a(2b + 5)$ h $g(9 - 3t)$ i $2z(5 + 3y)$

**35** Use the diagram to help you complete the statement below.
Each box represents an expression. The first one has been done for you.

$4(x + y + 5)$ = Area A  +  Area B  +  Area C

= $\boxed{4x}$  +  $\boxed{\phantom{xx}}$  +  $\boxed{\phantom{xx}}$

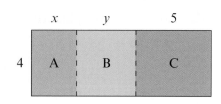

**36** Expand the brackets in these expressions.

    **a** $5(p + q + 3)$         **b** $3(2a + b - 6)$         **c** $4(12 - m + 2n)$

    **d** $10(2h + 5 - k)$       **e** $6(5 - 3c - 4d + 2e)$    **f** $3n(2p + 3q - 3)$

> explanation 9

**37** Expand the brackets and simplify the expressions.

    **a** $3(x + 5) + 2x$        **b** $4(2n - 3) - n$        **c** $2(4 - 5t) + 6$

    **d** $7(2a + 3) - 6a - 11$    **e** $8(w + 2q) + w - 9q$    **f** $4h + 3(h + 5)$

**38** Expand the brackets and simplify the expressions.

    **a** $5(3t + 1) + 2(4t + 3)$       **b** $4(m + 2n + 3) + 3(m + 4n) + 6$

    **c** $14 + 3(7k + 2h + 5) - 9k - 10$    **d** $11 - 5x + 6(x + 2y) - 3y$

> explanation 10

**39** Solve these equations by expanding the brackets first.

    **a** $3(x + 2.5) = 19.5$         **b** $4(x + 3) + 7 = 51$

    **c** $36 = 4(x + 3.5) + 6$      **d** $15 = x + 4(2x - 3)$

    **e** $3x + 2(x + 7) = 59$      **f** $5(x + 1) - 2x - 26 = 0$

    **g** $2(3x + 1) = x + 7$       **h** $7x - 3 = 5(x + 1)$

    **i** $2(3x - 8) = 3x - 7$       **j** $3(x + 1) = 2(x + 4)$

# Functions and mappings

- Completing a mapping diagram
- Using algebra to describe a mapping

Keywords

You should know

explanation 1a    explanation 1b

**1** Here is a partly completed mapping diagram.

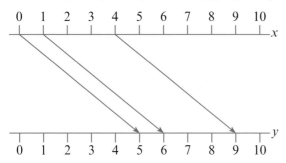

**a** Copy and complete the diagram.

**b** Copy and complete these statements.
The rule for the mapping may be written as

**i** $y = \square$          **ii** $x \rightarrow \square$

**2 a** Copy and complete this mapping diagram.

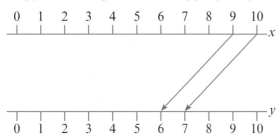

**b** Find the ouput for each of these input values.

**i** 16      **ii** 21      **iii** 38

**c** Copy and complete these statements.
The rule for the mapping may be written as

**i** $y = \square$          **ii** $x \rightarrow \square$

149

**3** Look at this function machine $x \rightarrow$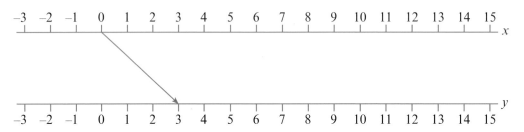

  **a**   **i**   Write the rule for the function machine in the form $y = \square$.

      **ii**   Write the rule for the function machine in the form $x \rightarrow \square$.

  **b**   Find the output for each of the following input values.

      **i**   0       **ii**   1       **iii**   2       **iv**   10       **v**   −2

  **c**   Find the input for each of the following output values.

      **i**   15      **ii**   63      **iii**   20      **iv**   50      **v**   −3

  **d**   Copy and complete this mapping diagram for values of $x$ from −3 to 6.

-3 -2 -1  0  1  2  3  4  5  6  7  8  9  10  11  12  13  14  15   $x$

-3 -2 -1  0  1  2  3  4  5  6  7  8  9  10  11  12  13  14  15   $y$

**4** This function machine uses the same instructions as in question **3**, but in reverse order.

$$x \rightarrow \boxed{+ 3} \rightarrow \boxed{\times 2} \rightarrow y$$

  **a**   Explain why the rule for this function machine *can't* be written as $y = x + 3 \times 2$.

  **b**   Write the rule correctly in the form $y = \square$.

  **c**   Find the values of $y$ when $x$ is −4, −3, −2, −1, 0, 1, 2, and 3.

  **d**   Draw a mapping diagram for this function. Use values of $x$ from −4 to 3.

explanation 2

**5** **a**   Aisha is using the values of $x$ from −2 to 4 to draw this simple mapping diagram for the mapping $x \rightarrow 4x - 3$.

      Copy and complete her diagram.

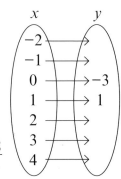

  **b**   Draw similar mapping diagrams for the following mappings.

      **i**   $y = 3(x - 1)$      **ii**   $x \rightarrow \dfrac{x}{2} + 1$      **iii**   $y = \dfrac{x + 8}{2}$

**6 a** Which partly completed mapping diagram belongs with which label?

$$y = 20 - 2x \qquad y = 10 - x \qquad y = 2(x - 5) \qquad y = 2x - 5$$

$$y = 2x + 3 \qquad\qquad y = x + 3$$

**i**

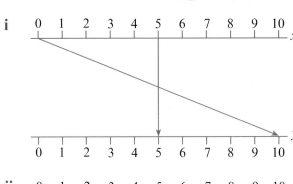

**ii**

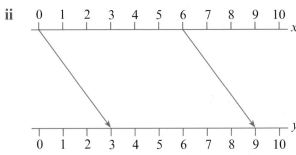

**iii**

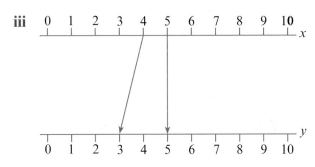

**iv**

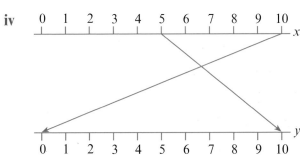

**b** Copy and complete each of the mapping diagrams in part **a** using the rules you chose.

151

explanation 3

**7 a** Find the rule for each mapping diagram.
Write each rule in two ways, as $y = \Box$ and as $x \to \Box$.

**i** 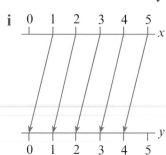    **ii**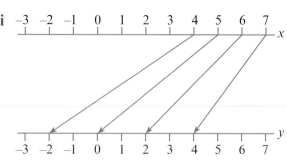

**iii**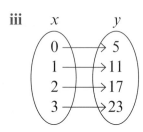

**b** For each diagram find, if possible, the number that is mapped to itself.

**8 a** Which of the following labels could match the partly completed mapping diagram below?

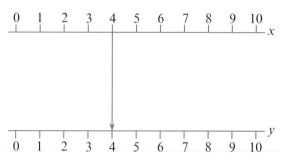

**b** Which of the labels in part **a** results in each of the following mappings?

**i** $3 \to 5$         **ii** $10 \to 10$         **iii** $5 \to 6$

**9** This question is about the mapping $x \to 4x - 12$.

**a** Find the value of $x$ that is mapped to itself.

**b** Find the value of $x$ that is mapped to twice itself.

# Measures

- Approximating sizes of everyday objects in metric units
- Reading scales on a variety of instruments
- Converting between different metric units

Keywords

You should know

explanation 1a | explanation 1b

**1** Copy the table and put a tick in one column for each unit.
The first one has been done for you.

| Unit | Length | Area | Capacity | Mass |
|------|--------|------|----------|------|
| Metre | ✓ | | | |
| Centilitre | | | | |
| Centimetre | | | | |
| Square millimetre | | | | |
| Gram | | | | |
| Litre | | | | |
| Square centimetre | | | | |
| Millimetre | | | | |
| Kilogram | | | | |

**2** The abbreviation for centimetre is cm. Write the abbreviation for each of the following units.

a millimetre      b centilitre      c square metre

d square centimetre      e kilometre      f gram

g metre      h kilogram      i millilitre

**3** Copy and complete.

a $10\,\text{mm} = 1\,\square$      b $100\,\square = 1\text{ litre}$      c $1000\,\text{g} = 1\,\square$

d $\square\,\text{cm} = 1\,\text{m}$      e $1000\,\square = 1\,\text{m}$      f $1000\,\square = 1\text{ litre}$

**4** What is the capacity of each container?

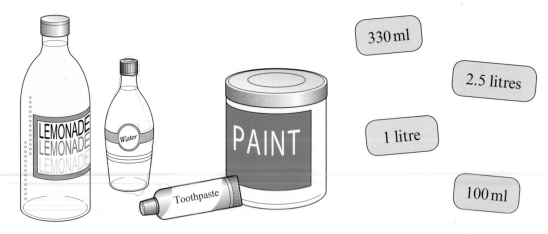

330 ml

2.5 litres

1 litre

100 ml

**5** What is the mass of each item?

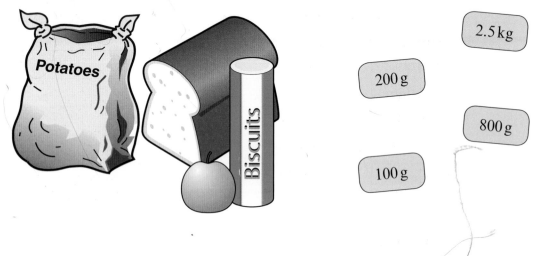

2.5 kg

200 g

800 g

100 g

**6** Carol does her shopping on the internet.
She has to be careful to order things in the right quantities.
List any of the following items and quantities that don't seem to be correct.

Butter (500 g)                    Milk (40 litres)
Cheese (400 g)                   Potatoes (5 g)
Mushrooms (50 kg)            Broccoli (300 g)
Orange juice (1.5 ml)         Tomato sauce (330 litres)
Frozen peas (1.2 kg)          Carrots (2 kg)
Washing up liquid (500 litres)   Chocolate (100 g bar)

explanation 2

**7** Elliot is cooking spaghetti for five people.

He opens a 1 kg pack and uses the scales to measure out the amount he needs.

**a** How much spaghetti did he use for five people?

**b** How much spaghetti would each person get?

**c** How much spaghetti is left in the packet?

**8** A recipe requires 0.6 litres of stock, pine nuts, currants, onions and cinnamon.

**a** How many millilitres of stock are needed?

**b** A new 150 g packet of pine nuts is opened.

The scale shows the amount of pine nuts left after some have been used in the recipe.

What is the reading on the scale?

**c** How many grams of pine nuts have been used for the recipe?

**9** The diagram shows two scales.

**a** What is the mass of the cheese?

**b** Copy the second set of scales. Draw an arrow to show the mass of cheese.

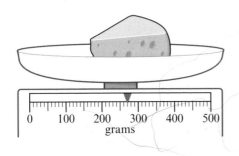

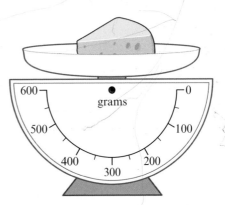

**10** The scales show the combined mass of three different types of cheese.

Find the mass of each type of cheese.

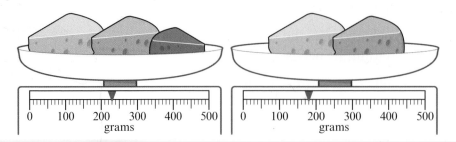

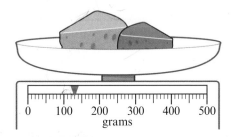

**11** Read the values shown on these instruments. Remember to include the units.

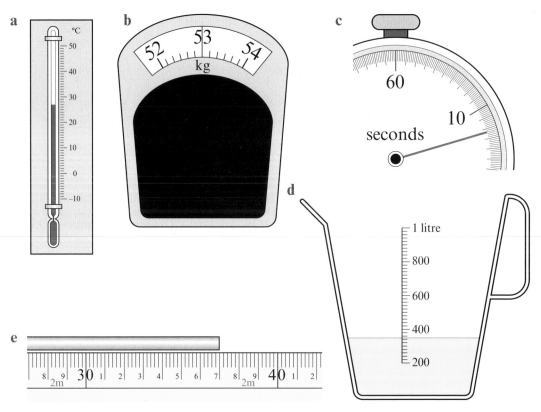

explanation 3

**12** Copy and complete.

    **a**  36 cm = ☐mm        **b**  24.8 cm = ☐mm

    **c**  900 mm = ☐cm       **d**  437 mm = ☐cm

    **e**  1.6 m = ☐mm        **f**  320 cm = ☐m

| 10 mm = 1 cm |
| 100 cm = 1 m |

**13** Copy and complete.

    **a**  75 cl = ☐litres       **b**  2.5 litres = ☐ml

    **c**  125 cl = ☐litres      **d**  330 ml = ☐cl

    **e**  3 litres = ☐cl        **f**  55 cl = ☐ml

| 10 ml = 1 cl |
| 100 cl = 1 litre |

**14** Copy and complete.

    **a**  2000 g = ☐kg        **b**  3.5 kg = ☐g

    **c**  625 g = ☐kg         **d**  0.7 kg = ☐g

    **e**  0.09 kg = ☐g       **f**  24 g = ☐kg

| 1000 g = 1 kg |

**15** Petrol is now sold in litres, but years ago it was sold by the gallon.
There are roughly 4.5 litres in 1 gallon.

    **a**  A typical family car will travel about 8 miles on 1 litre of fuel.
How many miles is this per gallon?

    **b**  A Lamborghini will only travel about 9 miles on 1 gallon of fuel.
How many miles is this per litre?

**16** A standard ruler used in schools is 12 inches long.
What is the length of a standard ruler in centimetres?

| 1 inch is |
| about 2.5 cm. |

**17** Michael has a hand span of 20 cm. What is this in inches?

**18** Look at the recipe for spicy pasta.

    **a**   What type of units are used in the recipe?

    **b**   Copy the recipe out and use the newspaper article to change the amounts to metric measures. Write your answers to an appropriate degree of accuracy.

> 2 oz butter
> 1 lb tomatoes
> 7 fl oz vegetable stock
> $\frac{3}{4}$ lb dried pasta
> 2 tsp tomato puree
> Onion, garlic, chilli, salt and pepper

## New for old

1 ounce (oz) = 28.4 g          1 pound (lb) = 16 oz

1 pint = 568.2 ml           1 pint = 20 fluid ounces (fl oz)

**19** Here are some motorway signs seen by a driver travelling at a constant speed of 72 mph in a car.

| Birmingham |
| 120 miles |

| Services 18 m |

mph is short for miles per hour.
1 mile = 1609 m
1 km = 1000 m

$$\text{speed} = \frac{\text{distance}}{\text{time}}$$

    **a**   How long will it take to get to Birmingham?

    **b**   How far away are the services?

    **c**   How long will it take to get to the services for a drink?

    **d**   What are the distances on the signs to the nearest kilometre?

    **e**   What speed is the car moving at in kilometres per hour?

explanation 4a    explanation 4b    explanation 4c

**20**  How many hours are there in a week?

**21**  **a**  How many minutes are there in a day?

   **b**  How many minutes are there in a week?

**22**  It has been calculated that Bill earns $250 per second.
   How much does Bill earn in an hour?

**23**  Write these times using the 24-hour clock.

   **a**  7:21 a.m.          **b**  3:20 p.m.          **c**  10:24 p.m.

   **d**  5:15 p.m.          **e**  1:09 a.m.          **f**  1:36 p.m.

**24**  Write these times using the 12-hour clock.

   **a**  18:05             **b**  16:22             **c**  09:20

   **d**  11:30             **e**  23:55             **f**  10:42

**25**  Ben can walk to work in 22 minutes. He wants to arrive at
   8:10 a.m. to prepare for a meeting. What time should Ben
   leave for work?

**26**  Suzie is travelling from Stafford to Cambridge and has to change trains at
   Nuneaton. Her arrival time at Nuneaton is 07:48 and her departure time is
   08:03. How long does Suzie have to wait at Nuneaton?

**27**  The new high speed Channel Tunnel rail link makes it possible to travel from
   London to Paris in 2 hours 15 minutes and from London to Brussels in
   1 hour 51 minutes.

   **a**  A train leaves London at 14:47. What time will it arrive in Paris?

   **b**  A train arrives in Brussels from London at 16:24. What time did the train
   leave London?

# Triangles

- Recognising and naming different types of triangle
- Which information is needed to define a triangle
- Constructing a triangle using SAS, ASA or SSS

Keywords

You should know

explanation 1a    explanation 1b

**1** Pick the best label for each of the following triangles from the ones given below.

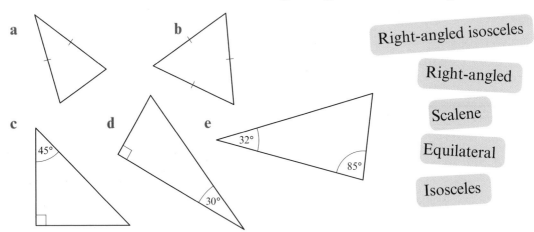

Right-angled isosceles

Right-angled

Scalene

Equilateral

Isosceles

**2** The triangles in the diagram are drawn on isometric paper.

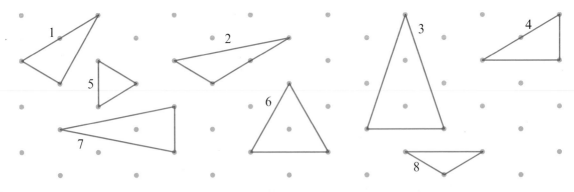

List the triangles that are:

**a** Equilateral

**b** Isosceles

**c** Right-angled

**d** Obtuse-angled

**e** Scalene

**f** Acute-angled

**3** Pupils were asked to draw a right-angled triangle ABC with AB = 4 cm and BC = 5 cm. The triangles that Inez and Declan drew are shown.

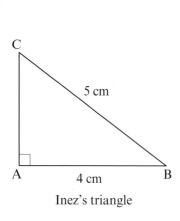

Inez's triangle

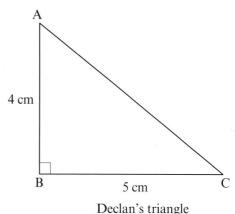

Declan's triangle

   **a** Are the triangles the same?

   **b** Who is right? Explain.

( explanation 2a ) ( explanation 2b ) ( explanation 2c ) ( explanation 2d )

**4** You are given the lengths of two sides of a triangle. Which angle do you need to complete the information for **SAS** when you are given the lengths of the following pairs of sides?

   **a** XY and YZ      **b** AC and AB

   **c** PR and QR?

> It's a good idea to sketch the triangles first.

**5 a** Use the information in these sketches to construct the triangles.

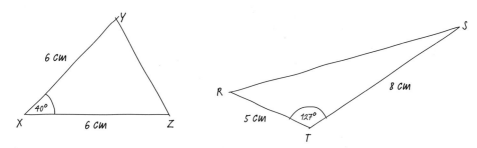

   **b** Measure the following lengths on your diagrams.

      **i** YZ       **ii** RS

   **c** Use capital letters to describe the two angles of 40° and 127°.

   **d** Sanjeev needs to draw triangle RST for homework, but he hasn't got the sketch of this triangle. What instructions would you give him over the phone?

**6** Construct triangle ABC where AC = 8.6 cm, AB = 3.9 cm and angle
BAC = 120°.
Measure BC and angle ABC.

Sketch the triangles first.

**7** ABCD is a rhombus. AC and BD cross at their midpoints.
AC = 8 cm and BD = 6 cm.

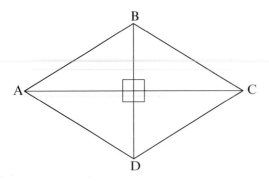

Construct a triangle and use it to work out the perimeter of the rhombus.
Explain how you did it.

**8 a** Make an accurate drawing of the rhombus PQRS shown in this sketch.

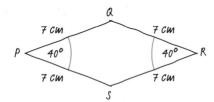

**b** Measure the length of the diagonals PR and QS.

explanation 3a  explanation 3b  explanation 3c  explanation 3d

**9** You are given the size of two angles in a triangle. Which side do you need to
complete the information for **ASA** when you are given the following pairs of
angles?

**a** ∠ABC and ∠ACB    **b** ∠FHG and ∠FGH    **c** ∠JKL and ∠KLJ

**10 a** Use the information in the following sketches to construct the triangles.

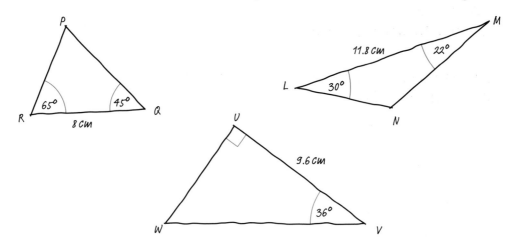

**b** Measure the following lengths on your diagrams.

**i** PR     **ii** PQ     **iii** UW     **iv** VW     **v** LN     **vi** MN

**11** Construct triangle DEF where DE = 9.2 cm, ∠DEF = 45° and ∠FDE = 57°. Measure DF.

**12** Construct triangle KLM where LM = 11.3 cm, ∠KLM = 38° and ∠KML = 64°. Measure KL.

**13** Daniel, Emily and Farah are trying to find the width of a river.
Emily stands to face Daniel on the opposite side of the river.
Farah measures 10 m along the river bank from Emily.
She measures the angle between the directions of Daniel and Emily as 53°.

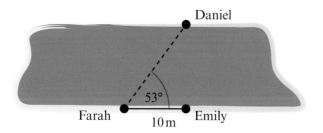

You don't need to draw a line 10 m long! Use centimetres to represent metres.

Construct a triangle to show this information. How wide is the river?

**14** The diagram shows two coastguard
stations D and E, 8 km apart.
A distress flare F is set off at the
position shown.

Construct an accurate scale drawing
using this information.

Measure the distance of the flare from
each of the coastguard stations.

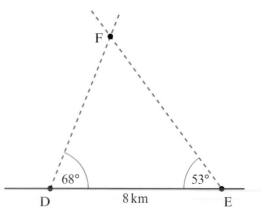

**15** A group of ramblers
cannot walk straight from
Anford to Briarbridge as
they usually do.
Instead they have to go
through Cranley, to avoid
a conservation area.
Cranley is 7.2 km from
Anford and 5.6 km from
Briarbridge, as shown in
this sketch map.

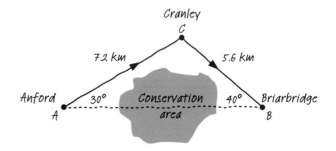

**a** Nadia is drawing a scale diagram of the walk but she cannot get started.
   What instructions would you give her?

**b** Construct an accurate scale drawing of the route.

**c** How much further did the ramblers walk, compared with the direct route
   from Anford to Briarbridge?

explanation 4a    explanation 4b    explanation 4c    explanation 4d

**16 a** Use the information in the following sketches to construct the triangles.

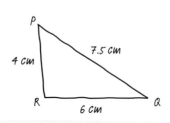

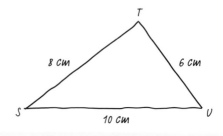

**17** Measure the following angles from the diagrams you drew in question **16**.

    **a**   RP̂Q              **b**   ∠SUT

**18** Construct the triangle UVW where UV = 6.5 cm, UW = 8 cm and VW = 8 cm. Measure the two equal angles.

**19** Construct the rhombus ABCD shown in this sketch.
The length of the diagonal AC is 9 cm and all the sides are 5 cm.

Measure the length BD.

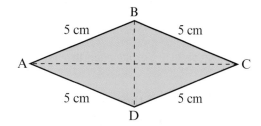

**20** Construct the arrowhead PQRS shown in this sketch.
PR = PQ = QR = 6 cm and PS = RS = 3.5 cm.

Measure QS.

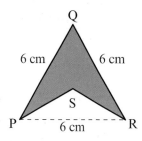

**21** This diagram shows the school cross-country course.

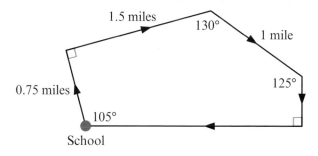

    **a**   Draw the course accurately using 4 cm to 1 mile.

    **b**   What is the length of the course in miles?

# Nets and 3-D shapes

- Constructing a net for a 3-D shape
- Finding the surface area of a 3-D shape
- The relationship between the number of vertices, faces and edges of a 3-D shape

Keywords

You should know

explanation 1a   explanation 1b

**1  a**  Which of these diagrams could be used as a net for a cube?

1     2 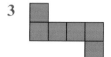    3     4

**b**  Draw two other nets that fold into a cube.

**c**  How many *vertices* does a cube have?

**d**  How many *faces* does a cube have?

**e**  How many *edges* does a cube have?

**2**  The diagram shows a partly completed net for a cuboid drawn on a grid of 1 cm squares.

**a**  What shape is needed to complete the net? Include its size.

**b**  There are a number of options for where to place the missing part. Make a list of the edges where it could be attached.

**c**  When the cuboid is made, which of the labelled points will meet A?

**d**  Give the dimensions of the completed cuboid.

**e**  Find the area of each of these rectangles.

   **i**  ABKL    **ii**  CDEB    **iii**  BEHK

**f**  Work out the total surface area of the cuboid.

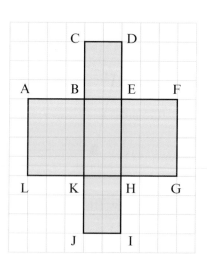

**3** Copy this net for a cube onto paper or card and add any necessary flaps.
The cube is to be made into a dice.

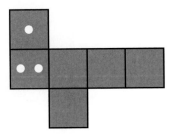

   **a** Label it so that numbers on opposite faces add up to 7. In how many ways
can this be done?

   **b** Make the dice.

**4** The diagram shows a partly completed net for a cuboid on a grid of
centimetre squares.

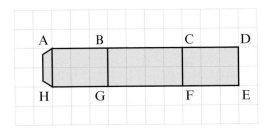

   **a** Copy the diagram and complete it by drawing rectangles on the edges
BC, DE and FE.

   **b** The net has a flap on the edge AH.
How many flaps are needed altogether?
Add the necessary flaps to your net.

   **c** Work out the surface area of the cuboid.

**5** Draw nets without flaps and use them to find the surface areas of these shapes.

   **a** A cube with side 2.5 cm

                                 **b** A cuboid 6 cm by 3 cm by 2 cm

2.5 cm

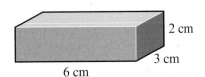

2 cm

3 cm

6 cm

explanation 2

6   Here is a partly completed sketch of a net for a
    triangular prism.

    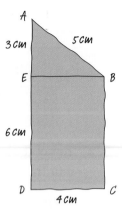

    a   Copy and complete the sketch by adding a triangle
        to the edge DC and rectangles to ED and BC.

        Include the measurements on your sketch.

    b   Work out the surface area of the triangular prism.

    c   Which of the labelled points will be furthest from A
        when the prism is complete?

    d   Find the number of vertices, faces and edges of a
        triangular prism.

7   Kerry found the surface area of the triangular prism in question 6 by working
    out $3 \times 4 + 6(3 + 4 + 5)$

    a   Explain why Kerry's method works.

    b   Write an expression to find the surface area of a prism twice as long, but
        otherwise the same as the one in question 6.

    c   Use your expression to calculate the area.

8   a   Use a ruler and protractor to draw the triangle shown on a piece of card.
        Check that each side is 3 cm long.

        Read the whole  of question 8 before you do part a.

    b   Use your triangle as part of a net for a triangular
        prism of length 5 cm.

    c   Cut out the net and make the prism.

    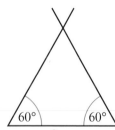

**9** The sketch shows a partly completed net of a triangular prism.

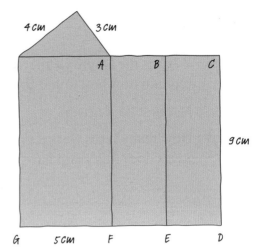

**a** Write down the length of:

  **i** AB  **ii** BC

**b** Copy the sketch and complete it by adding a triangle to the edge GF. Label the lengths of its sides.

**c** Repeat part **b** but, this time, attach the triangle to the edge FE.

**d** Work out the surface area of the triangular prism.

**10** The diagram shows the net of a prism.

**a** Which of the labelled points will be joined to A when it is complete?

**b** Write down the lengths of the following edges.

  **i** AB  **ii** BC

  **iii** CD  **iv** DE

  **v** EF  **vi** FG

**c** Copy and complete the following expression for the surface area of the prism.
Each ☐ stands for a number.

$2 \times (5^2 - ☐^2) + ☐ \times (5 + ☐ + ☐ + ☐ + ☐ + ☐)$

**d** What is the surface area of the prism?

**e** Find the number of vertices, faces and edges of the prism.

**11** Describe the smallest solid shape that can be combined with the prism in question **10** to make a cuboid.

**12 a** Draw the net of the ramp shown in this diagram, starting with the rectangular base.

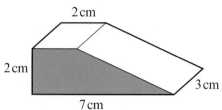

**b** What is the length of the slope? Explain how you found this length.

**c** Is this solid a prism?

**d** How many faces, vertices and edges does this ramp have?

**13 a** Construct the net shown for a square-based pyramid and add any flaps as necessary.

**b** Cut out the net and make the pyramid.

**c** The angle at the base of the triangle is 70°. What would happen if this angle was 45°?

**d** Find the number of vertices, faces and edges of the pyramid.

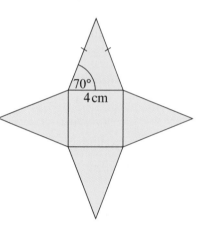

**14 a** Construct the triangle shown.

**b** Join the midpoints of the sides of the triangle to make the net of a tetrahedron of side 3 cm. Add the flaps.

**c** Cut out the net and fold to make the tetrahedron.

**d** Find the number of vertices, faces and edges of the tetrahedron.

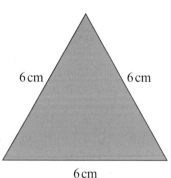

**15 a** Look at the sketch of solid A shown below. Copy and complete the following table to show how many vertices, faces and edges solid A has.

Extend the table to include the solid shapes from questions **1, 6, 10, 12, 13** and **14**. Show the number of vertices, faces and edges for each shape.

| Solid shape | Vertices (V) | Faces (F) | Edges (E) |
|---|---|---|---|
| Solid A | 8 | 6 | |

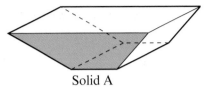

Solid A

**b** Try to find a formula connecting the values of V, F and E.

**16** Find the length of each edge of a cube if its surface area is:

**a**   $96\,cm^2$ **b**   $216\,cm^2$ **c**   $486\,cm^2$

**17 a** Find the surface area of a cube with side 3 cm.

**b** Find the surface area of a cube with sides twice as long. Is the surface area twice as big?

**18** The first cuboid has length $x$ cm, width $y$ cm and height $z$ cm.
The sides of the second cuboid are twice as long as the first cuboid.

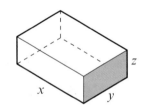

**a** Explain why the area of the base of the smaller cuboid is $xy\,cm^2$.

**b** Write down an expression for the total surface area of the smaller cuboid.

**c** Explain why the area of the base of the larger cuboid is $4xy\,cm^2$.

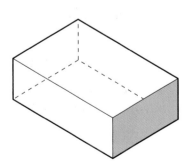

**d** Write down an expression for the total surface area of the second cuboid.

**e** Compare your answers to parts **b** and **d**.

# Geometry and measures GM3.4

## Representing 3-D shapes

- Drawing solid shapes on plain paper
- Drawing solid shapes on isometric paper

Keywords

You should know

explanation 1a · explanation 1b · explanation 1c

**1** Write down the more usual name for each of these solid shapes.

a A circular-based pyramid  b A rectangular prism

c A circular prism  d A triangular-based pyramid

**2** Match each of the following solid shapes to its label.

Cone  Cylinder  Square-based pyramid  Cube

Triangular prism  Cuboid  Tetrahedron

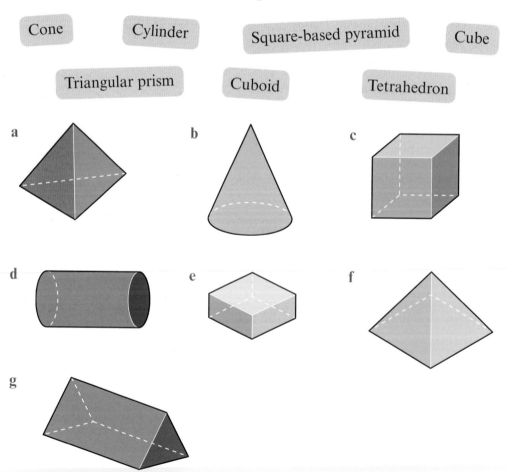

**3** Here are some partly completed sketches of 3-D objects.
Copy and complete them.

a 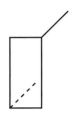    b 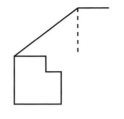    c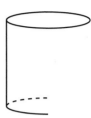

d     e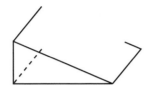

**4** Look at this diagram representing a solid made from glass so that you can see all of its edges.

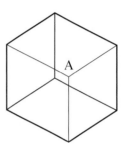

It is actually a flat pattern of lines, but you could visualise it in either of the following ways.

- A cuboid with the vertex at A closest to you.
- A cuboid with the vertex at A furthest from you.

The hard part is to try to switch between the two possible views!

**a** Copy the diagram but replace three of the solid lines with dotted lines to represent a cuboid with the vertex at A closest to you.

**b** Make another copy of the diagram but, this time, replace three different solid lines with dotted lines to represent a cuboid with the vertex at A furthest from you.

**5** This diagram represents a cone positioned slightly below your point of view.

Copy the diagram but make one change so that the cone is slightly above your point of view.

**6** Look at this diagram representing a prism.

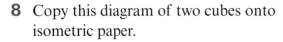

 **a** Does the shaded end appear closer or further away than the unshaded end?

 **b** Copy the diagram but change which lines are dotted so that the opposite end of the prism appears closer.

explanation 2a   explanation 2b

**7** This diagram shows two cubes drawn on isometric paper.

 **a** Copy the diagram onto isometric paper. Add an extra cube to make a block of three cubes in a straight line.

 **b** Is it easier to add the extra cube to the near end or the far end? Explain why.

**8** Copy this diagram of two cubes onto isometric paper.

 Add two extra cubes to make a block of four cubes in a straight line.

**9** This diagram shows one cube stacked on top of another.

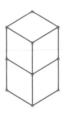

 **a** Copy the diagram an add a third cube to the stack.

 **b** Is it easier to add the third cube above or below the two cubes shown?

**10** Eight cubes can be placed together to make a larger cube. Show how this would look on isometric paper.

Use your answers to questions **8**, **9** and **10** to plan the order in which you draw the cubes.

**11  a**  Copy these three solids onto isometric paper.

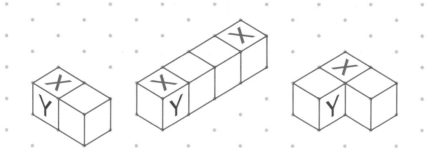

    **b**  Draw another diagram to show what each shape will look like if you place one cube on top of each face labelled X and one cube next to each face labelled Y.

**12**  Copy and complete this diagram to represent two layers of six cubes. Use isometric paper.

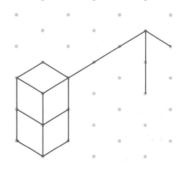

**13  a**  Copy and complete this drawing of a cuboid measuring 4 cm by 3 cm by 2 cm. Use isometric paper.

    **b**  Draw on isometric paper a cuboid measuring 2 cm by 2 cm by 5 cm.

    **c**  Draw on isometric paper a cuboid measuring 5 cm by 1 cm by 4 cm.

**14**  How many 1 cm by 1 cm by 1 cm cubes would be needed to make each of the cuboids in question **13**?

**15** The diagram below shows shape A and a partly completed shape B.

The two shapes fit together to make a cuboid.

    **a**  Copy and complete shape B.

    **b**  Draw shapes A and B fitted together to make the cuboid.

    **c**  What are the dimensions of the cuboid?

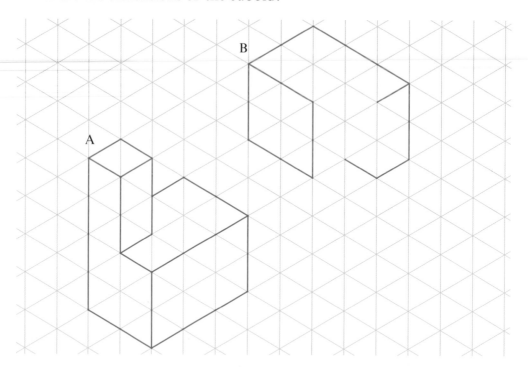

**16** The diagram shows one possible way of making a solid from four cubes.
Each cube is 1 cm by 1 cm by 1 cm.

The surface area of this solid is $18 \text{ cm}^2$

    **a**  Draw all the possible solids that can be made
from four cubes.

    **b**  Which solid has the smallest surface area?

**17** Use isometric paper to draw as many different cuboids as you can that can be
made using twelve 1 cm by 1 cm by 1 cm cubes.
Which has the smallest surface area?

# Fractions and percentages of amounts

- Calculating a fraction of an amount
- Calculating a percentage of an amount

Keywords

You should know

explanation 1

**1** Here are some diagrams divided into smaller parts.

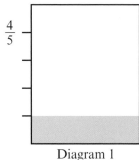
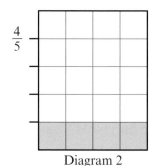
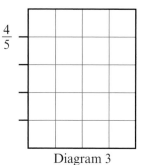

Diagram 1          Diagram 2          Diagram 3

**a** What fraction of Diagram 1 is blue?

**b** Copy Diagram 2 and write the missing fractions on the vertical scale.

**c** Copy and complete.
The number of blue squares in Diagram 2 is $\dfrac{\square}{\square}$ of 20 = $\dfrac{20}{\square}$ = $\square$.

**d** Copy Diagram 3 and shade $\dfrac{4}{5}$ of the squares.

**e** Copy and complete.
The number of shaded squares in Diagram 3 is $\dfrac{4}{5}$ of 20 = $\square \times \dfrac{1}{5}$ of 20 = $\square$.

**2 a** $\dfrac{1}{5}$ of a number is 23. What is $\dfrac{2}{5}$ of the number?

**b** $\dfrac{1}{11}$ of a number is 32. What is $\dfrac{3}{11}$ of the number?

**c i** Copy and complete: $\dfrac{1}{3} = \dfrac{\square}{9}$

**ii** $\dfrac{1}{9}$ of a number is 42. What is $\dfrac{1}{3}$ of the number?

**d i** Copy and complete: $1 = \dfrac{\square}{5}$

**ii** $\dfrac{1}{5}$ of a number is 61. What is the number?

**3** Work these out.

a i $\frac{1}{5}$ of 40      ii $\frac{2}{5}$ of 40      iii $\frac{3}{5}$ of 40

b i $\frac{1}{12}$ of 36      ii $\frac{5}{12}$ of 36      iii $\frac{11}{12}$ of 36

c i $\frac{1}{7}$ of 28      ii $\frac{2}{7}$ of 28      iii $\frac{5}{7}$ of 28

**4** What are the missing numbers?

a $\frac{\square}{5}$ of 20 = 12      b $\frac{3}{8}$ of $\square$ = 21      c $\frac{11}{\square}$ of 24 = 22

d $\frac{5}{\square}$ of 27 = 15      e $\frac{7}{20}$ of $\square$ = 35      f $\frac{\square}{50}$ of 200 = 52

**5** A theatre has a maximum capacity of 800 seats. On the last performance only $\frac{1}{10}$ of the seats are empty and it is estimated that $\frac{4}{9}$ of the audience have a programme.

a How many people are in the audience?

b How many programmes have been sold?

**6** Every 10 weeks a mushroom farm produces 240 boxes of mushrooms. $\frac{3}{4}$ of the boxes go to the supermarket and the rest are sold locally. $\frac{2}{3}$ of the boxes that go to the supermarket are graded as Class 1 mushrooms.

a How many boxes go to the supermarket?

b How many boxes that go to the supermarket are Class 1?

explanation 2a    explanation 2b

**7** Work these out.

a $\frac{2}{5} \times 30$      b $\frac{3}{4} \times 64$      c $\frac{6}{25} \times 75$

d $20 \times \frac{7}{10}$      e $32 \times \frac{11}{16}$      f $21 \times \frac{3}{7}$

**8** Write these fractions as mixed numbers.

a $\frac{1}{3}$ of 8      b $15 \times \frac{1}{4}$      c $\frac{2}{3}$ of 11

d $\frac{3}{5} \times 9$      e $\frac{3}{4}$ of 21      f $44 \times \frac{5}{8}$

explanation 3

**9  a**  Copy the diagram and fill in the missing values.

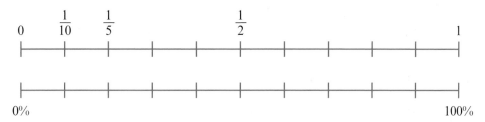

**b**  Use your diagram to write these fractions as percentages.

  **i**  $\dfrac{1}{10}$      **ii**  $\dfrac{3}{5}$      **iii**  $\dfrac{9}{10}$      **iv**  $\dfrac{2}{5}$

**c**  Use your diagram to write these percentages as fractions.

  **i**  20%      **ii**  50%      **iii**  70%      **iv**  60%

**10**  Copy and complete.

  **a**  30% of 40 = $\dfrac{3}{\Box}$ of 40 = $\Box$        **b**  80% of 30 = $\dfrac{\Box}{\Box}$ of 30 = $\Box$

**11**  Work these out by first writing the percentages as fractions.

  **a**  20% of 60      **b**  50% of 86      **c**  25% of 36

  **d**  10% of 3000      **e**  75% of 140      **f**  90% of 1200

  **g**  50% of 65      **h**  25% of 24      **i**  60% of 25

explanation 4a   explanation 4b

**12**  Find 10% of each of these amounts.

  **a**  £80      **b**  £300      **c**  £1700      **d**  £25 000

  **e**  £92      **f**  £7      **g**  £234      **h**  £67.50

  **i**  £9.40      **j**  £27.80      **k**  £0.70      **l**  £1.50

**13** Oskar is working out $7\frac{1}{2}$% of £6.80 without a calculator. He starts by finding 10%.

> $10\% = \dfrac{1}{10}$
>
> 10% of £6.80 = £6.80 ÷ 10
>
> = £0.68
>
> 5% of £6.80 = £0.34

   **a** Explain what he has done next.

   **b** What else should he do to work out $7\frac{1}{2}$% of £6.80?

   **c** How could he work out $22\frac{1}{2}$% of £6.80?

   **d** Use a similar method to work out 15% of £8.20.

**14** Work out these percentages.

   **a**  **i**  10% of 46 kg        **ii**  20% of 46 kg

       **iii**  30% of 46 kg      **iv**  15% of 46 kg

   **b**  **i**  10% of £24          **ii**  5% of £24

       **iii**  2.5% of £24       **iv**  17.5% of £24

   **c**  **i**  50% of 60 m         **ii**  5% of 60 m

       **iii**  45% of 60 m       **iv**  55% of 60 m

   **d**  **i**  50% of 84 g          **ii**  25% of 84 g

       **iii**  12.5% of 84 g      **iv**  85% of 84 g

**15** Use the methods of questions **13** and **14** to work out these percentages.

   **a** 20% of £70         **b** 5% of 80 cm       **c** 25% of 140 mm

   **d** 30% of £16         **e** 12.5% of 48 g     **f** 45% of 40 litres

   **g** 15% of 32 km       **h** 7.5% of 120 people   **i** 55% of 800 tonnes

**16**  **a** Copy and complete.

      $3 \times 33\frac{1}{3} = 3 \times (33 + \square) = 99 + \square = \square$

   **b** Write $33\frac{1}{3}$% as a fraction in its lowest terms.

**17** Find the sale price for each of these marked prices.

   **a** Boots £57          **b** Jumper £25.80

SALE

Everything must go

$33\frac{1}{3}$% off

**18** A top sprinter can run at a speed of about 10 m/s.

A little-known fact is that some crocodiles can reach up to 40% of this speed.

How fast can these crocodiles run?

**19** The prices shown below for the DAB radio and the 19-inch LCD TV do not include VAT at $17\frac{1}{2}\%$.

Without using a calculator find the total cost, including VAT, of each item.

a

£68

b

£180

( explanation 5a )   ( explanation 5b )

**20** Write the decimal equivalents of these percentages.

| | | | | |
|---|---|---|---|---|
| **a** 6% | **b** 7% | **c** 10% | **d** 14% | **e** 17.5% |
| **f** 25% | **g** 30% | **h** 45% | **i** 94% | **j** 87.4% |

Use a calculator for questions **21** to **30**.

**21** Work these out.

| | | |
|---|---|---|
| **a** 7% of 83 kg | **b** 62% of £118 | **c** 90% of 23.4 mm |
| **d** 120% of £85 | **e** 19.5 % of £2000 | **f** 4.8% of £302 |

**22** Look at the information on this yoghurt pot.
Find the amount of each food type.

**a** Fat

**b** Sugar

**c** Protein

Low Fat Yoghurt
125 g

Sugar 9%
Fat 2.5%
Protein 4%

**23** Research has shown that 13% of all males and 11% of all females are left-handed. In a school there are 130 girls and 120 boys aged 15.

    **a** How many 15-year-old girls would you expect to be left-handed?

    **b** How many 15-year-old pupils would you expect to be left-handed?

**24** A dog weighs 35 kg. The vet says it needs to lose 16% of its body weight. How many kilograms is this?

**25** Jenny is paid £6.50 per hour but has been offered a pay rise of 12%. To find her new rate of pay she finds 12% of £6.50 and adds this on. What is her new pay rate?

**26** The prices shown do not include VAT.
Find the total cost including VAT at 17.5%.

    **a** Radiator at £109     **b** Lamp at £35     **c** Computer at £460

**27** A bus company increases its prices by 8%. At the moment the bus fare to town is 70p. Calculate the new fare.

**28** Find the sale price of each item.

**29** Paige is buying a DVD online.

    **a** Find how much she pays.

    **b** Find 65% of £19.99 and comment on your answer.

> **Latest DVDs**
> Normally £19.99
> Save 35%
> You pay: £?

**30** A 2-disc DVD usually costs £24.99. It is now a special offer item and you save 56%.

    **a** Explain two ways of finding the new price.

    **b** The shop price of a CD is £14.95. Calculate the online price if you save 18%.

# Ratio and proportion

- Expressing a proportion as a fraction, decimal or percentage
- Comparing proportions
- Comparing two quantities using a ratio
- Simplifying a ratio and sharing an amount in a given ratio

Keywords

You should know

explanation 1

**1** The proportions of the main gases that make the atmosphere on Earth are shown below. Unfortunately, they are mixed in with the proportions for the planet Mars.

| Other 1% | Nitrogen 3% | Carbon dioxide 95% |

| Oxygen 21% | Nitrogen 78% | Other 2% |

Copy and complete these tables by working out which information must go where.

We need ... to breathe.

| Planet | Gas | Proportion |
|--------|-----|------------|
| Earth  |     |            |
|        |     |            |
|        |     |            |
|        | Total | 100%     |

| Planet | Gas | Proportion |
|--------|-----|------------|
| Mars   |     |            |
|        |     |            |
|        |     |            |
|        | Total | 100%     |

**2** In a football match, Team A had 25 shots at goal with 17 on target. Team B had 20 shots at goal with 13 on target.

**a** Write the proportion of shots on target for each team as a fraction and as a decimal.

**b** Which team seems to be more accurate?

**c** Which expression of a proportion did you find the most useful when answering part **b**?

**3** The table shows the choices made by a class of 30 pupils going on a school trip.

| | Boys | Girls | Total |
|---|---|---|---|
| Bowling | 9 | 12 | |
| Cinema | 3 | 6 | |
| Total | | | 30 |

  **a** Copy and complete the table.

  **b** What proportion of boys want to go bowling?

  **c** What proportion of girls want to go bowling?

  **d** What proportion pupils want to go bowling?

  **e** What proportion of pupils going bowling are girls?

  **f** Is bowling more popular among boys or girls?

**4** Look at the statements written on these cards.

> Nine out of the top twenty fencers are left-handed.

> 88% of people are right-handed.

> Six of Europe's best ten table-tennis players are right-handed.

> Five out of the top twenty-five tennis players are left-handed.

  **a** Use the statements to write the following proportions as percentages.

> Assume that everyone is either left-handed or right-handed.

    **i** Left-handed people out of all people

    **ii** Left-handed tennis players in the world's top twenty-five

    **iii** Left-handers among Europe's best ten table-tennis players

    **iv** Left-handed fencers out of the top twenty in the world

  **b** What do your answers to part **a** suggest? Give a possible reason for this.

**5** What proportion of each square is shaded?

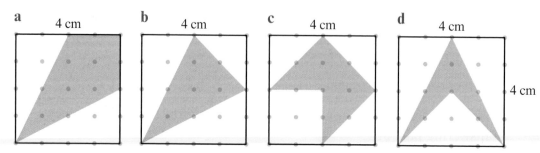

  **a** 4 cm    **b** 4 cm    **c** 4 cm    **d** 4 cm    4 cm

**6** The table gives some information about typical brain weight and body weight for several species.

| Species | Brain weight | Body weight |
| --- | --- | --- |
| Dolphin | 1700 g | 170 000 g |
| Elephant | 4000 g | 4 000 000 g |
| Horse | 420 g | 350 000 g |
| Human | 1400 g | 70 000 g |
| Rabbit | 12 g | 2400 g |
| Rat | 2.5 g | 200 g |

a Do you think that brain weight is a good way to compare intelligence across species?
Explain your answer.

b Write brain weight as a proportion of body weight for each species.
Give your answers as fractions in their lowest terms.

c Write the proportions found in part **b** as percentages.

d Use your answers to part **c** to list the species in order, highest first.

e Do you think that your list gives the species in order of intelligence? Explain your answer.

explanation 2a   explanation 2b

**7** Danny and Mira are going to share some sweets.

a What is the ratio of blue sweets to orange sweets?

b What is the ratio of orange sweets to blue sweets?

c What is the ratio of blue sweets to the total number of sweets?

d Danny eats one of the orange sweets.

What is the new ratio of blue sweets to orange sweets in its simplest form?

e Mira then eats three sweets, making the ratio of blue sweets to orange sweets 2:1.
How many blue sweets did Mira eat?

**8** Write each of these ratios in its simplest form.

    **a**   8:12        **b**   27:9        **c**   24:30        **d**   30:25

    **e**   62:31        **f**   24:32        **g**   7:21        **h**   45:30

    **i**   42:56        **j**   120:270        **k**   55:132        **l**   68:51

**9** Write each of these ratios in its simplest form.

    **a**   £1:2p        **b**   25cm:1m        **c**   10cm:1mm

    **d**   1km:200m        **e**   £1.45:£2.90        **f**   40mm:3cm

    **g**   16cm:1m        **h**   12mm:6cm        **i**   97m:97km

**10** Find the missing quantities.

    **a**   £2:☐p = 4:1           **b**   ☐mm:15cm = 1:5

    **c**   3kg:☐g = 50:1        **d**   ☐cm:1m = 2:5

    **e**   0.5m:☐cm = 2:1     **f**   1.2km:☐m = 3:4

**11 a**   In a survey, 55% of students in their first year at university said that they could drive a car. Write the ratio of drivers to non-drivers in its simplest form.

    **b**   In their final year the ratio of drivers to non-drivers is 7:2. Explain what this means and write down the fraction of non-drivers.

**12** A bracelet is made from red and green beads.

   **a** What is the ratio of red to green beads?
   Explain this ratio.

   **b** A matching necklace needs 15 green beads.
   How many red beads are required?

**13** An internet company found that $\frac{7}{8}$ of its customers had access to broadband.
What is the ratio of broadband users to non-broadband users?

**14** Taha mixes blue and yellow paint in the ratio $13:7$ to make a shade of green.

   **a** What percentage of the paint Taha uses is yellow?

   **b** Find the amount of blue paint he should use to make the following
   amounts of green paint.

   **i**  60 litres  **ii**  140 litres  **iii**  10 litres.

**15 a** Draw two rectangles: the length and height of one rectangle should be
   twice as big as the length and height of the other.
   What is the ratio of the areas?

   **b** Draw a rectangle 4 cm long and 8 cm high. What is the ratio of length to
   height?

   **c** A rectangle is 4 cm long. The ratio of length to height is $1:1.6$. What must
   its height be? Draw this rectangle.

   **d** Look at your rectangles from parts **b** and **c**. Which rectangle looks better?

explanation 3a    explanation 3b    explanation 3c

**16** Jack and Nadia share £400 in the ratio $5:3$. How much does each receive?

**17** In the diagram $AP:PB = 8:5$. Find the distance AP.

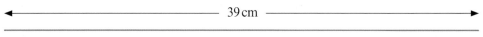

| A | P | B |

**18** A shade of magenta is made by mixing blue and red paint in the ratio $8:7$. Calculate the amount of each colour needed to make the following the following quantities.

    **a**  30 litres           **b**  75 litres           **c**  7.5 litres

**19** The ratio of girls to boys on a school trip is $5:4$.
Find the number of girls when there are these numbers of pupils.

    **a**  56 boys           **b**  72 boys           **c**  189 pupils altogether

**20** Bronze is made from copper and tin in the ratio $3:1$.

    **a**  How much copper and tin is needed to make 600 g of bronze?

    **b**  How much tin is needed if 2.4 kg of copper is used?

    **c**  How much copper is required if 1.2 kg of tin is used?

**21** Mortar that is used for building interior walls is a mixture of sand, lime and cement in the ratio $9:2:1$.

    **a**  How much sand, lime and cement is needed to make 60 kg of mortar?

    **b**  Martha needs six buckets of mortar. How many buckets of sand, lime and cement are needed?

    **c**  To mix a different amount of mortar Martha uses four shovelfuls of lime. How many shovelfuls of sand and cement will she need?

**22** A basic curry powder is a mixture of coriander, cumin and chilli. They are in the ratio $6:3:1$.

    **a**  How much of each spice is in a 400 g bag of curry powder?

    **b**  How much cumin and chilli powder are needed if you have 30 g of coriander?

    **c**  How much curry powder is made if 75 g of cumin is used in the mixture?

# Adding and subtracting fractions

- Adding fractions
- Subtracting fractions

Keywords

You should know

explanation 1a    explanation 1b

**1** Copy and complete the fraction calculations shown by these diagrams.

a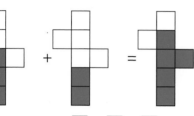

$$\frac{\square}{7} + \frac{\square}{\square} = \frac{\square}{\square}$$

b

$$\frac{\square}{8} - \frac{\square}{\square} = \frac{\square}{\square}$$

$$= \frac{\square}{2}$$

**2** Copy and complete these diagrams and fraction calculations.

a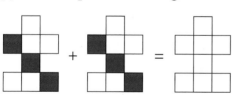

$$\frac{\square}{\square} + \frac{\square}{\square} = \frac{\square}{\square}$$

$$= \frac{\square}{4}$$

b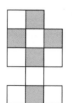

$$\frac{\square}{\square} - \frac{\square}{\square} = \frac{\square}{\square}$$

$$= \frac{\square}{3}$$

**3** Simplify these calculations as far as possible.

a  $\frac{5}{9} + \frac{2}{9}$

b  $\frac{7}{12} - \frac{1}{12}$

c  $\frac{3}{10} + \frac{5}{10}$

d  $\frac{7}{16} - \frac{4}{16} + \frac{1}{16}$

e  $\frac{9}{20} + \frac{10}{20} - \frac{7}{20}$

f  $\frac{21}{26} - \frac{3}{26} - \frac{5}{26}$

**4** Copy and complete these diagrams and fraction calculations.

**a**

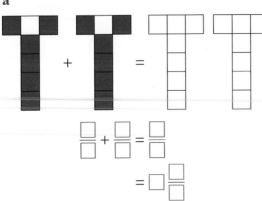

$$\frac{\square}{\square} + \frac{\square}{\square} = \frac{\square}{\square}$$

$$= \square\frac{\square}{\square}$$

**b**

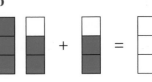

$$1\frac{\square}{\square} + \frac{\square}{\square} = \square\frac{\square}{\square}$$

$$= \square\frac{\square}{\square}$$

**5** Simplify these calculations as far as possible.

**a** $\dfrac{7}{9} + \dfrac{6}{9}$

**b** $\dfrac{9}{12} + \dfrac{4}{12}$

**c** $\dfrac{2}{7} + \dfrac{5}{7}$

**d** $\dfrac{7}{8} + \dfrac{3}{8}$

**e** $\dfrac{4}{6} + \dfrac{5}{6}$

**f** $\dfrac{17}{20} + \dfrac{8}{20}$

**g** $\dfrac{7}{8} + \dfrac{7}{8}$

**h** $\dfrac{13}{16} + \dfrac{9}{16}$

**i** $\dfrac{11}{12} + \dfrac{5}{12}$

**6** Simplify these calculations as far as possible.

**a** $1\dfrac{2}{5} + \dfrac{2}{5}$

**b** $2\dfrac{1}{8} + \dfrac{5}{8}$

**c** $1\dfrac{2}{5} + \dfrac{4}{5}$

**d** $1\dfrac{5}{8} + \dfrac{6}{8}$

**e** $2\dfrac{5}{12} + \dfrac{8}{12}$

**f** $1\dfrac{3}{8} + \dfrac{7}{8}$

**g** $1\dfrac{11}{12} + \dfrac{7}{12}$

**h** $2\dfrac{9}{10} + \dfrac{5}{10}$

**i** $3\dfrac{5}{6} + \dfrac{4}{6}$

**7** Simplify these calculations as far as possible.

**a** $\dfrac{8}{9} - \dfrac{5}{9}$

**b** $\dfrac{10}{12} - \dfrac{1}{12}$

**c** $\dfrac{13}{15} - \dfrac{3}{15}$

**d** $1 - \dfrac{2}{5}$

**e** $1 - \dfrac{7}{10}$

**f** $2 - \dfrac{3}{8}$

**g** $7 - \dfrac{4}{11}$

**h** $9 - \dfrac{3}{20}$

**i** $16 - \dfrac{9}{25}$

**8** Simplify these calculations as far as possible.

a $1\frac{1}{3} - \frac{2}{3}$

b $2\frac{1}{4} - \frac{3}{4}$

c $2\frac{4}{9} - \frac{7}{9}$

explanation 4

**9** Copy and complete these diagrams and fraction calculations.

a  +  =

$$\frac{\square}{5} + \frac{\square}{\square} = \frac{\square}{10} + \frac{\square}{\square}$$

$$= \frac{\square}{\square}$$

b 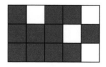 −  = 

$$\frac{\square}{\square} - \frac{\square}{3} = \frac{\square}{\square} - \frac{\square}{\square}$$

$$= \frac{\square}{\square}$$

c  −  =

$$\frac{\square}{\square} - \frac{\square}{\square} = \frac{\square}{\square} - \frac{\square}{\square}$$

$$= \frac{\square}{\square}$$

$$= \frac{\square}{\square}$$

d  + = 

$$\frac{\square}{\square} + \frac{\square}{\square} = \frac{\square}{\square} + \frac{\square}{\square}$$

$$= \square \frac{\square}{\square}$$

**10** Simplify these calculations as far as possible.

a $\frac{1}{2} + \frac{3}{8}$

b $\frac{3}{4} + \frac{7}{16}$

c $\frac{11}{12} - \frac{1}{6}$

d $\frac{17}{20} + \frac{4}{5}$

e $\frac{11}{15} - \frac{2}{3}$

f $\frac{9}{25} - \frac{14}{75}$

g $\frac{9}{10} + \frac{3}{5}$

h $\frac{5}{6} + \frac{7}{24}$

i $\frac{41}{50} + \frac{6}{25}$

j $2\frac{3}{5} + \frac{1}{10}$

k $3\frac{7}{12} - \frac{1}{3}$

l $9\frac{1}{4} - \frac{5}{12}$

m $\frac{9}{10} + \frac{7}{20} + \frac{3}{5}$

n $\frac{2}{3} + \frac{7}{12} - \frac{1}{6}$

o $\frac{23}{25} - \frac{9}{50} + \frac{7}{10}$

> Remember to make the denominators the same before you add or subtract.

explanation 5a   explanation 5b

**11** Work out these calculations. Write your answer in its simplest form.

a $\frac{2}{3} + \frac{1}{4}$

b $\frac{3}{8} + \frac{7}{10}$

c $\frac{4}{9} + \frac{3}{5}$

d $\frac{5}{6} - \frac{3}{10}$

e $\frac{7}{9} - \frac{3}{4}$

f $\frac{6}{7} - \frac{1}{2}$

g $\frac{1}{2} + \frac{2}{3} - \frac{1}{6}$

h $\frac{3}{8} + \frac{1}{4} - \frac{1}{3}$

i $\frac{11}{12} - \frac{3}{5} + \frac{1}{4}$

**\*12** Work out these calculations. Write your answer in its simplest form.

a $2\frac{1}{2} + 1\frac{3}{4}$

b $5\frac{2}{3} + 2\frac{1}{8}$

c $1\frac{3}{5} + 1\frac{1}{2}$

d $5\frac{2}{3} - 3\frac{1}{2}$

e $10\frac{3}{4} - 8\frac{2}{5}$

f $3\frac{1}{6} - 1\frac{3}{7}$

**\*13** Tim is driving to Barnsley. Along the way he sees two signs.

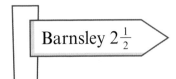 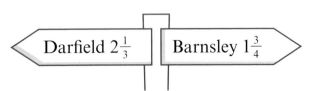

a What is the distance between the two signs?

b How far is it from Darfield to Barnsley?

**\*14** Tara spends $\frac{1}{5}$ of her pocket money on

sweets and $\frac{2}{3}$ on clothes. She saves the rest.

What proportion of her pocket money
does Tara save?

Sweets

Clothes

Save

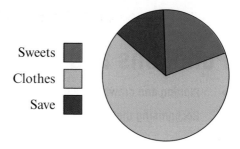

**\*15** Calculators and computers store numbers in binary form which only uses the digits 0 and 1.

Peter writes the headings for numbers in base 10 and Sunita writes similar headings for numbers in base 2 (binary).

They then use the table to work out how to write the binary number $1001.101_2$ in base 10.

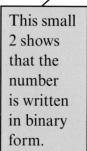

This small 2 shows that the number is written in binary form.

Column headings for base 10.

| Thousands | Hundreds | Tens | Units | tenths | hundredths |
|-----------|----------|------|-------|--------|------------|

Column headings for base 2.

| Eights | Fours | Twos | Units | halves | quarters | eighths |
|--------|-------|------|-------|--------|----------|---------|
| 1 | 0 | 0 | 1 | 1 | 0 | 1 |

$$1001.101_2 = 8 + 0 + 0 + 1 + \frac{1}{2} + 0 + \frac{1}{8}$$

$$= 9 + \frac{4}{8} + \frac{1}{8}$$

$$= 9\frac{5}{8}$$

**a**  Convert these binary numbers to base 10.

   **i**  $1.1_2$      **ii**  $1.111_2$      **iii**  $10.011_2$

   **iv**  $11.11_2$      **v**  $1.0011_2$      **vi**  $110.1101_2$

**b**  Write these numbers in binary.

   **i**  $1\frac{5}{16}$      **ii**  $5\frac{11}{16}$

# Functions and graphs

- Plotting and drawing the graph of an equation
- Recognising the graph of an equation

Keywords

You should know

explanation 1

**1 a** Write the coordinates of A, B, C and D.

**b** Describe in words what the coordinates have in common.

**c** What is the equation of the red line?

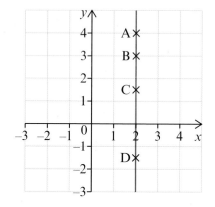

**2 a** Write the equation of each line.

**b** What is the equation of the line that lies on top of the $y$-axis?

**c** Write the equation of the line that is halfway between lines **1** and **2**.

**d** Write the equation of the line that is halfway between lines **2** and **3**.

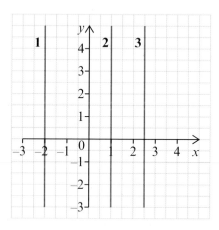

**3 a** Write the coordinates of A, B, C and D.

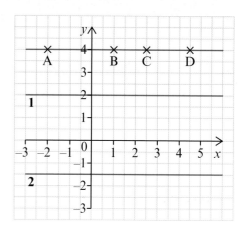

**b** What is the equation of the line passing through the labelled points?

**c** Write the equations of lines **1** and **2**.

**d** What is the equation of the line that lies on top of the $x$-axis?

**e** Write the equation of the line that is halfway between lines **1** and **2**.

**4** The diagram shows a set of axes and the line $x = 4$.

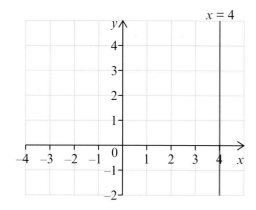

**a** Copy the diagram and draw the lines $x = -3$, $y = 0$ and $y = 3$.

**b** Shade in the rectangle enclosed by the lines in **a**.

**c** Write the coordinates of each corner of the rectangle and the coordinates of the centre of the rectangle.

**5 a** Draw a set of axes with each axis ranging from $-5$ to 5. Mark and label the point P(2, 1).

**b** Draw two vertical lines and two horizontal lines that form a square, 6 units by 6 units, with the point P at its centre. Write the equation of each line.

explanation 2a    explanation 2b

**6 a** Copy these axes and draw the line $y = x$.
Write the equation next to the line.

**b** Copy and complete the table for the
equation $y = x + 1$.

| $x$ | −4 | −3 | −2 | −1 | 0 | 1 | 2 | 3 |
|---|---|---|---|---|---|---|---|---|
| $y$ | −3 | | | | | | | |

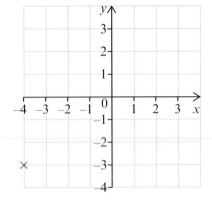

**c** Plot the $x$ and $y$ pairs from the table as
coordinates.

**d** Draw the line $y = x + 1$ through your
plotted points.
Write the equation next to the line.

> Your plotted points should
> lie on a straight line.

**e** Compare the line $y = x + 1$ to the line
$y = x$. What is the same and what is different?

**f** What would the lines $y = x + 2$, $y = x + 3$ and $y = x − 3$ look like?

Draw them on your diagram and label each line.

**g** Describe in words what the lines $y = x + 10$ and $y = x − 8$ look like.

**7** The diagram shows the graph $y = −x$.

**a** Copy the table and use the graph to fill
in the missing values of $y$.

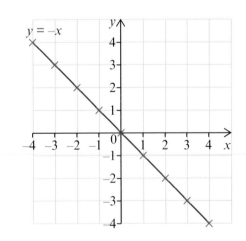

| $x$ | −4 | −3 | −2 | −1 | 0 | 1 | 2 | 3 | 4 |
|---|---|---|---|---|---|---|---|---|---|
| $y$ | | | | | | −1 | | | −4 |

**b** What would the graphs of $y = −x + 2$
and $y = −x + 4$ look like?

Copy the diagram and draw these two
lines on the same axes.

**c** Is $y = −x + 10$ the same as $y = 10 − x$?

**d** Describe in words what the graph of $y = 10 − x$ looks like.

explanation 3a   explanation 3b

**8** Here are some equations shown on cards.

$y = x$

$x = -2$

$y = 4$

$y = 2 - x$

$y = x + 1$

Which equation matches each pair of points?

a   A and B
b   A and E
c   B and D
d   E and C
e   A and D

**9** The diagram shows a hexagon.

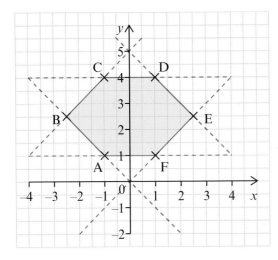

The equation of the line passing through A and F is $y = 1$.

Write the equation of the line passing through each pair of points.

a   F and E
b   D and E
c   C and D
d   B and C
e   A and B

**10 a** Draw a set of axes and these lines.

$y = x$,  $y = -x$,  $x = 3$,  $x = -3$,  $y = 6$

**b** Shade the shape that is enclosed by the five lines.

**c** Write the coordinates of each corner of the shape.

**11** Sketch each of the lines below on a separate set of axes. Write the coordinates of the points where each line cuts the $x$-axis and the $y$-axis.

**a** $y = x + 7$    **b** $y = x + 9$    **c** $y = 6 - x$

**12 a** Copy the diagram for the line $y = 5 - x$.

**b** Copy and complete the table for the equation $y = 2x - 1$.

| $x$ | $-1$ | 0 | 1 | 2 | 3 | 4 |
|-----|------|---|---|---|---|---|
| $y$ |      |   |   |   |   | 7 |

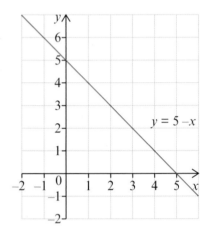

$y = 5 - x$

**c** Plot the values from your table as coordinates on your copy of the axes.

**d** Draw and label the line $y = 2x - 1$.

**e** Write the coordinates of the point where the lines cross.

**13 a** Copy and complete the following coordinates of points on the line $y = 3 - x$.

**i** $(-2, \square)$    **ii** $(0, \square)$    **iii** $(1, \square)$    **iv** $(5, \square)$

**b** Plot the points on a set of axes, where $x$ goes from $-3$ to 6 and $y$ from $-3$ to 10.

**c** Draw and label the line $y = 3 - x$.

**d** Copy and complete the table for the graph $y = 2x + 6$.

| $x$ | $-3$ | $-2$ | $-1$ | 0 | 1 | 2 |
|-----|------|------|------|---|---|---|
| $y$ |      |      | 4    |   |   |   |

**e** Plot the values from your table as coordinates to draw the graph $y = 2x + 6$.

**f** Write the coordinates of the point where these two lines meet.

**14 a** Copy the diagram.

**b** Copy and complete the table for the equation $y = 2x$.

| $x$ | 0 | 1 | 2 | 3 | 4 | 5 |
|---|---|---|---|---|---|---|
| $y$ | 0 | | | | | |

**c** On your diagram draw and label the line $y = 2x$.

**d** What point do $y = x$ and $y = 2x$ have in common?

**e** Find the value of $y$ when $x = 2$ for each equation.

    **i** $y = 3x$         **ii** $y = \frac{1}{2}x$

**f** Draw and label the lines on your graph.

**g** Describe what lines in the form $y = mx$ are like ($m$ represents any number).

**15 a** Copy and complete these coordinates of points on the line $y = \frac{1}{2}x + 2$.

    **i** $(-2, \square)$     **ii** $(0, \square)$     **iii** $(2, \square)$     **iv** $(6, \square)$

**b** Plot the points on a set of axes, where $x$ goes from $-3$ to 7 and $y$ from $-8$ to 7.

**c** Copy and complete the table for the line $y = 3x - 8$.

| $x$ | 0 | 1 | 2 | 3 | 4 | 5 |
|---|---|---|---|---|---|---|
| $y$ | | | | | | |

**d** Draw and label the graph $y = 3x - 8$ on the axes used in part **b**.

**e** Where do the two lines meet?

**16 a** Draw a set of axes where $x$ goes from $-4$ to 4 and $y$ ranges from $-2$ to 7.

**b** Copy and complete the table for the line $y = 7 - 2x$.

| $x$ | 0 | 1 | 2 | 3 | 4 |
|---|---|---|---|---|---|
| $y$ | 7 | | | | |

**c** Copy and complete the table for the line $y = x + 4$.

| $x$ | $-4$ | $-3$ | $-2$ | $-1$ | 0 | 1 | 2 | 3 |
|---|---|---|---|---|---|---|---|---|
| $y$ | 0 | | | | | | | |

**d** Draw and label the line $y = 7 - 2x$ and the line $y = x + 4$ on your diagram.

**e** Draw the line $y = 3$ and shade the triangle enclosed by the three lines.

**f** Write the coordinates of each corner of the triangle and find its area.

# Using graphs

- Using a graph to convert one quantity into another
- Using a graph to solve an equation

Keywords

You should know

explanation 1

**1** This graph shows the stopping distances for cars travelling at different speeds.

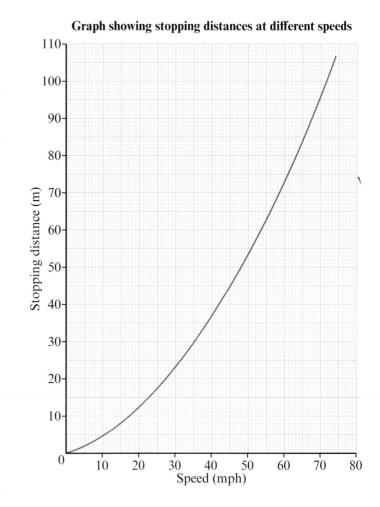

Graph showing stopping distances at different speeds

**a** What is the stopping distance for 30 mph?

**b** A camp site has a speed restriction of 10 mph. What is the stopping distance when travelling at this speed?

**c** What is the difference between the stopping distance of a car travelling at 70 mph and a car travelling at 40 mph?

**d** At what stopping distance is the stopping distance, in metres, equal to the speed, in miles per hour? Explain how you arrived at your answer.

**2**  A teacher uses this graph to convert test marks to percentages.

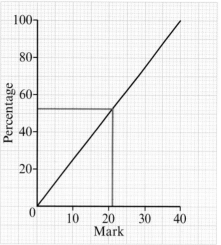

**Graph converting tests marks to percentages**

  **a**  Use the red lines to help you write a mark of 21 as a percentage.

  **b**  Write each of these marks as a percentage.

  **i**  28        **ii**  14        **iii**  17.5

  **c**  What was the highest possible test mark?

  **d**  The lowest percentage scored was 20%. How many marks did this pupil score?

  **e**  The highest percentage scored was 90%. How many marks did this pupil score?

**3**  You can use this graph to convert between temperatures in degrees Celsius (°C) and degrees Fahrenheit (°F).

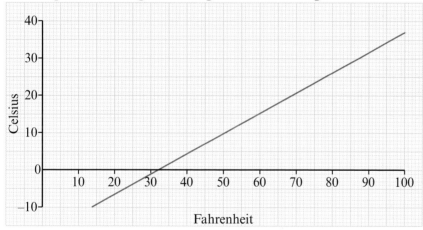

**Graph for converting between degrees Celsius and degrees Fahrenheit**

  **a**  A typical classroom temperature is around 20 °C. Write this temperature in Fahrenheit.

  **b**  On a summer's day, the temperature might be 86 °F. Write this temperature in Celsius.

  **c**  At what temperature in Fahrenheit does the graph cross the horizontal axis? What is significant about this temperature?

  **d**  The temperature one morning in winter is −5 °C. Write this temperature in Fahrenheit.

  **e**  Human body temperature is 98.4 °F. Write this in Celsius to the nearest degree.

**4**  **a**  $6\frac{1}{4}$ miles is approximately 10 km.

What does the red cross on the graph indicate?

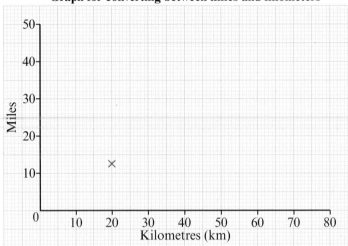

Graph for converting between miles and kilometers

**b**  Copy the diagram and plot three more points. Draw a graph through the plotted points.

**c**  Copy and complete the cards. Give each answer to the nearest whole number.

**i**

Marathon
(26.2 miles) $= \square$ km

**ii**

Channel Tunnel
51 km long $= \square$ miles

**iii**

Pisa to Florence
43 miles $= \square$ km

**d**  Explain how you could use this graph to convert 140 km to miles.

explanation 2

**5**  The diagram shows the graph of $y = 2x - 3$.

**a**  Use the red lines to help you solve the equation $2x - 3 = 5$.

**b**  Use the graph to solve these equations.

   **i**  $2x - 3 = 1$       **ii**  $2x - 3 = 0$

   **iii**  $2x - 3 = -3$     **iv**  $2x - 3 = -1$

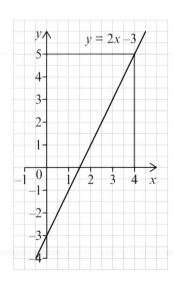

**6** The diagram shows the graph of $y = \frac{1}{2}x + 5$.

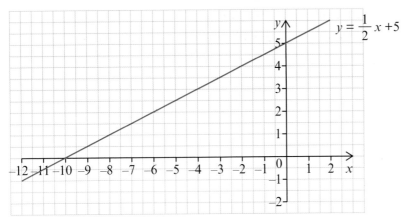

**a** Use the graph to solve these equations.

**i** $\frac{1}{2}x + 5 = 4$  **ii** $\frac{1}{2}x + 5 = 1$  **iii** $\frac{1}{2}x + 5 = 0$

**iv** $\frac{1}{2}x + 5 = 2.5$  **v** $\frac{1}{2}x + 5 = 5$  **vi** $\frac{1}{2}x + 5 = -1$

**b** Which equation in part **a** is equivalent to the equation $\frac{1}{2}x + 17 = 16$?

**c** Copy and complete:  $\frac{1}{2}x + 21 = 19.5$

$$\frac{1}{2}x + 5 = \square$$

$$x = \square$$

**7 a** Copy and complete the table for the equation $v = \frac{t + 3}{2}$.

| t | −5 | 0 | 5 |
|---|----|---|---|
| v | −1 |   |   |

**b** Plot the points and use them to draw the line $v = \frac{t + 3}{2}$.

**c** Use your graph to solve these equations.

**i** $\frac{t + 3}{2} = 3$  **ii** $\frac{t + 3}{2} = 1.5$  **iii** $\frac{t + 3}{2} = 0$

**d** Copy and complete:  $\frac{t + 3}{2} + 7 = 6$

$$\frac{t + 3}{2} = \square$$

$$t = \square$$

**8** The diagram shows the graph of $y = x^2$.

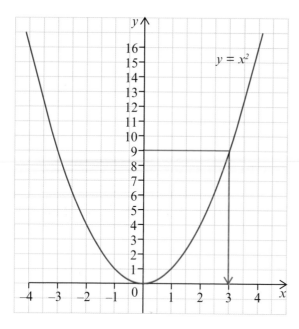

**a**  Find $y$ for these values of $x$.

    **i**  1                    **ii**  2                    **iii**  3                    **iv**  4

**b**  Peter says the answer to $x^2 = 9$ is $x = 3$.
    Mary says there are two answers. What are the two answers?

**c**  Use the graph to solve these equations.

    **i**  $x^2 = 4$           **ii**  $x^2 = 7.5$           **iii**  $x^2 = 1$           **iv**  $x^2 = 2.5$

**d**  Use the graph to solve $x^2 - 6 = 0$.

**e**  Solve these equations.

    **i**  $x^2 = 100$           **ii**  $x^2 = 169$           **iii**  $x^2 - 25 = 0$

**f**  Why can you not solve $x^2 + 4 = 0$?

**g**  What other equations can you solve using this graph?

# Reflection

- Reflecting points and lines in a variety of mirror lines

Keywords

You should know

explanation 1

**1** Copy the diagrams and show the image of each of the labelled points after a reflection in the black mirror line.

Label the images A', B', C', D' and E'.

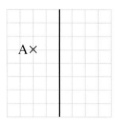 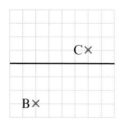 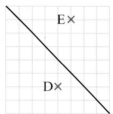

**2** Copy the diagrams and draw a mirror line in the correct position for each one.

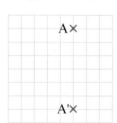 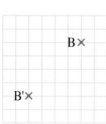 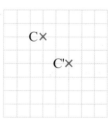

explanation 2

**3** Copy the diagrams and reflect each labelled line in the black mirror line. Label the end points of each reflection.

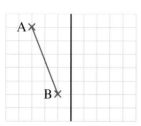 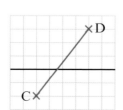

**4** Copy these diagrams and reflect the shapes in the black mirror lines.

a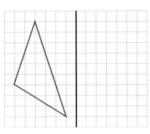

b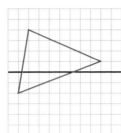

c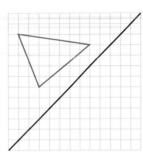

d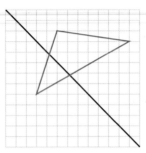

**5** Copy the diagrams and draw a mirror line in the correct position for each one.

a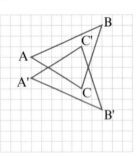

b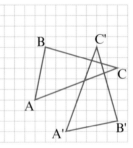

**6** Copy the diagram onto squared paper.

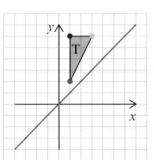

a Draw the image of triangle T under a reflection in the *y*-axis. Label this T'.

b Reflect triangle T in the red mirror line *y* = *x* and label this image T".

c Reflect T" in the *x*-axis and label this T'''.

d What is the connection between the triangles T' and T'''?

explanation 3

**7 a** The image of A(3, 1) after reflection in the red line $x = 4$ is A'(5, 1). Write down the image of each of the other labelled points under a reflection in $x = 4$.

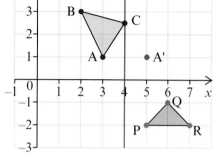

**b** Copy the diagram and draw the image of each triangle under a reflection in $x = 4$.

**c** Copy this diagram again and add the red horizontal line $y = 1$. Draw the image of each triangle under a reflection in the line $y = 1$.

**8** Write down the equation of the mirror line for each mapping.

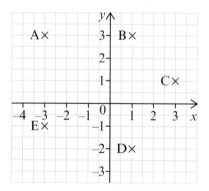

**a** $A \rightarrow B$      **b** $B \rightarrow C$

**c** $B \rightarrow D$      **d** $B \rightarrow E$

**9** Write down the coordinates of a point that maps to itself under a reflection in $x = 2$.

**10** Write down the coordinates of the point that $(3, -1)$ maps to under a reflection in these lines.

**a** $x = 5$     **b** $x = -1$     **c** $y = -1$     **d** $y = 4$

**e** $y = x$     **f** $y = 2 - x$     **g** $y = -x$     **h** $y = 4 - x$

**11** On a set of axes which go from $-2$ to 9, draw the line $y = 2x$ and the triangle ABC with A(3, 1), B(4, 3) and C(7, 4). Reflect the triangle in the line and label the reflected image A'B'C'.

# Rotation

- Describing a rotation
- Rotating a shape using tracing paper
- Rotating a shape on a grid
- Mapping one point to another under a rotation

Keywords

You should know

explanation 1a    explanation 1b

1 Copy the diagram. Show the new position of the shape after a clockwise rotation of 90° with each of these centres of rotation.

   a  P                    b  Q

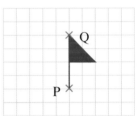

2 Copy these diagrams. Show the new position of each shape after an anticlockwise rotation of 90° with centre P.

   a 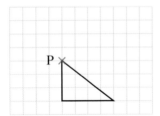    b 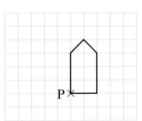    c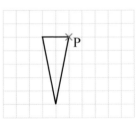

3 Copy these diagrams. Show the new position of each shape after a clockwise rotation of 90° with centre P.

   a 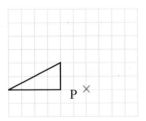    b 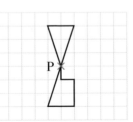    c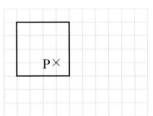

**4** Copy the diagram and rotate the triangle through 180° with centre P.
Explain why it isn't necessary to give the direction of rotation.

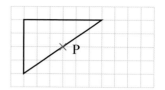

**5** Describe the rotation that maps shape A to shape B in each of these diagrams.

a
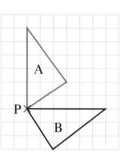

b
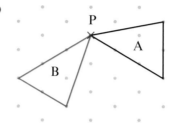

Every line of shape A is rotated through the same angle to make shape B.

Choose the simplest pair of matching lines to work out the angle.

**6** Copy the diagram.

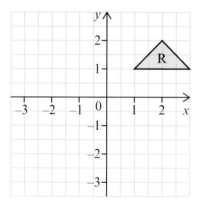

   **a** Rotate the triangle R through 90° clockwise, with centre of rotation at the origin. Label this R'.

   **b** Rotate triangle R through 180° about the origin. Label this R".

   **c** Reflect R" in the x-axis and label this R"'.

   **d** What transformation maps R to R"'?

209

**7** Copy the diagram.

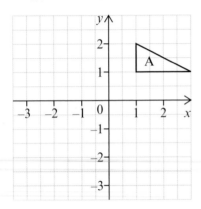

a Rotate triangle A through 90° clockwise with centre (0, 0). Label the image B.

b Reflect triangle A in the y-axis. Label this C.

c Rotate triangle C through 90° anticlockwise with centre (0, 0). Label the image D.

d What transformation maps B to D?

**8** Describe the rotation such that

a A→B          b A→C          c B→D          d A→D

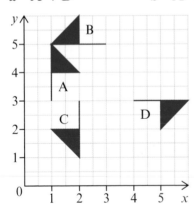

**9** Draw the triangle ABC with coordinates A(3, −1), B(5, 1) and C(3, 5) on squared paper where the axes range from −7 to 7.

a Rotate ABC through 90° anticlockwise with centre (0, 2) to make the triangle A' B' C'.

b Rotate ABC through 180° about the point (0, 2) to make the triangle A" B" C".

Write down the coordinates of A' B' C' and A" B" C".

# Translation

- Describing a translation
- Applying a translation to a shape
- Using vectors to describe a translation

Keywords

You should know

explanation 1

1 Describe the translation for each of these mappings.

a A→B          b A→C

c B→A          d C→A

e D→A          f A→E

g A→D          h E→A

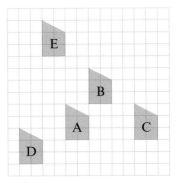

2 P is mapped to Q by the translation 3 units right and 2 units down.
Describe the translation that maps Q to P.

3 In the diagram, each shape may
be mapped to *one* other by a
translation.

Copy and complete the following
and describe each translation.

a A→□          b □→F

c J→□          d □→I

e B→□

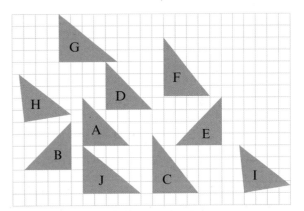

**4** In the diagram, triangle ABC is mapped to triangle A'B'C' by a translation.

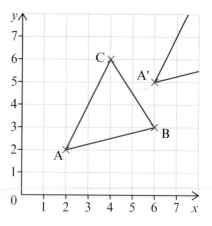

**a** Write down the coordinates of A and A'.

**b** Describe the translation.

**c** Find the coordinates of B' and C'.

**d** The point A" is not shown on the diagram but has coordinates (2, −4). Describe the translation that maps A to A".

**e** Write down the coordinates of B" and C".

**5** Copy the diagram showing the arrowhead A with one vertex labelled P.

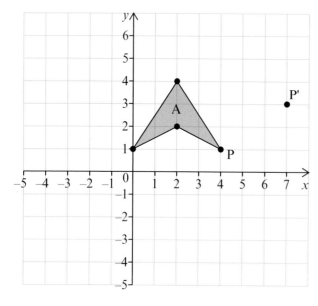

**a** Write down the translation that maps P to P'.

**b** Draw the image of A under this translation. Label this image B.

**c** Find the image of the arrowhead A under a translation 5 units to the left. Label this image C.

**d** Rotate shape C through 90° anticlockwise about the origin. Label this image D.

**e** Explain why shape A cannot be mapped to D by a translation.

explanation 2

**6** Copy the diagram but extend both axes to range from −7 to 7.

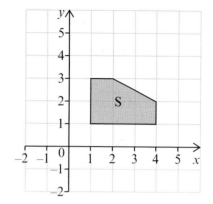

   **a** Draw the image of S under each translation.

   **i** $\begin{pmatrix} 0 \\ 4 \end{pmatrix}$, label this T.

   **ii** $\begin{pmatrix} 3 \\ 2 \end{pmatrix}$, label this image U.

   **iii** $\begin{pmatrix} 0 \\ -5 \end{pmatrix}$, label this image V.

   **iv** $\begin{pmatrix} -6 \\ 3 \end{pmatrix}$, label this image W.

   **b** Plot the points (−5, 0), (−5, 2), (−4, 2), (−2, 1), (−2, 0) and join them to form the shape R. What translation maps S to R?

**7** Copy the diagram showing the triangles S and T.

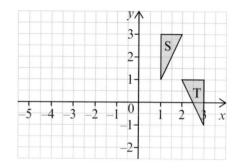

   **a** Draw the line $x = -1$.

   **b** Reflect triangle T in the line $x = -1$ and label this image T'.

   **c** What translation maps T' to S?

   **d** What translation maps S to T'?

**8** The diagram shows a triangle and two mirror lines M1 and M2.

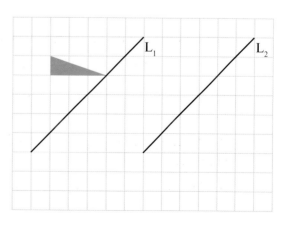

   **a** Reflect the triangle in M1.

   **b** Reflect the image in M2.

   **c** Describe the translation equivalent to the two reflections.

# Comparing data

- Comparing data using charts
- Comparing data using an average and the range
- Understanding the limitations in using averages to compare data

Keywords

You should know

explanation 1a    explanation 1b

**1** The pie charts show the percentages of people recorded as using different methods of transport to get to work in two cities in England.

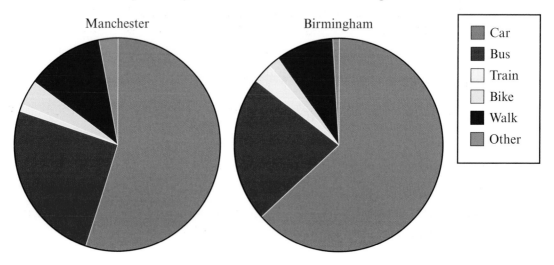

Manchester                    Birmingham

| | Car |
| | Bus |
| | Train |
| | Bike |
| | Walk |
| | Other |

**a** Approximately what percentage of people used the car in each of the cities?

**b** Which category of transport was used by a similar percentage of people in both cities?

**c** In which city did most people walk to work? Explain your answer.

**d** If 32 000 people used the bus in Manchester about how many people were involved in the Manchester survey?

**2** This compound bar chart shows car ownership per household for the regions of England.

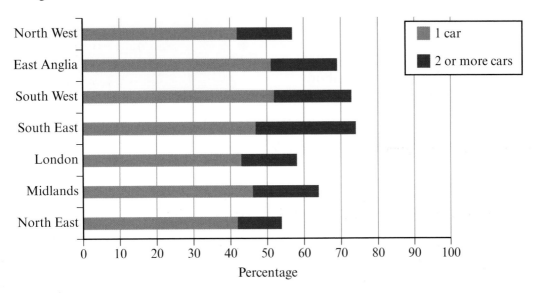

**a** What percentage of households in the South East owned only one car?

**b** What percentage of households in the South West owned two or more cars?

**c** What percentage of households in London had no car?

**d** Which area had the same percentage of households with two or more cars as the Midlands?

**e** In which area was the percentage of one-car households over three times greater than the percentage of households with two or more cars?

explanation 2a    explanation 2b

**3** Sarah and Rifat have been running. Their trainer records their pulse rates every minute during the next few minutes.

Sarah's median pulse rate is 120 with a range of 70.
Rifat's median pulse rate is 110 with a range of 40.

> Your pulse rate increases with exercise and reduces again as you recover.

**a** Suggest possible values for the highest and lowest pulse rates of each runner.

**b** Who do you think had the lower pulse rate at the end of the run? Explain your answer.

**c** Who is showing the greater rate of recovery? Explain your answer.

**4** This diagram shows a section of dual carriageway passing through a village.

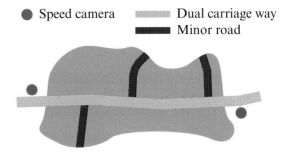

● Speed camera    Dual carriage way
▬ Minor road

The speed limit is 40 mph, but many motorists do not slow down. The villagers are concerned about safety.

A survey found that the mean speed of cars on the dual carriageway was 53 mph. The range of speeds was 32 mph.

Police then set up speed cameras, as shown by red dots, and put up signs to warn motorists.

  **a** What effect do you think this had?

  **b** Explain the likely effect on the range and mean speed.

  **c** What would you expect the modal speed to be?
     Explain your answer.

**5** A small firm has an owner and eight employees. The annual pay of the owner and his employees is shown in the table.

| Person | Annual pay |
|---|---|
| Owner | £68 000 |
| Manager | £37 000 |
| Worker 1 | £23 000 |
| Worker 2 | £21 000 |
| Worker 3 | £20 000 |
| Worker 4 | £18 000 |
| Worker 5 | £18 000 |
| Worker 6 | £15 000 |
| Worker 7 | £14 000 |

  **a** Work out the mode, the median and the mean annual pay.

  **b** The workers say their pay is too low, but the owner disagrees.

    Which value from part **a** would each use to support their opinion?

# Statistics S3.2

# Using statistics

• Applying your knowledge of statistics to solve problems

Keywords

You should know

explanation 1a  explanation 1b

This is an example of a simple question to investigate, although there are other things you have to consider before you can begin the investigation.

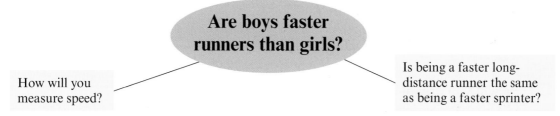

An example of a more complicated question is shown below.
There are lots of different things you can investigate to answer this question.
A sample of these smaller investigations is shown here.

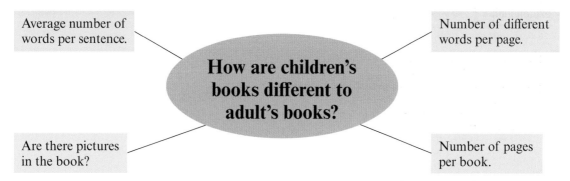

**1** Choose a question to investigate. You could investigate one of the examples above or find an example of your own.
Can you answer your question with a single investigation or does it have lots of smaller questions to answer?

explanation 2a explanation 2b

**2** What sort of data can you collect for your question?

Will you use primary data or secondary data? You might need to use more than one sort of data to answer your question.

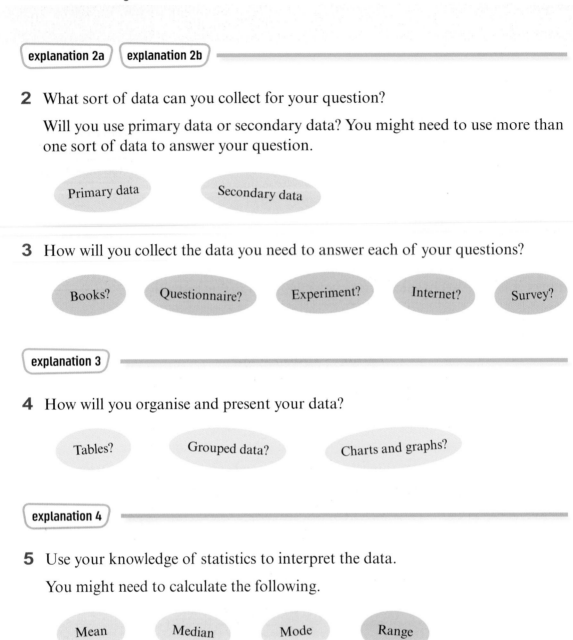

Primary data

Secondary data

**3** How will you collect the data you need to answer each of your questions?

Books?    Questionnaire?    Experiment?    Internet?    Survey?

explanation 3

**4** How will you organise and present your data?

Tables?    Grouped data?    Charts and graphs?

explanation 4

**5** Use your knowledge of statistics to interpret the data.

You might need to calculate the following.

Mean    Median    Mode    Range

**6** Interpret your results. Have you answered your original question?

**7** Display your work.

# Fractions of integers

- Multiplying a fraction by an integer and an integer by a fraction without a diagram

- Cancelling when multiplying a fraction by an integer

- Multiplying an integer by a faction and then by a second fraction

Keywords

You should know

explanation 1

**1 a** Copy and complete this fraction calculation to match the diagrams.

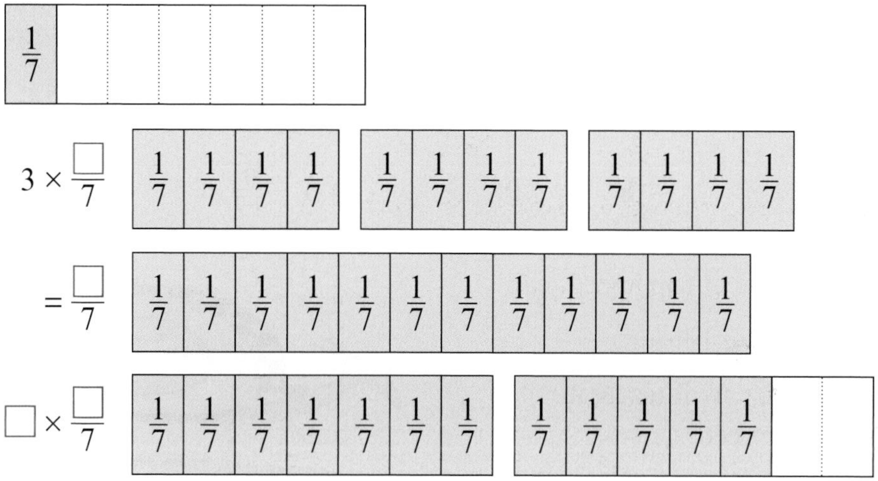

**b** Copy and complete these fraction calculations.

$$\text{i} \quad 2 \times \frac{3}{7} = \frac{\Box \times \Box}{7}$$
$$= \frac{\Box}{7}$$

$$\text{ii} \quad 4 \times \frac{2}{5} = \frac{\Box \times \Box}{5}$$
$$= \frac{\Box}{5}$$
$$= \Box\frac{\Box}{5}$$

$$\text{iii} \quad \frac{4}{9} \times 2 = \frac{\Box \times \Box}{9}$$
$$= \frac{\Box}{9}$$

$$\text{iv} \quad \frac{5}{8} \times 3 = \frac{\Box \times \Box}{8}$$
$$= \frac{\Box}{8}$$
$$= \Box\frac{\Box}{8}$$

**2** The twelve cards below each have a calculation written on them.
There are four sets of three cards. Each card in a set gives the same answer.
Find the four sets and work out the answer for each set.

| A | B | C | D | E | F |
|---|---|---|---|---|---|
| $5 \times \dfrac{3}{4}$ | $\dfrac{5}{9} \times 27$ | $3 \times \dfrac{4}{5}$ | $\dfrac{2}{7}$ of 8 | $\dfrac{3}{4} \times 5$ | $\dfrac{4}{5}$ of 3 |

| G | H | I | J | K | L |
|---|---|---|---|---|---|
| $8 \times \dfrac{2}{7}$ | $\dfrac{4}{5} \times 3$ | $\dfrac{3}{4}$ of 5 | $27 \times \dfrac{5}{9}$ | $\dfrac{2}{7} \times 8$ | $\dfrac{5}{9}$ of 27 |

**3** Work out these calculations. Give your answers as mixed numbers.

a  $2 \times \dfrac{2}{3}$    b  $3 \times \dfrac{4}{7}$    c  $5 \times \dfrac{3}{8}$

d  $\dfrac{5}{9} \times 4$    e  $\dfrac{3}{5}$ of 6    f  $9 \times \dfrac{1}{3}$

g  $\dfrac{2}{11}$ of 12    h  $\dfrac{3}{10} \times 9$    i  $\dfrac{4}{17}$ of 5

**4** A snail, travelling at top speed, can
cover about $\dfrac{2}{3}$ m in 1 hour.

How far would a snail travel in
4 hours at this speed?

**5** A bakery uses $\dfrac{3}{4}$ of a sack of flour each day.

How much flour is used in 5 days?

explanation 2

**6** Copy and complete these calculations.

a  $12 \times \dfrac{5}{8} = \dfrac{\cancel{12} \times 5}{\cancel{8}_2}$

   $= \dfrac{\square}{\square}$

   $= \square \dfrac{\square}{\square}$

b  $\dfrac{7}{16} \times 20 = \dfrac{7 \times \cancel{20}^{\square}}{\cancel{16}}$

   $= \dfrac{\square}{\square}$

   $= \square \dfrac{\square}{4}$

**7** Simplify these expressions as much as you can. Give your answers as mixed numbers.

a $\dfrac{9}{16} \times 24$

b $27 \times \dfrac{11}{18}$

c $8 \times \dfrac{9}{20}$

d $30 \times \dfrac{7}{25}$

e $\dfrac{3}{14}$ of 21

f $\dfrac{5}{24}$ of 32

**8** $\dfrac{7}{40}$ of the cost of an item is paid as VAT. Calculate the VAT paid on these amounts.

a £60

b £20

c £24

d £8

e £30

f £50

**9** A grizzly bear may eat up to $\dfrac{3}{20}$ of its body weight in salmon each day.

Find how much salmon might be eaten if the bear weighs these amounts.

a 100 kg

b 150 kg

c 250 kg

**\*10** Use the formula $F = ma$ to find $F$ for these values of $m$ and $a$.

a $m = 10$ and $a = \dfrac{3}{4}$

b $m = 25$ and $a = \dfrac{7}{10}$

c $m = \dfrac{2}{3}$ and $a = 60$

**\*11** Use the formula $v = u + at$ to find $v$ for these values of $u$, $a$ and $t$.

a $u = 12$, $a = \dfrac{3}{5}$ and $t = 15$

b $u = 3$, $a = \dfrac{7}{8}$ and $t = 20$

c $u = 10$, $a = -\dfrac{7}{100}$ and $t = 50$

d $u = -1$, $a = 6$ and $t = -\dfrac{3}{4}$

explanation 3

**\*12** Work out these products. Give your answers as mixed numbers in their simplest form.

a $14 \times \dfrac{3}{7} \times \dfrac{5}{6}$

b $15 \times \dfrac{2}{3} \times \dfrac{3}{4}$

c $25 \times \dfrac{4}{5} \times \dfrac{2}{7}$

d $16 \times \dfrac{7}{8} \times \dfrac{5}{9}$

# Direct proportion

- Recognising direct proportion
- Calculating unknown values using direct proportion
- The connection between direct proportion and graphs
- Finding the equation connecting two quantities that are in direct proportion

Keywords

You should know

explanation 1

**1** The tables below show pairs of values of $x$ and $y$.
Which tables show $x$ and $y$ in direct proportion?

**a**

| $x$ | 1 | 2 | 3 |
|---|---|---|---|
| $y$ | 3 | 6 | 9 |

**b**

| $x$ | 1 | 3 | 5 |
|---|---|---|---|
| $y$ | 7 | 9 | 11 |

**c**

| $x$ | 4 | 12 | 20 |
|---|---|---|---|
| $y$ | 2 | 6 | 10 |

**d**

| $x$ | 1.5 | 2 | 2.5 |
|---|---|---|---|
| $y$ | 3.5 | 4 | 4.5 |

**e**

| $x$ | 10 | 20 | 30 |
|---|---|---|---|
| $y$ | 4 | 8 | 12 |

**f**

| $x$ | 50 | 75 | 100 |
|---|---|---|---|
| $y$ | 15 | 20 | 25 |

**2** Copy and complete these tables so that $x$ and $y$ are in direct proportion.

**a**

| $x$ | 5 | 7 | 9 |
|---|---|---|---|
| $y$ | 10 | | |

**b**

| $x$ | 8 | 9 | |
|---|---|---|---|
| $y$ | 24 | | 33 |

**c**

| $x$ | 10 | 18 | |
|---|---|---|---|
| $y$ | | 9 | 15 |

**d**

| $x$ | 15 | 21 | 27 |
|---|---|---|---|
| $y$ | | | 9 |

**e**

| $x$ | 7 | | 19 |
|---|---|---|---|
| $y$ | 3.5 | 8 | |

**f**

| $x$ | 1.2 | 1.5 | |
|---|---|---|---|
| $y$ | | 4.5 | 5.1 |

explanation 2

**3** Leroy is pouring water into his fish
tank. It took 18 litres of water to fill
the tank to a depth of 15 cm.

**a** How much water was needed to
make the depth 5 cm?

**b** Leroy wants the depth to be 25 cm.
How much water will there be in
the tank?

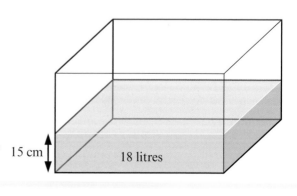

15 cm

18 litres

**4** A regional television company charges advertisers £15 900 for 30 seconds of air time in the late evening.

    **a** How much would it cost for 10 seconds of air time at this rate?

    **b** An advertiser buys 8 evening spots of 20 seconds each. How much does this cost?

    **c** The cost to advertise across all regions is £45 000 for 30 seconds of air time. Find the cost for 8 spots of 20 seconds across all regions.

**5** A skip hire company charges the amounts shown in the table.

| Size (cubic yards) | Cost to hire |
|:---:|:---:|
| 2 | £125 |
| 3 | £150 |
| 6 | £212 |
| 8 | £250 |
| 10 | |

    **a** Give an example to show that the cost to hire is not proportional to the size of the skip.

    **b** If the cost to hire *was* proportional to the size of the skip, how much would it cost for the 10 cubic metre skip, based on the 2 cubic metre price?

**6** Some carpet is on sale for £52 per square metre. The carpet is sold from a roll that is 4 m wide.

    **a** How much does it cost for each metre of carpet from the roll?

    **b** The diagram shows the measurements of Sharon's lounge.

        **i** What length of carpet must Sharon buy for her lounge?

        **ii** How much will the carpet cost?

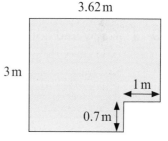

3.62 m

3 m

1 m

0.7 m

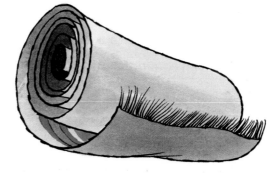

**7** Sean decides to swim a mile at his local swimming pool.

He has to swim 48 lengths of the pool.
He swims 30 lengths in 25 minutes.

How long does Sean take to swim 48 lengths at this speed?

**8** The ingredients for sticky toffee pudding are shown.
The amounts are based on a recipe for 6 people.

> **Sticky toffee pudding recipe**
>
> | Pudding | Sauce |
> |---|---|
> | 150 g dates | 180 g butter |
> | 250 ml hot water | 360 g brown sugar |
> | 60 g butter | 250 ml double cream |
> | 50 g caster sugar | |
> | 2 eggs | |
> | 150 g self-raising flour | |

**a** Work out the amounts needed to serve 3 people.

**b** How much brown sugar is needed if the recipe is adapted for 9 people?

**c** How much butter is needed, in total, if the recipe is adapted for 5 people?

**9 a** Copy and complete the table to show that
$S$ is directly proportional to $t$.

| $t$ | 0 | 2 | 4 |
|---|---|---|---|
| $S$ | | | 8 |

**b** Copy the diagram and plot the values from the
table as coordinates.

**c** Join the points with a straight line.

**d** Write an equation connecting $S$ and $t$.

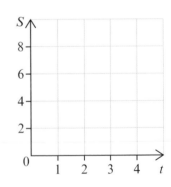

**10 a** Copy and complete the table for the equation
$S = 3t + 2$.

| t | 0 | 2 | 4 |
|---|---|---|---|
| S |   |   |   |

**b** Is $S$ directly proportional to t in this case?

**c** Copy the diagram and plot the points from your table as coordinates.

**d** Join the points with a straight line.

**e** What difference do you notice between this straight line and the one in question **9**?

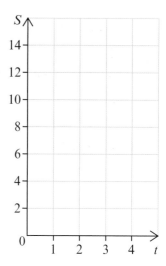

explanation 3

**11** Which of the following graphs show direct proportion? Explain how you know.

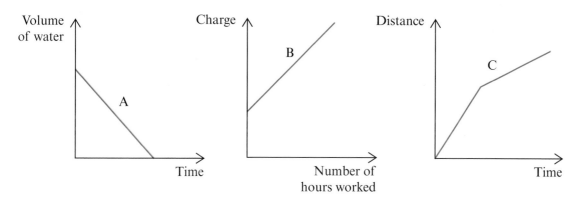

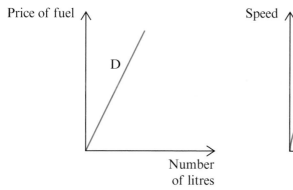

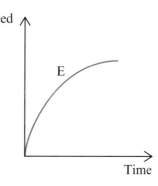

**12** Draw graphs for each of the following tables of values.
Write down the equation of the line for each graph.
Which graphs show direct proportion?

a

| x | 2 | 3 | 5 | 8 |
|---|---|---|---|---|
| y | 10 | 15 | 25 | 40 |

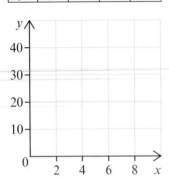

b

| t | 1 | 4 | 6 | 10 |
|---|---|---|---|---|
| S | 1.5 | 6 | 9 | 15 |

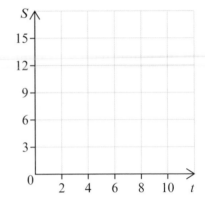

c

| b | 4 | 8 | 12 | 16 |
|---|---|---|---|---|
| a | 5 | 10 | 15 | 20 |

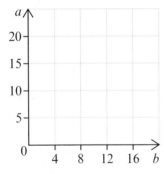

d

| m | 1 | 2 | 3 | 4 |
|---|---|---|---|---|
| n | 1 | 3 | 5 | 7 |

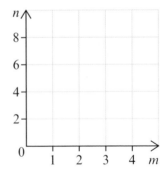

e

| Q | 2 | 4 | 6 | 8 |
|---|---|---|---|---|
| P | 1 | 2 | 3 | 4 |

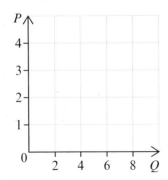

# Deriving expressions and formulae

- Finding expressions and formulae in a variety of situations

Keywords

You should know

explanation 1a    explanation 1b

**1** Write an expression for each of these numbers.

   **a** 3 more than *m*      **b** 5 less than *m*      **c** twice as big as *m*

   **d** half as big as *m*     **e** *m* more than 7      **f** *m* less than 11

**2** Write an expression for each of these numbers.

   **a** the product of *m* and *n*   **b** the sum of *m* and *n*   **c** *m* more than *n*

   **d** *n* less than *m*         **e** *m* less than *n*         **f** *m* times as big as *n*

**3** *n* is an odd number. Write an expression for each of these numbers.

   **a** the next odd number         **b** the next even number

   **c** the previous even number    **d** the previous odd number

**4 a** Sam draws three shapes that can fit into a 6 by 6 number square.
Copy each shape and write expressions for the rest of the squares
in terms of the letter given.

   **i**    **ii** 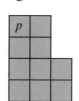   **iii**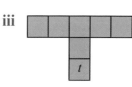

| 1 | 2 | 3 | 4 | 5 | 6 |
|---|---|---|---|---|---|
| 7 | 8 | 9 | 10 | 11 | 12 |
| 13 | 14 | 15 | 16 | 17 | 18 |
| 19 | 20 | 21 | 22 | 23 | 24 |
| 25 | 26 | 27 | 28 | 29 | 30 |
| 31 | 32 | 33 | 34 | 35 | 36 |

   **b** Find the sum of all the numbers in shape **i** in
terms of *n*. Comment on your answer.

   **c** What is the sum of all the numbers in a 3 by 3 square
if the middle number is 20?

**5**  Each card shows an expression representing a number.

$n + 2$     $n - 1$     $n + 5$

  **a**  Write the numbers shown on the cards in order, smallest first.

  **b**  What is the median of the numbers?

  **c**  Find and simplify an expression for the sum of the numbers.

  **d**  Write an expression for the mean of the numbers.

  **e**  What is the range of the numbers?

---

explanation 2 ─────────────────────────────────────

**6**  Write an expression for the number midway between the following pairs of
values.

  **a**  $n, n + 2$         **b**  $n - 1, n + 1$         **c**  $3n, 5n$

  **d**  $n, 5$             **e**  $n + 1, 8$             **f**  $m, n$

**7**  The numbers represented by
the expressions on these cards     $t + 2$     $2t$     $2t + 6$     $3t + 4$
are in order, smallest first.

  **a**  Write an expression for these amounts.

   **i**  The median of the numbers.       **ii**  The range of the numbers.

   **iii**  The sum of the numbers.       **iv**  The mean of the numbers.

  **b**  What do you notice about the median and the mean?

**8**  In the diagram, P has coordinates (5, 5) and
the yellow square has each side length $b$.

  **a**  Peter says the coordinates of A are $(5 - b, 5)$.

   Explain why Peter is correct.

  **b**  Which point has coordinates of $(5, 5 - b)$?

  **c**  Write down the coordinates of the rest of
the points.

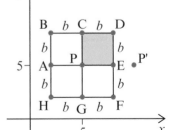

  **d**  What are the coordinates of P′, which is the reflection of P in the line DF?

**9** P', Q' and R' are the images of P, Q and R after a reflection in $y = x$.

a Write the coordinates of these points.

  i P and P'

  ii Q and Q'

  iii R and R'

b S has coordinates $(x, y)$.
Write the coordinates of the image of S after a reflection in $y = x$.

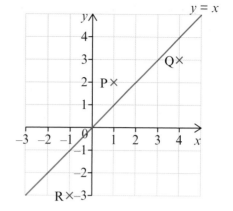

---

explanation 3

**10** Write a formula for $y$ in terms of $x$ for each of these function machines.

a $x \rightarrow \boxed{\div 3} \rightarrow \boxed{+ 1} \rightarrow y$     b $x \rightarrow \boxed{- 4} \rightarrow \boxed{\times 7} \rightarrow y$

**11** To find $T$, start with $n$, double it, add on 5 and divide the answer by 3.
Write a formula for $T$ in terms of $n$.

**12** The area of the rectangle is $A$.
The perimeter of the rectangle is $P$.

a Find a formula for $A$ in terms of $a$, $b$ and $h$.

b Find and simplify a formula for $P$ in terms of $a$, $b$ and $h$.

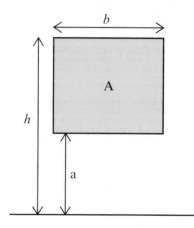

**13** Find and simplify a formula for the sum, $S$, of three consecutive numbers with middle value $m$.

explanation 4a  explanation 4b

**14** Copy and complete the table.

| Sequence | Going up by | Part of $n$th term | Correction | $n$th term |
|---|---|---|---|---|
| 5, 7, 9, 11... | +2 | $2 \times n$ | Add 3 | $2n + 3$ |
| 4, 8, 12, 16... | +4 | $4 \times n$ | None | $4n$ |
| 1, 9, 17, 25... | | | | |
| 9, 16, 23, 30... | | | | |
| 50, 47, 44, 41... | −3 | $-3 \times n$ | | |

**15** **a** Write the first five odd numbers.

**b** Find the $n$th term for the sequence of odd numbers.

**16** For each sequence find the $n$th term and then use it to find the 30th term.

**a** 2, 4, 6, 8 ...    **b** 10, 20, 30, 40 ...    **c** 7, 8, 9, 10 ...

**d** 5, 8, 11, 14 ...    **e** 10, 15, 20, 25 ...    **f** 1, 5, 9, 13 ...

**17** For each sequence write the next two terms and find the $n$th term.

**a** 100, 90, 80, 70 ...    **b** 37, 35, 33, 31 ...

**18** Here are some matchstick patterns.

**a** Copy and complete the table.

Pattern 1          Pattern 2          Pattern 3

| Number of triangles ($t$) | 1 | 2 | 3 | 4 | 5 |
|---|---|---|---|---|---|
| Number of matches ($m$) | | | | | |

**b** Find a formula for $m$ in terms of $t$.

**c** How many matches are needed to make 15 triangles?

**d** Which pattern contains 301 matches?

**19** When a cube is placed on a table there is one face you cannot see, the base. So one cube has only one hidden face.

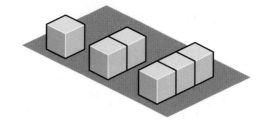

**a** Explain why the two cubes on the table have four hidden faces.

**b** Write down the number of hidden faces for three cubes in a line.

**c** Copy and complete the table of results for cubes in a line.

| Number of cubes $c$ | 1 | 2 | 3 | 4 | 5 | 6 |
|---|---|---|---|---|---|---|
| Number of hidden faces $f$ | 1 | 4 | | | | |

**d** Find a formula for $f$ in terms of $c$.

**e** Twelve cubes are placed in a line. How many hidden faces are there?

**20** The pattern shows the number of grey tiles needed to surround the red tiles.

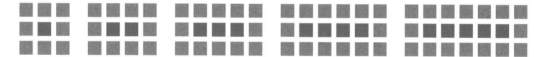

**a** Copy and complete the table.

| Number of red tiles ($r$) | 1 | 2 | 3 | 4 | 5 |
|---|---|---|---|---|---|
| Number of grey tiles ($g$) | | | | | |

**b** Find a formula for $g$ in terms of $r$.

**21** Two red tiles are surrounded by a border of 14 purple tiles. A second border of yellow tiles is followed by a third border of purple tiles.

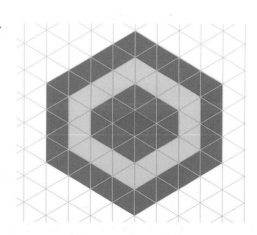

**a** How many tiles will be needed for the fourth border?

**b** Write a sequence describing the number of tiles in each border.

**c** Find the $n$th term and the number of tiles in the 30th border.

# Using equations

- Using an equation to represent a problem
- Using the solution of an equation to solve a problem

Keywords

You should know

explanation 1a    explanation 1b

**1** Solve these equations. Give your answers as mixed numbers.

    **a** $14 + 5r = 30$     **b** $15 + 3h = 20$     **c** $35 = 7d + 15$

    **d** $29 = 11x - 24$     **e** $9s - 23 = -4$     **f** $-9 = 4k - 18$

**2** Solve these equations. Give your answers as decimals.

    **a** $9 + 2g = 16$     **b** $25 - 4w = 16$     **c** $5x + 11 = 14$

    **d** $-8 + 10b = 81$     **e** $14m + 9 = 30$     **f** $31 - 6y = 4$

**3** Simplify and solve these equations.

    **a** $2x + 7 + 3x - 4 = 33$         **b** $x + (x + 1) + (x + 2) + (x + 3) = 34$

explanation 2a    explanation 2b

**4** You can use algebra to help you solve the puzzle shown on the scroll.

Use $x$ to represent Lucy's age in years.

    **a** Write an expression for Scott's age, using $x$.

    **b** How old is each parent in terms of $x$?

    **c** Write an expression for the sum of all four ages and simplify it.

    **d** Use the final piece of information from the scroll to write an equation.

    **e** Solve the equation.

    **f** How old is Scott?

**Age-old puzzle**

Scott is 3 years older than his sister Lucy.

Their parents are the same age, which is three times Lucy's age.

The sum of all four ages is 99 years. How old is Scott?

**5** The smallest angle of a quadrilateral is $x$. The other three angles are 10°, 20° and 30° larger than $x$ respectively.

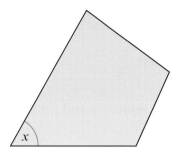

  **a**  Write the size of the other three angles in terms of $x$.

  **b**  What do the four angles of a quadrilateral add up to?

  **c**  Write an equation for the sum of the four angles.

  **d**  Solve the equation and write down the size of the four angles.

**6** The green addition pyramid starts off with the consecutive integers 5, 6 and 7.

The bottom three numbers of the purple pyramid start with a different set of consecutive integers, increasing from left to right.

What are the missing numbers?

Follow the steps below to solve the puzzle.

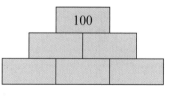

  **a**  Copy the second purple diagram and write expressions for the missing numbers in the bottom row.

  **b**  Use the rules for an addition pyramid to find expressions for the other missing numbers. Simplify them and write them in the spaces.

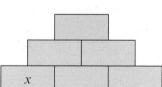

  **c**  Write an equation using what you know about the top number in the pyramid.

  **d**  Solve the equation.

  **e**  Copy the first purple diagram and fill in the missing numbers.

**7** Ravi added five consecutive integers to make a total of 2010. Let $n$ be the first number.

> If $n$ is the first number then the next consecutive number is $n + 1$ and so on.

  **a** Copy and complete.

    $n + (n + 1) + (\phantom{x}) + (\phantom{x}) + (\phantom{x}) = 2010$

  **b** Solve this equation to find the integers that Ravi used.

**8** An addition pyramid starts with three consecutive odd numbers and finishes at 68.

Let $y$ be the first number in the bottom row.

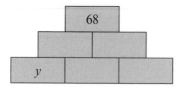

  **a** Copy and complete the addition pyramid by writing expressions for the missing numbers in the pyramid in terms of $y$.

  **b** Use your answers to **a** to write an equation for the number at the top of the pyramid (68).

  **c** Solve your equation and find the three odd numbers in the bottom row.

**9** The width of the rectangle is $x$ cm and the length of the rectangle is 1 cm longer than the width. The square is 3 cm by 3 cm.

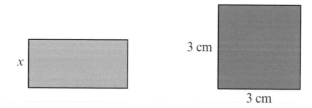

  **a** Write an expression for the length of the rectangle in terms of $x$.

  **b** The perimeter of the rectangle and the square are equal. Use this information to write an equation involving $x$.

  **c** Solve this equation and write the length and width of the rectangle.

**10**

The red square contains the numbers 20, 21, 22, 29, 30, 31, 38, 39 and 40.

The sum of the numbers in the four corners is 20 + 22 + 38 + 40 = 120.

The sum of the numbers in each diagonal is 90.

20 + 30 + 40 = 90 *and* 22 + 30 + 38 = 90.

| 0 | 1 | 2 | 3 | 4 | 5 | 6 | 7 | 8 |
|---|---|---|---|---|---|---|---|---|
| 9 | 10 | 11 | 12 | 13 | 14 | 15 | 16 | 17 |
| 18 | 19 | 20 | 21 | 22 | 23 | 24 | 25 | 26 |
| 27 | 28 | 29 | 30 | 31 | 32 | 33 | 34 | 35 |
| 36 | 37 | 38 | 39 | 40 | 41 | 42 | 43 | 44 |
| 45 | 46 | 47 | 48 | 49 | 50 | 51 | 52 | 53 |
| 54 | 55 | 56 | 57 | 58 | 59 | 60 | 61 | 62 |
| 63 | 64 | 65 | 66 | 67 | 68 | 69 | 70 | 71 |
| 72 | 73 | 74 | 75 | 76 | 77 | 78 | 79 | 80 |

The 3 by 3 red square can be drawn anywhere inside the grid.

Let $x$ be the number in the top left-hand corner.

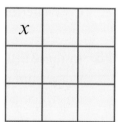

**a** Look at the pattern of numbers in the grid. Copy the large red square and write an expression in each of the spaces in terms of $x$.

**b** Write and simplify an expression for the sum of the numbers in the four corners.

**c** If the sum of the numbers in the four corners is 164, write down an equation and solve it to find the numbers in the red square.

**d** If the sum of the three numbers in the diagonal is 66, write down an equation and solve it to find $x$. What are the numbers in the red square this time?

**11** Fifty chocolates are arranged on a three-tier tray. The largest tray has three times as many chocolates as the smallest tray and the middle tray has 6 fewer than the largest tray.

Let $n$ be the number of chocolates on the smallest tray.

**a** Write expressions for the number of chocolates on each tray.

**b** Write down an equation and solve it to find $n$.

**c** How many chocolates are on each tray?

**12** A farmer wants to build a rectangular enclosure for his sheep. He wants the length of the enclosure to be 6 m longer than the width. He has 70 m of fencing.

x m

**a** Copy the sketch and write an expression for the length of the enclosure.

**b** Write and simplify an expression for the total length of fence needed.

**c** Write an equation to represent the problem.

**d** Solve the equation.

**e** Write the length and width of the enclosure.

**13** In these arithmagons the number in a square is equal to the sum of the two numbers inside the circles on either side.

2

5    9

3 — 10 — 7

The numbers inside the squares are 20, 23 and 27. What are the numbers in the circles?

Let $n$ be the number in the top circle.

**a** Explain why the number in the bottom-left circle is $20 - n$.

**b** Write an expression for the number in the bottom-right circle.

**c** Write an equation that involves the square containing 27.

**d** Simplify and solve this equation to find $n$.

**e** Write the three numbers that go in the circles.

20    23

27

**14** Use the same method that you used in question **13** to find the numbers that go in the circles.

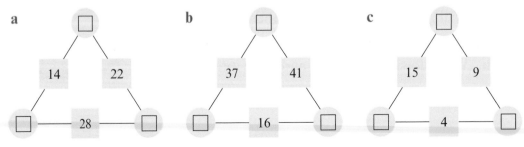

**a**

14    22

28

**b**

37    41

16

**c**

15    9

4

explanation 3

**15** Solve these equations.

a  $3(x + 11) = 48$        b  $4(x - 9) = 24$

c  $6(12 - x) = 18$        d  $5(x - 6) = -20$

**16** Solve these equations by expanding the brackets first.

a  $4(h + 2.5) = 30$        b  $5(r + 2) + 11 = 56$

c  $42 = 4(d - 1) + 6$        d  $34 = g + 4(2g - 5)$

e  $p + 3(p - 7) = 23$        f  $9(v + 1) - 2v - 44 = 0$

**17** Solve these equations.

a  $\dfrac{x + 11}{4} = 7$        b  $\dfrac{u}{5} - 9 = 2$

c  $14 = \dfrac{t + 23}{3}$        d  $\dfrac{y}{10} + 19 = 23$

e  $\dfrac{a - 7}{6} = 5$        f  $-7 = \dfrac{e}{5} - 11$

**18** I think of a number, subtract 2 and then multiply by 4. The answer is 14. Write this information as an equation and solve it to find my number.

**19** a  I think of a number, add 17 and then divide by 5. My answer is 5.4. Write this information as an equation. Solve the equation to find my number.

b  I think of a number, divide it by 6 and then subtract the result from 20. My answer is 11.5. Write this information as an equation and solve it to find my number.

explanation 4

**20** Solve these equations.

a  $2y + 3 = y + 8$        b  $5n - 7 = 2n + 17$

c  $6p - 2 = p + 43$        d  $4p + 7 = 42 - 3p$

**21** Paul has three children and he was 28 years old when his first child was born. The oldest child is 2 years older than the middle child who is 4 years older than the youngest.

Let $n$ be the age of the middle child.

    **a**  Write an expression for the age of the oldest and youngest child in terms of $n$.

    **b**  Write an expression for Paul's age in terms of n.

    **c**  Explain what the equation $n - 4 + n + (n + 2) = 30 + n$ means.

    **d**  Simplify this equation and solve it to find $n$.

    **e**  Write Paul's age and the age of each child.

**22** The length of each side of the grey square is $n$ centimetres.

Two shapes are made with four of these grey squares.

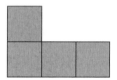 

    **a**  Write expressions for the perimeter of each shape in terms of $n$.

    **b**  The perimeter of the first shape is 18 cm more than the perimeter of the second shape.
       Write an equation that describes this fact in terms of $n$.

    **c**  Solve the equation to find the length of the side of the large grey square.

**23** The length of each side of the triangle is $x$ centimetres.

Two shapes are made using six of these triangles.

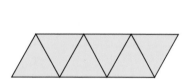 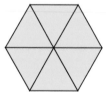

    **a**  Write expressions for the perimeters of each shape.

    **b**  The perimeter of the first shape is 5 cm more than the perimeter of the second shape.

       Use this fact to write down an equation in terms of $x$.

    **c**  Solve this equation to find the length of each side of the equilateral triangle.

# Graphs of real-life situations

- Interpreting information shown by a graph

Keywords

You should know

explanation 1

1  Danni sets off from home to take a walk.
   The graph shows her progress.

   a  Danni stopped for a rest at one point.
      What time did she stop?

   b  How long did she rest for?

   c  How far did she walk altogether?

   d  How long did her return journey take?

   e  What time did she get home?

   f  How much time did she spend
      walking?

2  Mike and Alex raced each other over
   two lengths of a swimming pool.
   The graph shows what happened.

   a  Who turned first?

   b  How long was the pool?

   c  What distance was left to go when
      they were level with each other?

   d  Who won the race?

   e  What did Alex do that was different
      to Mike?

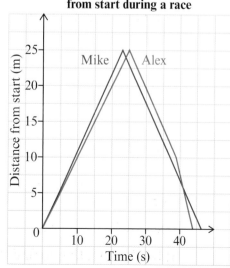

Graph showing distance
from home during a walk

Graph showing distance
from start during a race

**3**   The graph shows the first six seconds of a bungee jump off a tower.

**Graph showing height from ground during bungee jump**

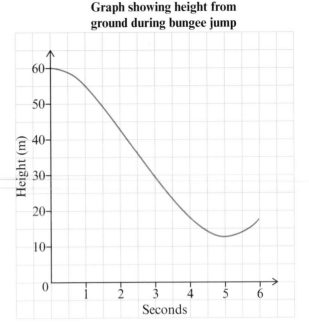

a   How high is the tower?

b   The unstretched length of the bungee cord is 11 m. For how many seconds was the bungee jumper in free fall?

c   How close to the ground did the bungee jumper get?

d   How many times its unstretched length did the rubber cord stretch?

explanation 2

**4**   The graph shows the speed of a rollercoaster during the first 50 seconds of a ride.

**Graph showing speed of a rollercoaster**

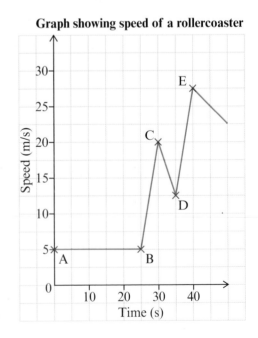

a   What can you say about the speed corresponding to the first section AB of the graph?

b   Which point on the rollercoaster do you think B corresponds to?

c   Describe what section BC shows.

d   Describe what section CD shows.

e   What is the greatest speed shown on the graph?

**5** A firework rocket is pointed vertically upwards. The graph shows how the speed of the rocket changes with time.

**Graph showing speed of firework rocket**

a Describe what is happening to the rocket during the first 3 seconds of its flight.

b What is the greatest speed of the rocket?

c Describe what the section AB of the graph represents.

d Which of the labelled points corresponds to the greatest height reached? Explain your answer.

e Kevin wonders how high the rocket went. His teacher said this could be worked out by finding the area under the graph. How high did the rocket go?

**6** Match each of the following situations to one of the sketches below.

a The speed of a train between two stops.

b The speed of a parachutist after leaving a plane.

c The speed of a car in a traffic jam.

d The speed of a plane as it lands.

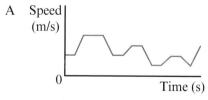

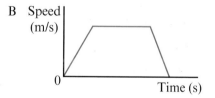

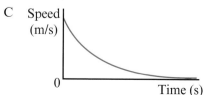

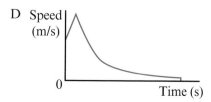

explanation 3

**7** Sally is going to have a bath. The graph shows the depth of water in the bath.

**Graph showing depth of water in a bath**

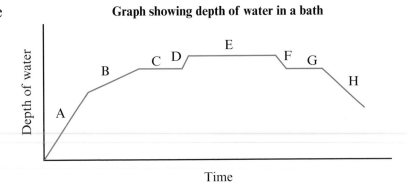

Describe each line on the graph. Here are some are some suggestions to get you started.

| The hot tap is on full. | Sally pulls out the plug. | Sally gets out of the bath. |

**\*8** The graph shows the height and horizontal distance made by a stunt rider who takes off at 35 km/h from a ramp that makes a 30° angle with the ground. His assistants have 1 metre cube boxes to build obstacles for him to jump over.

**Graph showing height of stunt rider during a jump**

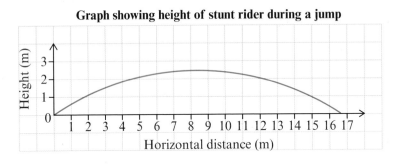

**a** What is the maximum height of his jump?

**b** What distance did he jump?

**c** How many boxes could his assistants line up side by side for him to jump over?

**d** Where would they place these boxes?

**e** How many boxes, two high, can they place in a line for him to jump over? Explain where they should be placed on the ground.

**\*9** 500 g of frozen carrots are dropped into a pan of boiling water. Draw a simple graph to show how the temperature of the water in the pan changes with time.

# Symmetry and transformations

- Finding the order of rotation symmetry
- Connecting line symmetry and reflection
- Using a vector to describe a translation
- Combining rotations, reflections and translations

Keywords

You should know

explanation 1a   explanation 1b

**1  a**  The shape shown is an equilateral triangle. O is
the centre of rotation.

    **i**  Explain why angle AOB must be 120°.

    **ii**  The triangle is rotated through 120° clockwise
about O. Sketch the triangle in this position.

    **iii**  How many more of these rotations are needed
to return the triangle to its original position?

    **iv**  What is the order of rotation symmetry of an equilateral triangle?

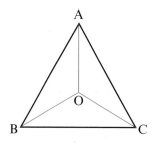

**b**  The shape shown is a regular pentagon.

    **i**  What is angle AOB?

    **ii**  The pentagon is rotated so that A moves to
where B originally was. How many rotations of
this size are needed to return the pentagon to its
original position?

    **iii**  What is the order of rotation symmetry of a
regular pentagon?

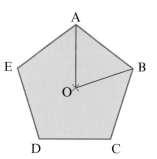

**c**  The shape shown is a regular octagon.
What is the order of rotation symmetry of a
regular octagon?

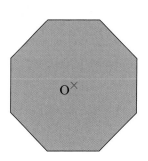

**2** Write down the order of rotation symmetry of each of these shapes.

a

Rectangle

b

Isosceles triangle

c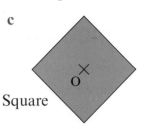

Square

d

Parallelogram

e

Trapezium

f

Hexagon

**3** Copy and complete these diagrams so that they have rotation symmetry of order 4 with centre at O.

a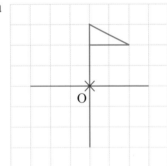

b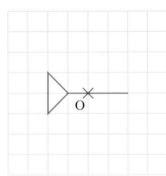

c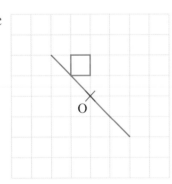

d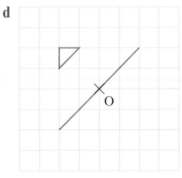

explanation 2

4  Copy the diagrams and reflect the shapes in the dotted lines.

a

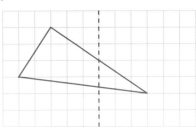

b

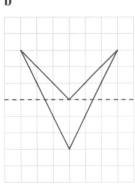

c

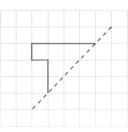

5  Copy these shapes and draw any lines of symmetry. If no line of symmetry
exists then write 'None'.

a

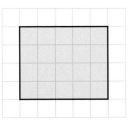

b

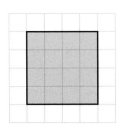

c

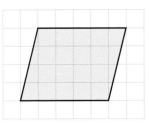

d

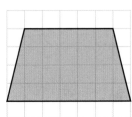

e

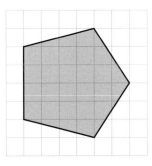

f

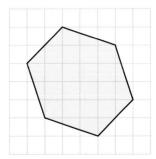

**6** State whether the shapes below have

    **A** line symmetry but not rotation symmetry
    **B** rotation symmetry but not line symmetry
    **C** both rotation symmetry and line symmetry

**a**

**b** %

**c** θ

**d** Ω

**e** ⌐

**f** ©

[explanation 3a] [explanation 3b]

**7** Give the translation vector that describes
the following translations.

    **a** A to B     **b** C to A

    **c** D to C     **d** B to D

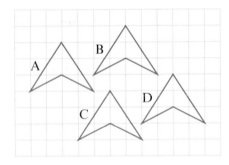

**8** The pattern shown in the diagram
continues forever in both directions.

    **a** Which of these translations will
map the whole pattern onto
itself?

       **i** 2 right      **ii** 4 right

      **iii** 8 left      **iv** 3 left

       **v** 1000 right     **vi** 4*n* right where *n* is an integer

    **b** Describe a reflection, followed by a translation, that maps the whole pattern
onto itself.

    **c** Describe a translation, followed by a reflection, that maps the whole pattern
onto itself.

**9** Copy the diagram.

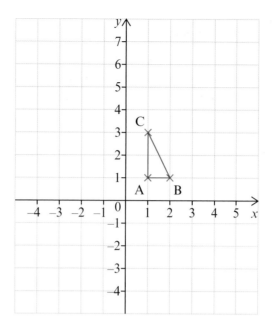

**a** Draw in the positions of triangle ABC after the following translations.

**i** $\begin{pmatrix} 1 \\ 5 \end{pmatrix}$  **ii** $\begin{pmatrix} -4 \\ 3 \end{pmatrix}$  **iii** $\begin{pmatrix} -3 \\ -5 \end{pmatrix}$

**b** Describe a way of working out the new positions of the shape without drawing diagrams.

**10 a   i** Translate triangle ABC using the translation vector $\begin{pmatrix} 5 \\ 2 \end{pmatrix}$.

**ii** Translate the answer to **i** using the translation vector $\begin{pmatrix} 2 \\ -6 \end{pmatrix}$.

**iii** What single translation would map triangle ABC to the position shown in the answer to **ii**?

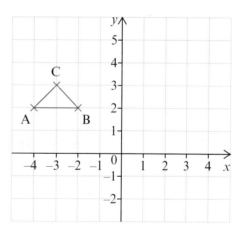

**b** Write the single translation that is the same as these combinations of translations.

**i** $\begin{pmatrix} 3 \\ -2 \end{pmatrix}$ followed by $\begin{pmatrix} -5 \\ 6 \end{pmatrix}$.

**ii** $\begin{pmatrix} -8 \\ -8 \end{pmatrix}$ followed by $\begin{pmatrix} -4 \\ -7 \end{pmatrix}$.

**iii** $\begin{pmatrix} 2 \\ -3 \end{pmatrix}$ followed by $\begin{pmatrix} 4 \\ 7 \end{pmatrix}$ followed by $\begin{pmatrix} -3 \\ -1 \end{pmatrix}$.

**iv** $\begin{pmatrix} -5 \\ 8 \end{pmatrix}$ followed by $\begin{pmatrix} 5 \\ -8 \end{pmatrix}$. What does the result mean?

**11**

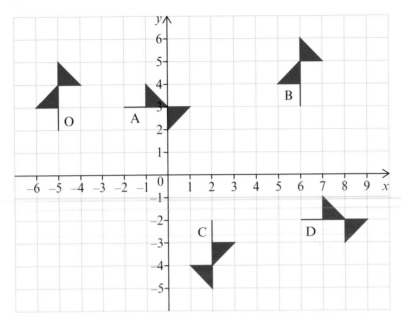

Describe the combinations of transformations that map the following.

a   O to A           b   O to B           c   O to C           d   O to D

There may be more than one way to do each one.

**12**   Copy the diagram.

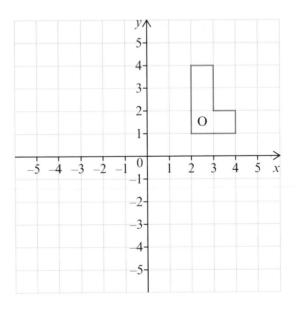

a   Reflect shape O in the *y*-axis. Call its new position 1.

b   Reflect the shape at 1 in the *x*-axis. Call its new position 2.

c   What single rotation would map shape O to position 2?

# Solving geometrical problems

- Applying your knowledge to solve problems

Keywords

You should know

explanation 1

**1** You have this rectangle and these two right-angled triangles.

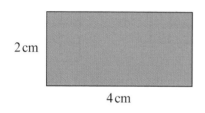

2 cm

4 cm

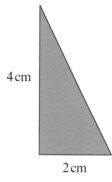

4 cm

2 cm

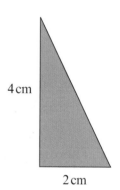

4 cm

2 cm

You can translate, rotate or reflect any of the shapes and combine them to build new shapes.

Draw diagrams to show how to build these shapes.

**a** A square
**b** Two different parallelograms
**c** Two different trapeziums
**d** Two different isosceles triangles
**e** A pentagon

**2 a** Show that this diagram contains two isosceles triangles.

**b** Calculate the distance AD.

Explain your method.

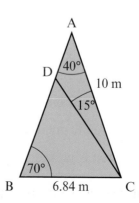

**3** In this diagram, ABCD is a rectangle.

The blue arc is a quarter of a circle with centre at D.

Find the length of AC and explain your reasoning.

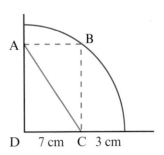

D     7 cm   C   3 cm

**4 a** Find the number of squares in each of these diagrams.

Count squares of different sizes and look for a pattern.

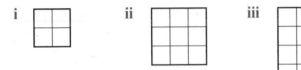

**b** A chessboard is an 8 by 8 square pattern. How many squares of different sizes are there altogether on a chessboard?

**5** This diagram shows a chessboard pattern with a pair of opposite corners removed.

You are given 31 domino-shaped tiles like the one shown here.

Each tile will exactly cover two squares of the chessboard.

Is it possible to place the tiles on the chessboard pattern so that it is completely covered?

- If it can be done, draw a diagram to show how.

- If it is impossible, explain why.

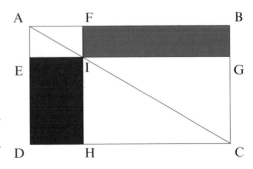

**6** This diagram shows a large rectangle with red and blue rectangles drawn inside.

Which of these statements is true?

- The blue area is greater than the red area.

- The red area is greater than the blue area.

- The blue and red areas are equal.

Explain your reasoning.

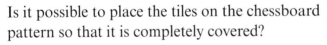